POMPEY THE GREAT

POMPEY THE GREAT

Pat Southern

TEMPUS

First published 2002

PUBLISHED IN THE UNITED KINGDOM BY:
Tempus Publishing Ltd
The Mill, Brimscombe Port
Stroud, Gloucestershire GL5 2QG

PUBLISHED IN THE UNITED STATES OF AMERICA BY:
Tempus Publishing Inc.
2 Cumberland Street
Charleston, SC 29401

British Library Cataloguing in Publication Data.
A catalogue record for this book is available from the British Library.

ISBN 0 7524 2521 8

Typesetting and origination by Tempus Publishing.
PRINTED AND BOUND IN GREAT BRITAIN.

Contents

Acknowledgements

Thanks are due to Peter Kemmis Betty and the Tempus staff who helped to produce this book, and to Jacqui Taylor and Jan Shearsmith for producing the drawings. Acknowledgement should also be made of the contribution of Cleo, our elegant black cat who helps with all the typing. Any unlikely errors and typos can be laid firmly at her paws.

In the late seventies and early eighties there was a rash of books on Pompey, by Leach, Seager and Greenhalgh; but that was over 20 years ago, so no apology is made for producing another. Having written about Pompey's contemporaries, Caesar, Antony and Cleopatra, it seemed neglectful to leave him out. Besides, though he appears in modern novels, he does not get his fair share of coverage in films; while the other characters have been made real in celluloid, Pompey is usually limited to a brief glimpse of a head being pulled out of a jar, so that no famous actor gets a chance to play him and bring him alive.

List of illustrations

1 Son of Strabo

On 28 September 48 BC a small boat set out from the harbour at Alexandria to meet a Roman ship which had arrived from nearby Pelusium. The occupants of the small boat were Achillas, the military adviser to the young King Ptolemy XIII of Egypt, and a Roman soldier called Lucius Septimius, who had probably been stationed in Egypt since the expedition of Aulus Gabinius in 56 in order to shore up the Egyptian royal family with Ptolemy XII Auletes at its head. The ostensible task of the passengers in the boat was to receive the Roman general from the ship that had just arrived. He had sought and been granted permission to land in Alexandria, and the boat party were to conduct him to Ptolemy for an audience. The general climbed down to the boat and greeted the occupants, attempting to engage Septimius in conversation; Gabinius' expedition to Egypt had been undertaken with the general's backing, so he tried to share a few pleasantries with a fellow Roman soldier, all to no avail. Since rapport and repartee were not forthcoming, he gave up and opened a little scroll that he carried, and he sat reading it as though rehearsing; this was the speech that he had prepared for his official audience. This was not a social or diplomatic visit; the general needed men, money and ships, and in his meeting with the Egyptian king, once the preliminaries were over, he would eventually have to introduce his requests. The occupants of the boat had already discussed with their ministerial colleagues the probable reasons for the general's arrival, and had come to the conclusion that he must be dealt with rapidly and efficiently, because close behind him there was another Roman general who had defeated him in battle, and who as the victor was more to be feared. 'Dead men don't talk', Achillas had said, when the Egyptian ministers discussed the matter of the visiting general. As the group stepped ashore, Septimius killed the general, in full view of his wife and son who were still aboard the ship. Pulling his cloak over his head, the general fell at the feet of his assassins. His head was cut off, to be carried to Ptolemy and pickled in a jar, and the body remained unburied on the shore until the general's freedman Philippus carried out the funeral rites, and sent the ashes to Rome.

The murdered general was Gnaeus Pompeius Magnus, once the foremost man in Rome, three times consul, a military hero from his early twenties, self-styled 'the Great', conqueror of the Mediterranean pirates, and of Rome's arch enemy Mithridates. He had never lost a war, until now. He had been defeated in his final campaign by Gaius Julius Caesar at the battle of Pharsalus. Pompey was 58 years old, and if he had survived one more day he would have been 59. He had lived through arguably the most eventful six decades of Roman history, some of which he had shaped and directed himself. It was to be another 25 years before his legacy and that of his enemies worked itself out and stability returned.

The man who met his end on the Egyptian shore was born 29 September 106, at a time when Rome was threatened by enemies from the north, the Celtic tribes chiefly known as the Cimbri and Teutones. There had been a continual presence of these tribesmen, sometimes menacing as they moved towards Italy, sometimes veering off in a different direction, for several years. They were unsettled, perhaps displaced, not given to prolonged residence in any lands. From about 113 until 105, Roman generals battled with them and often met defeat; it seemed that the tribes were never-ending and unbeatable, until Marius was elected consul and took the field against them. Marius was a highly capable soldier whose successes in the military sphere elevated him to the highest honours and repeated consulships. He and the young Pompey were enemies, but his military victories and the way in which he used them in the political realm, his popularity and above all his repeated tenure of the consulship in times of need, all served to set the precedent for Pompey's own career. There were always two consuls, theoretically to provide checks and balances and to avoid the domination of one individual, anathema to the Romans since the expulsion of the kings and the creation of the Republic. The consulship was held annually, and to achieve a second term of office was a signal honour indeed. Multiple consulships were hitherto unheard of, because the number of years that should elapse between consulships was expressly regulated by the *lex annalis* of 180 BC. Marius' first consulship was in 107, when he returned from the war in north Africa to stand for election, and then went back to take over the operation and achieve victory in a very short time. As the greatest war hero in Rome, when the Germanic tribes converged on northern Italy, Marius was elected consul every year from 104 to 100, such was his popularity and the faith of the people in his ability. He fought two great battles, in 102 at Aix-en-Provence and in 101 near Milan, when the Germans had broken through the Alps. He effectively put an end to the depredations of the Germanic tribes for many years; he was at the pinnacle of his career. Though Pompey was an infant at the time and too young to remember the details, the story of Marius would be familiar to him, and many of the principles behind leadership of the Roman state had been made crystal clear during the supremacy of Marius. Support of a loyal army could take a statesman further than statesmanship alone, support of the people could lead to the establishment of a military command, and promotion was rapid when there was a threat to the state that required a capable leader in whom the people of Rome had great faith. With these factors all acting in concert, the Senate could be circumvented; but its support oiled the wheels, and senators if not the Senate had to be cultivated from time to time.[1]

The Pompeii belonged to a hitherto undistinguished family. At some time before Pompey was born they had acquired lands and estates in Picenum in north-eastern Italy – this may not have been their ancestral homeland, but neither the origins nor the early history of the family are well-documented. The estates in Picenum formed the basis of Pompey's wealth and influence, which he used to advance himself after his father's death. The rest of his family did not provide him with much political support or social prestige. His father Pompeius Strabo was a successful general, but his career is not recorded in any detail. He had served as quaestor in Sicily in 104 and as praetor in Rome in 92, and reached the consulship in 89. He married Lucilia, whose family was perhaps even less distinguished than the Pompeii. She bore two children, Pompey and his sister Pompeia, though it is not known who was the elder. Lucilia's nephew was probably C. Lucilius Hirrus, tribune in 53 and supporter of Pompey at a time of political turmoil. Pompey's brother-in-law, Pompeia's husband C. Memmius, faithfully served Pompey in his early career, but was killed in Spain in 75.[2]

Pompeius Strabo achieved pre-eminence during the Social War, when the Italian allies (*socii*) took up arms against Rome. Throughout the wars with the Celtic tribes of the Cimbri and Teutones the Italian cities had supported Rome, contributed men to her armies and had bravely fought and died for her. Yet they had consistently been refused the grant of Roman citizenship, and the benefits and privileges that accompanied it; without it, although they paid local taxes to their own cities to support their contributions to the Roman army, they had no say in the debates about the wars that they were called upon to fight. Citizenship guaranteed a certain degree of protection and fair treatment before the law, and involved economic and social advantages as well. It was impossible to exercise the vote except by travelling to Rome; but the privileges alone satisfied some of the Italians, and those who wished for an active voice in Roman politics would at least not be denied the facility, provided that they were wealthy enough to travel and stay in the city. It was not ideal, but it was a facility that Rome had already bestowed on others, and the mechanism was already in place for the extension of citizenship to the Italians. What prevented it was not procedural difficulties but political obduracy in Rome itself.[3]

Various Roman politicians had tried to advance the cause of the allies without success, but when M. Livius Drusus introduced integrated legislation probably designed to cover all loopholes, it seemed that citizenship was within sight for the Italians. Drusus was tribune in 91. He was well-connected and acted more in the interests of the nobility than the common people or the allies. His programme has been much discussed because many of the details are still unclear; but what is certain is that his plans embraced much more than simply the enfranchisement of the Italian allies. He tried to reform the law courts by returning them to the control of the Senate, but he also intended to broaden the composition of the Senate by admitting men from the middle classes, the equites, to its ranks. An agrarian bill was also included in his programme, but not much is known of what he intended to do. It is possible that he wished to distribute corn either free or at below the market prices to the Roman mob, but there is no proof. His land allotment bill was closely bound up with his proposed enfranchisement of the Italian allies, because whenever land distribution was projected to relieve the pressure on the urban mob in Rome, it usually involved a loss of land for the Italian cities, when Rome declared that certain plots belonged to the Roman people (*ager publicus populi Romani*). The Italians might swallow the bitter pill of the land allotments if they could receive at the same time the privileges that came with citizenship. It was said that the leader of one of the strongest Italian tribes, the Marsi, was lodging with Drusus in Rome, which inflated the rumour that Drusus was to include enfranchisement of the Italians in his bill.

Such legislation never had an easy passage; land allotments were discussed many times in the late Republic, and the grant of citizenship was always jealously guarded by a narrow-minded Senate and people. It is probable that the bill never came before the Senate or the people for debate, because in a sudden attack in broad daylight, Drusus was assassinated. It was and is a mysterious affair, and to make matters worse for the Italians, there was no manhunt for the person or persons responsible for the murder. Lucius Marcius Philippus, who had opposed Drusus in the Senate, now urged the cancellation of all of his legislation. It seemed that the whole problem was to be brushed aside and ignored, a certain pointer to just how much the Romans cared about the situation of the allies. The Italians would have to begin all over again; and so they did, but this time in arms, in 90. The explosion was presumably premeditated, but perhaps held off until Rome had been given a chance to bestow citizenship voluntarily. When the war started, only the colonies that Rome had planted, and a few Italian cities, remained loyal.[4]

In this context Pompeius Strabo was appointed to a military command, in his own region of Picenum where his influence was strong. The rebels at Asculum had killed the Roman representatives sent to calm the area, and then slaughtered every single Roman in the town, so retribution was eagerly awaited for this outrage. Strabo set about raising an army. Rome did not possess a standing army at this period, so troops had to be specially recruited for the duration of campaigns and disbanded after the wars came to an end. Apart from calling up men from his estates, Strabo recruited Spanish cavalry, though it is not known how many. An inscription records the grant of Roman citizenship to about 30 of them as a reward for bravery. The eighth line of the inscription attests to the presence of Pompey, who would be about 16 years old, on his father's *consilium*, an informal group of friends and advisers that surrounded all Roman notables in daily life and business as well as on the battlefield. Several Picentines are also attested as members of Strabo's *consilium*, revealing that he looked for support close to home, and did not derive a following from among the great Roman noble families.[5]

Strabo may also have recruited soldiers from the Transpadane Gauls, Celtic tribes from beyond the river Po. His connection with these tribes was perhaps initially on a military basis, or at least it probably predated his legislative activity in granting them Latin rights, normally regarded as the preliminary step to full Roman citizenship. There was political kudos to be earned from taking up the cause of the Gauls, and it was an effective means of gaining a following that could be called upon for support. Many Roman politicians pursued this policy of cultivating clients outside Rome itself, and Strabo was just as concerned as anyone else to strengthen his position.[6]

Among the aspiring young Italians in Strabo's army was Marcus Tullius Cicero, who was the same age as Pompey. They may have met on both a formal and informal basis during the course of the war, but there is no evidence that they became friends or indeed took any notice of each other. It would have required a leap of faith to recognise the great general and the great orator in the two teenage soldiers, and perhaps no one could have predicted the upheavals that brought Pompey to fame and success at such a young age. Cicero in later years did not claim to have been a close personal associate of Pompey at this time, but he liked to remind people that he had served in the war; in the *Philippics*, written after Pompey's death to vilify Mark Antony, he describes what he saw of the meeting between Strabo and Vettius Scato, the leader of the Marsi.[7]

This fierce and hardy Italian tribe had provided many soldiers for Rome, and were noted as fearless warriors. They claimed that no Roman triumph had been held without their assistance, and none had ever been held over them, and at one point it required the combined forces of both Marius and Sulla to defeat them. The Marsi ensured that the campaign did not start auspiciously for Strabo. Before he could even approach Asculum (where the massacres of the Roman citizens had taken place), the tribesmen besieged him in Firmum. He broke out eventually, and at Rome this first dubious success of the war was celebrated by a return to civil dress instead of the mourning attire that had been decreed.[8]

Strabo's military success contributed to his election to the consulship for 89. He was the first of his family to rise to this high office, and his election implied that his son's future career would have a head start. In normal circumstances, the young Pompey would perhaps have made a name for himself in the law courts, and fulfilled a variety of administrative and military posts, starting with junior appointments and rising to more senior posts; he would have followed in his father's footsteps, as quaestor, then praetor, perhaps propraetor, and commander of troops if occasion demanded. He could look forward to a term of duty as one of the two annually-elected consuls, and perhaps even to attaining a second term as consul before retiring as an elder statesman, respected as a man whose opinion counted for something, asked to speak first in the Senate. But Pompey lived at a time when circumstances were far from normal, and he never for one moment followed what could have been considered a normal career path.[9]

It is generally assumed, without evidence one way or the other, that Pompey was present at the siege of Asculum, and took part in the battle with an enemy relieving force, learning the art of war alongside his father. Nothing is known of his activity or his achievements during and after the siege, but soldiering was only part of what he learned from Strabo. The other consul, Strabo's colleague Lucius Porcius Cato, was killed in a battle with the Marsi, and at Rome there was no time or organisational energy to spare to go through the process of electing another consul for the remaining term. Strabo was therefore sole consul for much of his term of office, an anomaly that would be repeated by his son some decades later, except that then the situation did not arise from the death of a colleague; Pompey was appointed sole consul because the political turmoil prevented the elections from being held. But the advantages of sole command without a colleague to negate ideas and activities, coupled with military success when others were defeated, would be as clear to the young Pompey as they were to his father.[10]

Another valuable lesson that required no emphasis, having been ably demonstrated by Marius, was that command of armies in tumultuous times could lead to a pre-eminence that carried over into political life, and after the wars were over there were potential personal benefits to be gained from the retention of an armed force, especially when the soldiers placed their trust in their commander and depended on him for their future subsistence. This mutual dependence of strong individual commanders and collectively strong soldiers was to shape the history of Rome for the next few centuries, even when standing armies had been formed with regular pay and compulsory savings and pension plans; but in Pompey's day the lack of a standing army with notional loyalty to the Emperor meant that a charismatic leader could play on the present needs of the soldiers for cash and provisions, as well as their future needs for lands or money after discharge, making himself the sole fount of pay and privileges. M. Licinius Crassus used to say that no man could count himself wealthy unless he could afford to equip and pay an army, an important consideration in an era when the state did not always fulfil its obligations in this respect. In a period when armies were raised from personal *clientelae* and the inhabitants of private estates, it was natural that commanders should develop a personal interest in the armies that they raised, and that the troops should look to their commanders rather than the state for their post-campaign livelihoods. Troops were required for the duration of the wars and then were disbanded, often without the firm promise of lands or pensions. Much of the legislative activity of the late Republic concerned veteran settlement, often combined with agrarian reforms to accommodate the land grants; had there been an easier and consistently organised path to the settlement of veterans, some of Rome's generals might not have had to resort to force, and to the acquisition of enormous powers to support that force.[11]

Strabo's troops were largely drawn from the inhabitants of his estates in Picenum, so he perhaps felt strongly proprietorial towards them, regarding them as his own personal army which he had put at the disposal of Rome, rather than Rome's army that had been entrusted to him to command. After his triumph in December 89, celebrating his services at Firmum and the successful siege of Asculum, Strabo passed from the office of consul, and became proconsul, still in command of his army, encamped in the countryside because a general was not allowed to enter Rome at the head of troops (except when he was celebrating his triumph).[12]

The consuls for 88 were Lucius Cornelius Sulla and Quintus Pompeius Rufus, who may have been a very distant relative of Strabo's family – so distant that the ancient authors did not bother to comment at length on it. Sulla was at odds with the war hero Marius because they were both determined to gain the command in the east against Mithridates, the king of Pontus, arch enemy of Rome. His full title was Mithridates VI Eupator Dionysus. He was descended from a long line of rulers, the majority of whom shared his name, as his title suggests. His mother ruled the kingdom while he was young but he seized power for himself probably in 115, and ruled until Pompey defeated him in 63. His constant ambition, like his ancestors before him, was to extend his territorial boundaries and to create an Empire at the expense of his neighbours. Previous kings of Pontus had taken over some of the Greek colonies founded on the Black Sea coast; others had absorbed the few cities of the interior. Remaining neighbours contiguous with Pontus were Galatia, Paphlagonia, Bithynia and Cappadocia. Mithridates VI co-operated with his neighbour Nicomedes II of Bithynia in a joint expansion programme, taking over

1 *The memory of Sulla and Quintus Pompeius Rufus, consuls in 88, was revived on the obverse and reverse of this coin by a descendant of Rufus in 54. This Quintus Pompeius Rufus was the grandson of the consul Rufus who was killed in Strabo's camp, and he was also directly descended from Sulla himself, being the son of Sulla's daughter.* Drawn by Jacqui Taylor and dividing most of Paphlagonia; but they quarrelled over Cappadocia, the strongest of all the neighbours of Pontus. Mithridates swapped his alliance with Nicomedes for a new one with Ariarathus of Cappadocia. This was possibly a scheme developed and encouraged by Marius, who was present in Asia Minor at the time, and would like nothing better than an excuse to go to war against Mithridates. Complications arose when Tigranes of Armenia invaded Cappadocia, and Parthia began to take an interest in her own western perimeters, that faced Rome's eastern borders. The end result of the scheming was that the Romans forced Mithridates to give up most of his Empire; it was Sulla who sorted it all out in 92, acting in concert with a representative from Parthia. No one could withstand pressure from both Rome and Parthia.[13]

Within a few years, Mithridates was active once again. Since the Social War seemed to occupy all Rome's attention, he chose this moment to strike into Bithynia and Cappadocia for another attempt at Pontic Empire building. The eastern territories, wealthy and exploitable as far as Rome was concerned, were now under direct threat from Mithridates, who exploited the hatred of Rome that united most of the eastern states; he encourage the indiscriminate massacre of both Roman and Italian officials and tax gatherers. Cappadocia and Bithynia were lost, and the murder of Romans and Italians demanded retribution. It was alarming that the eastern states seemed more ready to welcome Mithridates than they were reluctant to renounce Rome. The ruling classes in some of the Greek cities decided that life under Mithridates would be less difficult and less expensive than it was under Roman domination, and went over to him. Athens was one of them. Even though Athens offered few military advantages, morally this was a bitter blow to the Romans.[14]

Both Sulla and Marius were intent on leading the Roman armies against Mithridates. The command had already been granted to Sulla, but that did not deter Marius. He was prepared to go to extreme lengths to win the command, and the quarrel became violent when Marius recruited Sulpicius, one of the tribunes, to bypass the Senate and take direct to the popular assembly the proposal that the command should be wrested from Sulla and bestowed on Marius. Laws could be passed by the people in defiance of the Senate, so it was advisable to cultivate one or more of the ten tribunes to present bills to the assembly. Despite his age (he was in his seventies) Marius was still popular because his reputation as a general who had saved Rome was still intact after nearly 20 years; his appeal to the people therefore had a good chance of success. The measure was passed, but only by means of violent street riots organised by Sulpicius.

The consul Sulla withdrew to observe the heavens for portents, a well-used ploy because technically it meant that all public business should cease; but it was a ploy which enjoyed less and less effect. The only result this time was to increase the violence. Sulla was personally caught up in the riots, and whatever bodyguard he may have assembled did not save him from being hounded through the streets, until he dashed into a house for safety. It was Marius' residence. The ensuing scenario is ready-made for a modern novel. Marius offered his unexpected guest two choices: Sulla could leave his house, which meant taking his chance with the mob; or he could cease to observe the heavens and withdraw his obstruction to the passage of the bill through the assembly.[15]

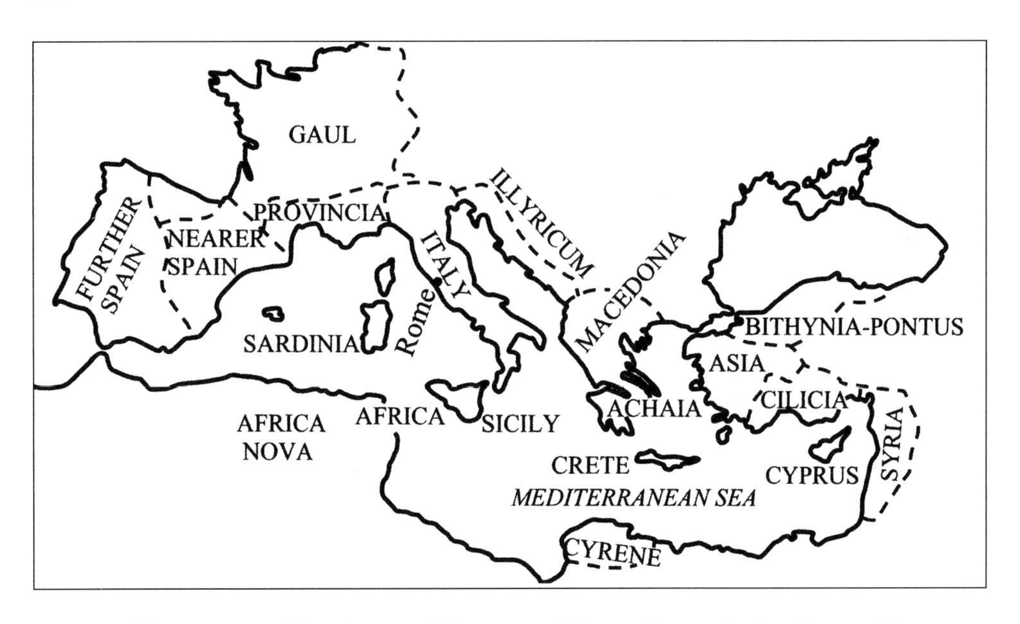

2 *Map of the Roman world at the time of Pompey and Caesar.* Drawn by Jan Shearsmith

Defeated by the machinations of Sulpicius and Marius, Sulla left the city and rounded up his old soldiers, pointing out to them that Marius, the new commander in the east, would probably recruit different troops, and so the opportunities for glory and booty would be given to other soldiers. Sulla asked them if they wanted him to lead them to victory in the east; they agreed, but first he would have to lead them to victory in Rome. When Marius' officers arrived to take charge of Sulla's men, they were stoned to death. With six legions, Sulla then set out on his infamous march on Rome, moving so fast that the Marians were unable to defend themselves or the city. Marius sailed to Africa, and the tribune Sulpicius was killed.[16]

Since he would be absent in Greece for some considerable time, Sulla was concerned to protect himself at home. He perhaps regarded Strabo and his army as a personal and political threat (Leach suggests that Sulla saw Strabo as a 'potent rival'), and he tried to counter the threat by having him recalled to Rome; but Strabo intrigued with Caius Herennius, one of the tribunes, who vetoed the proposal. Sulla's next move was to try to replace Strabo altogether, effectively making him redundant. Pompeius Rufus, Sulla's colleague in the consulship, was sent to take over Strabo's army. This was probably by decree of the Senate, though it is sometimes stated that Sulla himself sent Rufus to neutralise Strabo; at this stage, although his interests are clearly discernible behind the scheme, and he had armed force at his back, Sulla was not yet Dictator and would not have the power to make and carry out plans of that kind without at least the nominal consent of the Senate, even though he may have achieved it via coercion. Strabo did not protest or even react strongly when Rufus arrived to take charge of his army, a procedure that would convert him, a proven general now of consular rank, from independent proconsular commander answerable to the Senate, to a mere subordinate answerable to the new consul. Direct confrontation was not Strabo's way, especially since it would bring him into conflict with Sulla. Giving nothing away, Strabo had no doubt already reviewed the situation and made plans as soon as he heard that Rufus had been appointed to the command of his army. Perhaps only the most trusted members of his *consilium*, his group of intimate friends and advisers, were informed of his plans. Pompey himself was most likely taken into his father's confidence. Rufus must be removed, but it was essential that Strabo's hands should remain clean. The plan was simple. The morning after he had taken command, Rufus left his tent to conduct the sacrifices, and was murdered by the troops. Strabo had stood aside at the sacrifices because he was now in a subordinate position, and also no doubt so that he could be seen to be at a distance when the murder was committed. He went through the motions of extreme shock, horror, and anger, but immediately assumed command of the troops, seemingly unchallenged by either Sulla or the Senate.[17]

The assassination of a consul ought to have been an enormity, publicly decried and ruthlessly punished, but it was overshadowed by even more ghastly events in Rome itself. As soon as Sulla left for the war zone, Marius returned from exile. The consuls for 87 were C. Cornelius Cinna and Gnaeus Octavius. Trouble was inevitable, since the two mutually antagonistic consuls represented the factions of Marius and Sulla all over again, with Octavius prepared to uphold Sulla's principles and Cinna determined to undermine them. Octavius expelled Cinna, who returned in force with Marius himself. Strabo simply waited upon events. It was said that he negotiated with both sides, motivated of course by self-interest; no one imagined that this was an altruistic attempt to mediate between the two opposing parties. However Strabo clearly thought it important in this case not to act independently, but to wait until he was asked; it could have been a fit of pique because the Senate had been fully prepared to see him replaced, so now he wanted to be absolutely sure that he had the sanction of the Senate before he made a move. But by standing aloof, he incurred blame for the fact that Marius and his colleague Sertorius were granted time to recruit armies. There is an element of black comedy in the scenario of Strabo and Pompey watching from a distance, twiddling their thumbs until the inevitable happened and the Senate had to give in and ask for their help. This waiting game was something that Pompey developed to a fine art in his later career, always ensuring that there was a demand for his services before he took any overt action.[18]

It was probably at this juncture that the alleged plot to kill Strabo and Pompey was hatched, probably by Cinna, whose motives derived from his need for troops without the encumbrance of their commander. The story gains in the telling because it could be used as a vehicle for enhancing the reputation of the young Pompey, who emerges as the hero who saved the day, or rather the night. He was informed of the plot before he settled down for dinner with the assassin, his friend Lucius Terentius. He did not react at once, but feigning ignorance of the potential danger, he behaved normally, drank wine and conversed with Terentius and his friends, and pretended to retire to bed. Then he put a guard on his father's tent, and rigged his own sleeping quarters to watch and wait, arranging the bed to look as though it was occupied. Perhaps he wanted to be sure that the rumour was true, not wanting to accuse Terentius before he had proof of his guilt. As Strabo's son, it is probable that he had learned even at this early age not to trust anyone, but the knowledge that someone who professed to be his friend could even contemplate assassinating him was no doubt a bitter experience. He was only 19 years old, and had not yet embarked on an independent career; yet he was experiencing the sort of isolation that was the lot of princes and kings. It was a busy night. Terentius was overpowered as soon as he entered Pompey's quarters, but then there was a riot, which ended when Pompey toured the camp to persuade the men to remain loyal. Finally he lay down in front of the camp gateway so that anyone who left would have to trample over him first. Dramatic stuff, which may even be true. Plutarch says that the men loved Pompey as much as they feared his father. Only about 800 men deserted to Cinna; the rest waited for Strabo to act. Seager points out the apparent anomaly that just a short time before, the soldiers who now threatened to desert had permanently removed the consul Quintus Pompeius Rufus from command of the army on Strabo's behalf; but this is to imbue the collective mass with a unity of purpose and a consistency of opinion that is not generally present in human affairs. Only a small number of trusted men would be required to murder the consul, and likewise Cinna would require only a small number of infiltrators to attempt to stir up a mutiny. These groups could have been mutually exclusive, so there is probably no need to look for a massive change of heart among Strabo's men.[19]

By the time Strabo decided to take action, the situation was dire. Marius attacked Ostia, the port of Rome at the Tiber mouth, his ally Sertorius had also gathered an army, and Cinna marched on Rome. Strabo was summoned. He mobilised first against Sertorius, and came to Rome to help Octavius beat off Cinna, in a dreadful battle outside the Colline Gate. But Rome was still not safe nor saved; Marius persuaded a guard on the Janiculum hill to open the gates, and his troops and then Cinna's entered the city. The consul Octavius was within an ace of defeat, but Strabo arrived with part of his army and drove the Marians out.[20]

But the Marian victory could not be put off for ever, especially as there was no further military action to keep Marius and Cinna out of Rome and strengthen opposition to them. Strabo stands accused of trying to negotiate with Cinna while also co-operating with Octavius, thus preventing continuation of the war without gaining any advantage. If he imagined that he could somehow weld the two sides together and emerge supreme, having saved the state and avoided bloodshed, he was not given the opportunity to put his plans to the test.[21]

A plague broke out after the battles, and Strabo succumbed to it. The epidemic was probably caused by bad hygiene and crowded conditions, but there was a rumour that Strabo had been struck by lightning, dismissed by some modern authorities as a garbled rumour, perhaps started after lightning struck his tent. Three days before Strabo died, Caius Cassius took over command of his troops, ostensibly to keep order until Strabo recovered. But a battle-hardened, experienced army was obviously a valuable asset in these troubled times, and could also be potentially dangerous; on both counts it must be brought under the control of Cinna's party before the soldiers could be attracted to someone else's banner by the promise of money and rich rewards.[22]

Strabo was not granted a peaceful funeral by a grateful people. His body was dragged through the streets on a hook by the mob, until order was restored by the tribunes. Ancient sources agree that Strabo was universally hated, because of his avarice, and because he was greatly feared, and also perhaps as a result of his ambivalent attitude and his delay in taking action to save Rome. This last conjecture is probably a retrospective judgement, a product of inimical propaganda after the event, since in effect such a demonstration on this score would be tantamount to an open criticism of the new regime of Marius and Cinna, at a time when the two of them were settling old scores and hunting down adversaries. Any speculation as to what Strabo may have planned is redundant, but some authorities consider that he was aiming for a second consulship and was prepared to go to any lengths to reach it, joining no party or faction but attempting to play off one against the other. As a result neither Marius nor Cinna, nor the Senate trusted him, and he was not an ardent supporter of Sulla; self-interest was presumably his driving force.[23]

After his father's death, Pompey entered upon a difficult phase in his life. Cinna's men ransacked his house in Rome. He escaped the absolute carnage of Marius' proscriptions, either because of his youth and relative lack of importance, or possibly because Marius died soon after his return to Rome, and did not have a chance to add Pompey's name to the lists. More importantly, no one else added his name either, though it was a common practice to do so, in the expectation of taking over the property of the proscribed. Pompey escaped with his life, but not entirely without harrassment; he was prosecuted for extortion, accused of having illegal possession of some of the booty from Asculum. Fortunately he found new allies to defend him. These were the censor Lucius Marcius Philippus, and the orator Quintus Hortensius, later to be the great rival of Marcus Tullius Cicero in the law courts. Another politician who spoke for Pompey was Gnaeus Papirius Carbo, who was to be consul with Cinna in 85 and, within a short time after that, Pompey's adversary and finally victim. The young Pompey may not have enjoyed the support of a huge *clientela* in Rome, but he certainly had high-powered friends as he faced prosecution, even though it could be considered that each of his defendants might have been acting purely out of self-interest to advance their own careers. But Pompey's innate charm, and his youthful good looks that reminded people of Alexander the Great, coupled with real ability to also play a part in his defence. Antistius, the president of the court, was sympathetic, allegedly impressed with the way in which Pompey ably defended himself. One of Strabo's freedmen was found guilty of stealing some of the booty from Asculum; modern opinion differs as to whether he was really guilty, or whether there was some machination on Pompey's part to shift the blame. Ultimately it depends on perception of Pompey's character as an innocent and honest youth, or alternatively a scheming brat, a worthy successor to the avaricious Strabo. Before the trial came to an end, Pompey was already betrothed to Antistius' daughter, and though it was supposed to be a secret, when he was finally acquitted the crowd of spectators began to sing wedding songs. The marriage took place some time later.[24]

After the trial, nothing is known of Pompey for nearly three years. He would need to rebuild or repair his house, attend to his estates in Picenum, gather a following if he could, and amass wealth. Perhaps the political scene was not conducive to the regular career path via junior magistracies through the posts of quaestor and praetor, but whatever his reasons may have been, Pompey seemingly did not even think of pursuing that line of personal advancement. The city and the wider Roman world were dominated by Cinna, who held the consulship every year from 86 to 84, with Papirius Carbo as his colleague for the last two years. Pompey was indelibly dyed with the colours of Strabo, which did not make him a natural ally of the party of Marius and Cinna, so he presumably chose to keep a low profile, act circumspectly and wait for better times. There are signs that he had perhaps tried to join Cinna in an uneasy alliance by about 84, but there is a strange and probably garbled story, current in that year, that he feared for his life and left Rome for some time, possibly to his estates in Picenum. His disappearance gave rise to the rumour that Cinna had done away with him, and the soldiers in Cinna's army supposedly rioted because they thought that Pompey had been murdered. Once again this may be retrospective inflation of his importance. He was in his early twenties, held no specific posts or political office, commanded no troops, and headed no faction. He could not be a serious rival to Cinna, and as has been pointed out, there was no reason why Cinna's troops should care about him, dead or alive. Nor is there any mileage in the theory that when Cinna was killed in 84, Pompey was somehow implicated in his death. At that moment, he was not in any position to gain anything.[25]

Papirius Carbo remained in office as sole consul after the death of his colleague, but his star was waning. Sulla's was growing ever brighter. His victories against Mithridates, and his seeming invincibility against armies sent by Cinna to wipe him out far away from Rome, spread fear in the city. Soldiers were no longer willing to go and fight Sulla, especially since they would possibly have to fight Mithridates as well; the last troops that were sent to Greece never completed their journey, battered by storms at sea in which many lost their lives. The survivors returned to Italy in no mood to hear a speech by Cinna about discipline and the interests of the state; they killed him, and went home. Carbo did not attempt to raise another army to fight Sulla in Greece, but concentrated upon preparing to meet him in Italy. For Sulla was ready to come home; it was known in the first months of 83 that he had left Athens and was about to embark for Italy. The only reality in Roman life for the forseeable future was going to revolve around Sulla, and the 23-year-old Pompey quietly made a decision that was to shape the rest of his life. He gathered his friends and started to recruit troops in Picenum.[26]

When he began to raise troops he had no idea whether he would be annihilated before Sulla arrived in Italy, or whether Sulla himself might be defeated, and having declared for him so firmly it was doubtful that he would survive whatever regime arose after Sulla was gone. It was a gamble, but Pompey was not alone in taking it; Metellus Pius and Marcus Licinius Crassus were both recruiting from among their clients with the intention of bringing their armies to fight for Sulla. But Pompey was certainly the youngest and the least well-connected of the three. He started out at Auximum, with nothing but his own resources with which to pay and equip his troops. There was at first fierce competition from recruiting agents sent by Carbo to round up men for his own armies; but Pompey was more popular, and within a short time he was also the stronger. He was able to send Carbo's men packing, leaving the field clear for his own recruiting purposes. From Auximum he progressed to other towns, until he commanded about 6000 men, or roughly one legion. This modest beginning is perhaps more credible than Plutarch's account, in which it is suggested that Pompey raised three legions all at once. Certainly by the time he finished the campaign his army had grown to three legions, but this might have been a gradual process as his successes were reported, and as a consequence his reputation spread far and wide.[27]

It may have been during his first recruiting drive that Titus Labienus, Aulus Gabinius, and Lucius Afranius joined him. He appointed officers to command his troops, and these men, all from his home area of Picenum, were probably the among first to be offered posts in his army. They all enjoyed or endured a long association with him. Labienus became a trusted and capable officer of Caesar's army in Gaul, but returned to Pompey when the civil war broke out, to change from a somewhat ruthless but efficient officer to a downright bloodthirsty opponent of Caesar. Aulus Gabinius mounted an expedition to Egypt to restore Ptolemy Auletes to the throne, and later he was instrumental in gaining for Pompey the eastern command that sealed his reputation as the foremost general of the day. Gabinius became consul in 58, but ultimately gained little reward from Pompey for his services, being prosecuted and condemned for extortion whilst governor of Syria, even though Pompey hired Marcus Tullius Cicero to defend him. Lucius Afranius was with Pompey until the end. He was defeated by Caesar whilst holding Spain for Pompey during the civil war. He was allowed to go to join Pompey in Greece, and survived the battle of Pharsalus, but was captured and executed after Thapsus. Another Picentine who was older than these men was Marcus Petreius, who was already a soldier before the Social War. He may have been one of the officers in Strabo's army, though he is not named on the inscription listing the members of the general's *consilium*.[28]

When he was ready Pompey set out with his small army, moving not particularly hastily southwards to meet Sulla, who had landed at Brundisium and was marching to Rome, astonishingly unopposed for some considerable distance. Before he could join up with Sulla, Pompey had to fight the armies that Carbo sent against him, no less than three of them under three different generals. Before the three armies united, Pompey attacked the nearest one, taking an energetic part in the fighting. Carbo had recruited Celtic cavalry, and it was against these troops that Pompey launched an attack, leading it himself, and killing the commander. The three generals seem to have been dismayed by Pompey's early and rapid success, and could not agree on what to do next, thus losing the opportunity to act together and converge on him. Thus Pompey escaped defeat, but the presence of Carbo's troops delayed his march southwards, so that he remained in the north to consolidate his position.[29]

Sulla was finally blocked on his march towards Rome by two armies, one at the river Volturnus and the other near the town of Teanum. It was the first time that the

Marian troops had encountered Sulla and his experienced soldiers, and they failed to unite to meet him. Having carved his way relatively easily through the army attempting to hold the river line, Sulla moved on to Teanum, where he won hands down by a calculated ruse rather than by bloody fighting. The enemy were already disillusioned. They had seen how easily Sulla defeated the army on the Volturnus, and were not eager to fight. After a short armistice, while his men infiltrated the enemy ranks and spread more fear and discontent, Sulla pretended that the Marians had infringed the terms of the agreement, and drew up his army in battle order. But there was no battle. The enemy came over to him *en masse*.[30]

There remained vast tracts of Italy still loyal to the Marian cause, except around Picenum where Pompey was operating. It is not certain when Sulla heard of Pompey's successes against three different armies, but as soon as he could he marched to meet him. Plutarch reports the occasion. Pompey brought up his victorious troops, all well-equipped and looking splendid, and hailed Sulla very properly as Imperator, an honorary title bestowed on victorious generals by their soldiers, a name that would be absorbed into the titulature of the Emperors as part of the infrastructure of their power. It was not a word to be idly used, and it carried wide-ranging connotations; it therefore meant a great deal when Sulla dismounted, approached Pompey on foot, and returned the compliment by also hailing the young man as Imperator. He would have been fully aware of what he was doing, and once uttered for the benefit of Pompey's army, he could hardly retract the title. For Pompey it will have been a superb moment, one to savour until he topped it by other successes. His gamble had paid off superbly. Sulla approved and rewarded him, and the faith that his troops already had in him could only be enhanced when the soldiers saw how the great general favoured his young protégé. According to Plutarch, whenever Pompey approached, Sulla would rise and remove his headcovering as a mark of respect. He did this for only a few select people, so everyone in Sulla's immediate circle would be aware that Pompey was highly regarded and destined for greater things.[31]

At this point, when Sulla marched north to meet the little army that Pompey had raised, it was not at all certain that there would be an ultimate victory. The war in Italy had still to be won. Rome itself was not prepared to welcome Sulla, and most people acquiesced when Papirius Carbo and the young Marius, son of the dead general, were elected consuls for 82. One of their first acts was to declare *hostes*, enemies of the people of Rome, all those senators who had joined Sulla. Technically it meant that these men were now outlaws, to be denied fire, water, or shelter, and their property was confiscated. It was intended, probably successfully, to deter anyone else from declaring for Sulla.[32]

The two hostile forces moved in scattered groups around Italy. One of the Marian armies under Carbo faced Sulla's general Metellus Pius in the north of Italy, while another under the young Marius faced Sulla in Latium, in an effort to prevent him from reaching Rome. Pompey had joined Metellus Pius as a subordinate officer, alongside Marcus Licinius Crassus. There may be an element of truth in the story that Pompey dissuaded Sulla from appointing him as commander of the whole

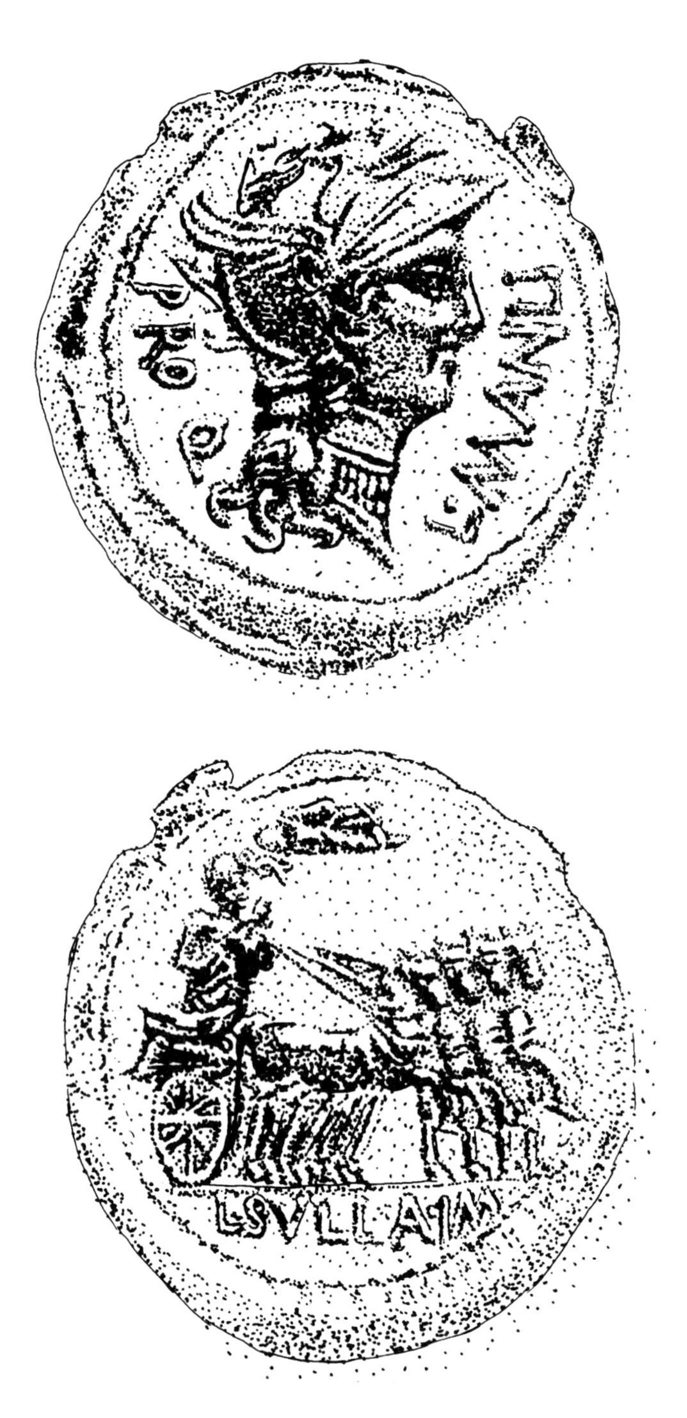

3 *Gold aureus, depicting on the obverse the head of Roma, or Rome personified, and a four horse chariot (*quadriga*) on the reverse. This coin was issued in 82, and the chariot relates to Sulla's triumph.*
Drawn by Jacqui Taylor

northern army, because Metellus Pius was of consular rank and therefore the most senior officer. Pompey wrote to Metellus, offering his services, thus avoiding ill feeling and also gaining in stature by his correct actions. It cost him nothing, not loss of face nor even loss of power, since he was not really relinquishing command of his soldiers. He still conducted military operations independently, chasing Carbo's army into Ariminum (modern Rimini), and defeating one of Carbo's legates, Gaius Marcius, at Sena Gallica. Sometime later, Pompey and Crassus defeated another legate, Carrinas, near the town of Spoletium, but although they killed many of Carrinas' men they failed to capture the legate himself, who slipped away at the dead of night. The same thing happened again when Pompey faced Gaius Marcius for the second time. Marcius commanded a much larger army at this encounter, but Pompey trapped him in a defile and then encircled him on the hill where his troops retreated. It ought to have been an easy victory, but Pompey was perhaps overconfident and did not prime his guards properly, since Marcius and his men left their camp fires burning while they evaded Pompey's lookouts and escaped. Instead of a battle next morning there was only disappointment, and perhaps not a little private rage; it was the oldest trick of all.[33]

The civil war between the Marians and Sulla began to spread out into the rest of the Roman world. One of the generals who had espoused the Marian cause, Quintus Sertorius, had begun to despair of success, and decamped to Spain, where he was eventually joined by others of like persuasion. He was an able administrator and a brilliant general, and was able to survive for many years without completely alienating the natives or being defeated by any of the armies sent against him, thus prolonging the war for at least another decade. Nearer to Rome, the civil war began to affect the tribes of Italy. The Samnites, a fierce and intransigent people, had refused to disarm after the Social War, and as a consequence their leaders had been executed by Sulla. They were therefore intent on revenge against him, and so declared for and marched to the aid of young Marius when Sulla ran him into Praeneste and besieged him there. It ought to have signalled defeat for Sulla, or at least forced him to raise the siege, but the approach to Praeneste was through a narrow pass, of which Sulla immediately gained control by placing men on the heights on either side of it. In several battles he prevented the Samnites from approaching the city, and also beat off attempts by Marius to break out.[34]

With Sulla tied down at Praeneste, Carbo chose this moment to attack Metellus in the north; but he abandoned the project when he discovered that the Gauls of northern Italy had joined Metellus. Finding the odds too great now that Metellus had been reinforced, and despairing of ever dislodging Sulla, Carbo gave up and fled to Africa, abandoning his soldiers, who were still willing to fight for him and indeed carried on doing so until Pompey defeated them. There were now two potential wars to which Sulla would have to turn his attention once the fighting in Italy was over, one with Sertorius in Spain and another with Carbo in Africa, where there were many veterans who had fought against Jugurtha under Marius himself. These men would no doubt rally to Carbo and provide him with another army. But before Sulla could attend to anything, there was a much more pressing problem nearer to home. The Samnites had diverted the focus of their attack, with an agenda now enlarged from revenge on Sulla to annihilation of what he stood for, namely Rome herself. They already had a head start, and Sulla was forced to race after them. He left Pompey in the north, and took Crassus and his men with him in a desperate march, engaging battle as soon as he arrived outside the city. He placed Crassus in command of the right wing, taking the left for himself, fighting immediately outside the Colline gate. His troops were tired and were steadily overrun. They were forced back towards the city, with the Samnites so close behind them that the enemy almost managed to force their way in, before the gates were closed in their faces. It seemed that all was lost. The Samnites were probably ready to besiege Rome, and Sulla was cut off from the northern troops. He had only a depleted army to defend the city, and he was not especially welcome there; his enemies inside Rome might ally with his enemies outside the city, and bring about his downfall.[35]

He had no idea what had happened to Crassus. During the battle it had been impossible to keep in touch with the right wing, and so he probably assumed that Crassus had been defeated, possibly even killed. In the evening some of Crassus' men arrived, not with dire news but a request for supplies for the men's dinner. Crassus had driven the enemy off and routed them, and maybe was not aware that Sulla had so nearly met with disaster. He had saved the day, and perhaps Sulla rewarded him with the same praise that he bestowed on Pompey; but he did not give him independent commands or promote him as he had Pompey, and there, perhaps, the seeds were sown of the famous rivalry between the two men.[37]

Pompey had been just as successful fighting against the abandoned army of Carbo, which he encountered and defeated near Clusium. The ones who escaped simply deserted; there was no army left. The soldiers and civilians of Praeneste now had no hope of any relief from an outside source, so they surrendered. The young Marius committed suicide, and his head was sent to Rome; Sulla watched while it was raised up on a spike, quoting bitterly from Aristophanes: 'First learn to row before you take the helm'. Marius was only in his twenties, yet he had been elected consul, flouting all custom. Sulla disapproved, and would pass laws to prevent such an occurrence. As Greenhalgh points out, Pompey was even younger than Marius – but then he was merely the leader of a privately-raised and very successful army. He had not yet committed the unforgivable sin of seeking the highest office, so Sulla could condone the actions of his favourite, while condemning those of his enemy.[37]

2 *Adulescentulus carnifex*

Pompey's career might have been stopped in its tracks or at least stunted if Sulla had not actively promoted him. Sulla could perhaps have achieved all that he desired without Pompey's military contribution, and the young general had no political weight on his own account. He could have been quietly dropped at this point, with the repeated vague promise, never quite honoured, of further commands. But instead Sulla chose to bind Pompey to himself even more firmly by marriage ties, offering him his step-daughter Aemilia as his wife. Her mother was Metella, whose previous husband, before she married Sulla, was Marcus Aemilius Scaurus. Thus Aemilia was the daughter of a consul and the step-daughter of the most important and influential man in Rome, and through her mother she was connected to the powerful family of the Metelli: it was a good match for Pompey. The fact that Aemilia was already married to Marcius Acilius Glabrio, and was several months pregnant, was brushed aside. A divorce was speedily arranged, facilitated by the fact that it was Sulla who authorised it and simplified because there would be no problems over the true fatherhood of the child that Aemilia was carrying. Octavian married Livia in the same circumstances several years later, when she was already pregnant with Tiberius.[1]

Pompey has been criticised for divorcing his first wife Antistia. The contrast with the young Caesar, who steadfastly refused to divorce his wife and to comply with Sulla's wishes, will not have been especially marked at the time, but it was no doubt elaborated upon by later historians who wished to tarnish Pompey's reputation and enhance Caesar's. Antistia's case is particularly poignant, since as far as is known she had hardly given Pompey cause for complaint, and she had been recently orphaned: her father had been killed in a riot for his suspected Sullan sympathies, and her mother had committed suicide when she saw her husband's body floating down the Tiber. Perhaps the marriage to Antistia had never been anything more than a political convenience, which was now outmoded and overshadowed by more tempting alliances. There had been no children born of the marriage, and when Pompey was not fighting battles, his amorous attentions were lavished on the courtesan Flora, and there is no reason to suppose that his association with this lady ceased as soon as he married Aemilia. It was a firm proclamation of his alliance to the house of Sulla and to the Metelli, not a love match. He probably did not feel overwhelmed with emotion when the marriage ended only a few months later; Aemilia miscarried and died.[2]

Pompey probably hardly noticed her absence. The political developments in Rome were intense and unprecedented. After the civil wars in Italy and the turmoil in the city, there was much damage to be repaired, starting with the establishment of a firm and longer-lasting government. This was Sulla's main aim. He knew how to provide the stability that Rome needed, but his problem was how to gain the requisite power and hold on to it, with some semblance of legality. Though he had the influence, backed by armed force, to secure repeated election to the consulship, and perhaps to secure also the election of compatible colleagues, he decided against this method. That was what Cinna had done, so the tactic was to be avoided. Besides, Sulla had no intention of seeking an office that expired after one year; if he failed to be elected again, his opponents could seize the opportunity to eradicate all that he had achieved so far. Sulla needed supreme power for an indefinite period; and in this he found himself in diametric opposition to the unwritten Roman constitution. Since the time of the kings the Roman government had actively shunned the awful concept of supreme power in the hands of one man.[3]

Since the two legally appointed consuls were both dead, the normal procedure in such a circumstance was to appoint an *interrex* who would then in turn appoint two suffect consuls to take the place of the deceased for the remaining term of their office. The Senate chose its leading member, Lucius Valerius Flaccus, to fill the post of *interrex*, but he was not afforded the chance of selecting suffect consuls. Instead Sulla proposed a Dictatorship, but one that departed on several counts from the normal variety, which strictly speaking had gone out of use after 202 BC. The original Dictatorship was intended to be an office with supreme power, but of short term tenure, reserved for great emergencies or specific tasks, usually embraced under a generic heading *rei gerendae caussa*, meaning in loose translation 'to direct affairs'. Once the danger or emergency was resolved, the office was then formally laid down so that normal government could be restored. Sulla needed more than the consulship, more even than the strictly conventional Dictatorship offered; so the people of Rome were brought into play, ironically for the last time as far as Sulla was concerned, because he intended to abolish such procedures in the future. Valerius Flaccus presented a bill to the popular assembly to make Sulla *Dictator rei publicae constituendae* or Dictator to reconstitute the Republic. It was a turn of phrase that Antony, Octavian, and Lepidus reused several years later, in their titulature as *Triumviri rei publicae constituendae*, when they too were empowered to repair the government that had been torn apart by civil war. Sulla set the precedent, but his power was potentially greater than the so-called Triumvirs (which is a modern term, not an ancient one), whose power was supposedly limited to five years. Sulla's had no temporal or political limits. Whilst the *lex Valeria* did not specifically engender the proscriptions, which were authorised by Sulla's own legislation under a *lex Cornelia*, it was the start of a legalised tyranny.[4]

One of the new Dictator's first concerns was to rid himself of past, present, and potential enemies. Though he originally proscribed only 80 men, the total of those killed in the proscriptions continued to rise to many times that number as men added names to the lists for various reasons, including pure and simple greed for control of the estates of the proscribed men. It was a free-for-all and a time to settle old scores. Sulla looked on with indifference, doing nothing to prevent anyone from adding new names to the proscription lists, and notoriously selling the property of the victims at ludicrously cheap prices to his friends.[5]

4 *Coin of Sulla, dating to 81. The head of Roma is shown on the obverse, and an equestrian statue of Sulla appears of the reverse. The legend reads L. SULLA FELI. DIC. referring to the Dictatorship of Sulla with the name Felix, which he adopted after his triumph.* Drawn by Jacqui Taylor

The political programme that Sulla set in motion was probably already worked out in broad general detail before he even became Dictator, for it was driven by the many problems that the state had encountered. From Sulla's point of view the Senate had to be augmented and strengthened so that it could govern the city and the growing Empire of Rome. The way in which he addressed this problem is known in outline, but not in detail, and the chronology of his various measures is not established. He is primarily remembered for his attack on the tribunate, which has perhaps assumed a disproportionate importance in later years, in comparison with his other legislation. The problems with the tribunate were bound up with the other main areas of contention. The original brief of the tribunes, in the historical past, was to save the plebeians from oppression by the magistrates, and this function was not altered by Sulla. In the later years of the Republic the tribunes had become inextricably associated with the great generals of the day, firstly in seeking prestigious military commands for certain generals, by taking bills direct to the popular assembly, and secondly in attempting to force through more legislation to allocate lands to the returning veterans when the generals came home. It ought to have been the Senate that chose generals for specific campaigns, and the Senate which ratified the post-war administrative arrangements and saw to the settlement of veterans; but since the track record of this august body had been woefully inadequate, especially with regard to the second of these considerations, the generals themselves had been led to enter the political arena in order to provide for their men, and they allied themselves with the tribunes in order to achieve their ends. The solution to this particular problem would have been to set up a pension scheme for the soldiers, as Augustus managed to do much later; but this was vastly expensive, and the Romans always seemed to expect defence at cheap rates. Instead of tackling this issue directly by improving the provision for veterans, thus removing the need for alliances between tribunes and generals, Sulla strangled the tribunate, by removing from the tribunes the right to initiate legislation without the approval of the Senate, and by ruling that anyone who became tribune was barred from holding any further office. No ambitious young man or aspiring politician would be able to launch himself into politics by this route; the office would be filled by nonentities. Sulla also pre-empted any attempt to establish a permanent body of tribunes, which would have enabled the interested generals to recruit suitable men who were not interested in political advancement to make a career out of occupying the tribunate and nothing else. Sulla decreed that there must be ten years between each tenure of the tribunate, so no one could choose that path as a career, to become the mouthpiece of any keen military men.[6]

There is uncertainty about Sulla's legislation against the use of the tribunician veto, and whether it was abolished altogether, or merely curtailed, although the mechanism by which this may have been brought about is not known. As a political tool, the veto was just as useful to the Senate, or at least it was as much an arm of the aristocracy within the Senate, as it was to the populace, and if Sulla did in fact abolish this primary tribunician right, his motives will have embraced the desire to curb the use of it by individual senators to achieve their own ends or obstruct the aims of others. In the end, the controversy over the abolition or otherwise of the veto and the general crippling of the tribunate is largely academic, because while the intent of the Sullan legislation was far-reaching and radical, and of obvious importance to Sulla himself, the effects were so short-lived that it hardly matters what the details were. As soon as Sulla was dead various politicians started to unravel his work, so that there was very little left to do by the time Pompey and Crassus, as consuls in 70, fully restored the tribunate.[7]

With regard to the Senate, Sulla worked to strengthen it, and to return control of the Roman world to the aristocracy. One of his most important contributions was his restoration of the control of the jury courts to the senators. This had been a contentious issue ever since the time of Gaius Sempronius Gracchus, who reformed the standing jury court to try cases of extortion (*quaestio de repetundis*). The provinces ruled by Rome were too often regarded as a means of increasing personal wealth, and the court had been established in 149 with a view to allowing the provincials some redress at Rome for the wrongs done to them by grasping governors and their staffs. The jury panels were drawn exclusively from senators, but since the men who came before this court were also senators, convictions were made only rarely and reluctantly. Gracchus handed over membership of the jury panels to equites; but since they were just as interested, if not more so, in making profit from the government of the provinces, their bias led to the conviction of clearly innocent governors who had curbed the extortionate practices of the tax-gatherers and businessmen. Sulla removed the equites from the juries and reinstated senators; but since he had elevated some equites to the Senate, there would be a supply of ex-equestrians with experience of the courts who would still be eligible to serve on the juries.[8]

Sulla's policies were not wholly detrimental to the equites. There was always a number of them who were quite content to remain in equestrian circles, pursuing their business interests that would have been forbidden to them if they had become senators; but for those who wished to enter the political life of Rome, entry to the Senate was essential. By his elevation of certain equites to the rank of senators, Sulla gratified their ambitions and at the same time doubled the size of the Senate. In order to provide more junior administrative personnel, he increased the number of quaestors from about 10 (the original quota is not established beyond doubt) to 20 – this number is not in doubt, since an inscription found in Rome in the 16th century attests to the *lex Cornelia de XX quaestoribus*. In the past, election to this junior post did not carry with it guaranteed entry to the Senate. Sulla ruled that all the young men elected as quaestors should automatically become senators, thereby promoting the sustained growth of the Senate, and converting it eventually to an elected body, rather than an appointed body. In line with the increase in the number of quaestors, Sulla also increased the number of praetors to eight per annum, significantly providing, with the two consuls, ten ex-magistrates every year who could then govern the provinces of Rome. It is suggested that he tried to limit the term of office as provincial governor to one year, and the provision of a larger pool of magistrates was made in part to facilitate the rapid turnover of governors; but this suggested limitation on the duration of office is not fully attested or properly elucidated, and would have been impractical in times of war, when the selection of the right candidate and continuity of command were of prime importance.[9]

Having provided for the continued recruitment of senators, Sulla abolished the censorship. The post of censor was normally instituted every five years or thereabouts. Two senior officials with long experience were chosen to take the census of citizens and allocate them to their classes, which were defined by wealth. One of the major functions of the censors was the revision of the membership of the Senate, which entailed adlection of some men into the ranks and the ejection of others who had proved unsuitable. Sulla had provided for the first of these censorial functions by the election of 20 quaestors every year, but he could not directly provide for the second. Without the censors to exercise some control over senatorial conduct, Sulla laid down a rigid pattern for career development, stipulating that there should be several years between tenure of each office on the long road to the consulship, with the intended result that no one would be able to take up the reins of state until at least the age of 42. Few in Rome could be in any doubt that he meant what he said, and that he would brook no opposition to his rule. Sulla's reaction was extreme when he learned that Quintus Lucretius Ofella (some sources prefer the name Afella), one of his own officers who had done him good service in the civil wars, intended to stand as candidate for the consulship without having held any of the previous offices, and without having reached the correct age. At first, Sulla asked him nicely to withdraw his candidacy. After a short interval, when it became clear that Ofella would do no such thing, Sulla had him assassinated in the Forum. Perhaps when Pompey heard of this, he began to ponder about his own future. He was only in his twenties and could not hope to advance in the Sullan political arena for many years, two decades at least if he were to follow the prescribed path to the consulship. He needed special dispensation to rise any further, and it seemed that it would not be forthcoming from Sulla, unless there were special tasks requiring his particular talents; in those cases he could glide through the legal entanglements and put off any worries about his future until he had completed the tasks in hand.[10]

He was assured of employment at least for the time being, because there were wars to be fought against Marian sympathisers who had fled to Spain, Africa and Sicily. The governor of Sicily, Perperna, was a declared Marian. If it was Sulla's intention to limit provincial governors to one year of office and exercise tight control over his generals, then he was forced to make exceptions from the beginning. He sent Pompey to root out opposition in Sicily. Until this moment, Pompey had held no official post. He was too young to have been elected to any magistracy, and though he had commanded armies since he was 23 years old, he had never been legally appointed by the Senate. With Sulla now in control of Rome and intent on ironing out all anomalies of this sort, Pompey's position must be rationalised and legalised. As the treatment of Ofella had shown, for everyone else except Pompey there would be strict rules about the progression through the junior and senior administrative and military posts. In Pompey's case a legal fiction allowed him to take command of the expedition to Sicily. He had not served as praetor, and so could not legally progress from that office to a propraetorship; but with Sulla at their backs the senators dutifully bestowed propraetorian powers on Pompey. This meant that he would be equal in rank to Perperna.[11]

Pompey's military reputation went before him; Perperna did not stay to fight it out in Sicily. He turned up later as an adherent of Marcus Aemilius Lepidus, the consul of 78 who followed Sulla's example and marched on Rome. When Lepidus was defeated and the cause was lost Perperna took the troops who remained loyal and went to join Sertorius in Spain, where he faced Pompey again. As Pompey took possession of Sicily, Papirius Carbo, who had only just arrived there from Africa, also turned tail because he was not ready for a battle. He did not return to Africa, however; instead he lurked on the island of Cossyra (modern Pantellaria), achieving very little. First one of his senior officers was captured while on a scouting mission, and committed suicide, and then in an unrecorded encounter Pompey's squadrons found Carbo himself. He was brought to Pompey in chains and executed. It would have been far better for him if he had been killed in battle or had committed suicide, but instead his death was a sordid affair. He broke down and wept, and had to ask permission to relieve himself before the swordsman could do his work.[12]

Pompey earned his reputation as the boy butcher from this episode. Carbo had been one of his defenders at his trial for expropriation of goods from the siege of Asculum, and for his past services to the young man he perhaps hoped for mercy. According to Plutarch, Carbo was on the list of proscribed men whom Sulla wanted killed, which would hardly be surprising, but this is seen by some modern authors merely as an apology for Pompey's behaviour in having him summarily executed. Another claim is that Carbo was still consul when he died, but this is disputed, and on the whole seems unlikely. The date of his death is not established, but it is probable that whenever it occurred, his consulship would already have been annulled.[13]

There was no other end for Carbo except death. Even if Pompey had relented and sent him as a prisoner to Sulla, so that his own hands remained free of his blood, it is hardly likely that Sulla would have spared his enemy. He was implacable, and had shown no mercy to the captured Samnites after the desperate battle outside Rome; 6000 of them were killed in the Circus Maximus while Sulla calmly addressed the Senate, assembled in the Temple of Bellona, close enough for the screams of the victims to be clearly heard. Pompey's reputation for cruelty was an inevitable consequence of his acceptance of his command against the enemies of Sulla.[14]

The young Pompey does not compare well with Caesar and his famous *clementia*, and Caesar's later propaganda was eager to demonstrate and exaggerate this difference. Pompey's apologists fall back on counter arguments, highlighting his merciful actions. Plutarch says that he turned a blind eye and let many people escape unharmed from Sicily, especially the lesser known men. In dealing with one of the chief citizens of Himera, a man called Sthenius, Pompey was especially lenient. He had orders to punish the city because the inhabitants had supported the Marians, but Sthenius argued that the whole population should not suffer on account of the one person who was to blame for the current situation, namely himself . Pompey heard him out, and since he was impressed by this disarming attempt at self-sacrifice, he pardoned the city and Sthenius too, thereby earning long-lasting support from the people and in particular from Sthenius. Cicero endorses the story, and provides evidence that the association with Sthenius endured.[15]

With Carbo eliminated and Sicily pacified and brought into the Sullan fold, it was now decided to send Pompey to Africa to eradicate the Marians who had taken refuge there. Once again the appointment was legalised by a senatorial decree. Pompey appointed his brother-in-law Memmius to command in Sicily, and set sail as soon as he could. In Africa, the anti-Sullan Domitius Ahenobarbus had made himself governor after the death of the previous incumbent, whose harsh government had ended in a riot at Utica, in which he was burned to death. Domitius was not an officially-appointed representative of the Senate and People of Rome. Like Sertorius in Spain he had raised an army, and had made an alliance with a neighbouring tribe, in this case Hiarbas, king of the Numidians. The Roman world offered considerable opportunity for renegade refugees, who followed the same pattern in later civil wars; for instance after the murder of Caesar, the assassins Brutus and Cassius seized much of the east, taking over provinces and armies in readiness for the coming battle against Octavian and Antony. It demonstrated the ease with which troops could be persuaded or bought, and would readily fight for one man rather than for the abstract idea of Rome. A charismatic leader with a cause needed only the promise of rewards to rally an army. The phenomenon that Tacitus called the secret of Empire was already well known in Pompey's day, and it was Sulla who had shown the way.[16]

Domitius Ahenobarbus was in a strong position, and perhaps seemed stronger to Pompey, who did not underestimate the difficulties of invading Africa. Opposition might be fierce, so to increase his chances of gaining a foothold he split his forces into two groups, and landed at Utica and Carthage. Probably to his surprise there was no one to meet him with hostile intent, only a crowd of deserters coming to join him, 7000 in all, more than an entire legion. The terrain in Africa could assist defenders and hinder invaders, and Domitius made full use of it. According to Plutarch, Pompey outnumbered him, so the desertion of 7000 men must have tipped the balance; no doubt Domitius felt nervous of committing himself to battle except in the best of circumstances, in case more soldiers lost faith in his ability to defeat Pompey. For the first few days after the landings, Domitius was granted a short respite, and entrenched himself behind some rough ground until Pompey was prepared. The reason why he was not ready for this period was not due to lack of planning on his part, or in fact anything that he could have foreseen. One of his soldiers fortuitously dug up a pile of coins, and so the troops spent all their time and energy in digging lots of holes, with an enthusiasm in inverse proportion to their disinclination if they had been on latrine duty, in an intense search for what they imagined must be the rest of the treasure. All generals need to be at least amateur psychologists, and in the same circumstances most of them would probably have dealt with the situation just as Pompey did, by doing precisely nothing. No amount of harsh orders would have made the soldiers move on willingly; far better to let them exhaust themselves while Pompey watched, highly amused. Within a short time the men were sufficiently disappointed to stop the hard work and start the fighting.[17]

Domitius did not attack while Pompey's men were so preoccupied, but he did use the time to prepare. Sitting behind the shield offered by the difficult ground, he had no intention of moving. Pompey quickly assessed the problems of attacking

Domitius, realising that in order to do so he would probably have to resign himself to losing a lot of men. The two sides formed up ready for battle but before either could make a move, a rain storm blew in, and Domitius gave the order to return to camp. The last thing he expected was to be attacked now, so that is what Pompey did, while Domitius' men were totally unprepared. Pompey joined in the battle, sensibly wearing his helmet, but though it protected him, it also made him anonymous to his own men, and when he was challenged he was too slow in replying. As a result he was very nearly killed. Thereafter, in order that the same mistake should not be made again, he discarded his helmet. Domitius' men were forced back and it was clear to everyone that the victory was soon to be Pompey's. The army saluted the young general as Imperator, but he refused to accept the title because the war was not yet over. The survivors of Domitius' army had gathered in the camp, and must be eradicated. Pompey led the charge himself. He knew how to wring the maximum effect from the soldiers and their probably spontaneous salutation, without incurring too much opprobrium from Sulla, whose patience might not stretch to approval of another military hero in the Roman world.[18]

Domitius was killed, but no one knows how he met his death. Some later sources say that he died in battle, but it is more likely that Pompey had him executed, like Carbo. Domitius may or may not have been proscribed, but it was only a technicality. Pompey's apologists underline the fact that he acted as a representative of the Senate and People of Rome, and primarily of Sulla, and therefore the blame for the deaths of both Carbo and Domitius really rests with Sulla himself. Detractors prefer to portray Pompey as a bloodthirsty tyrant at the age of 24. In both cases where he executed the enemies of Sulla, he could have chosen to send them to Rome and let Sulla deal with them, but from the point of view of the campaigns that he had just led, the execution of the chief quarry rounded off the fighting and gave it some purpose. The soldiers might not fight so readily if they saw that the political ringleaders habitually went free while hundreds of men lay dead. They would probably reason that negotiation could achieve the same result and avoid all the bloodshed and hard work.[19]

Within a startlingly short time the campaign was over, and pacification could begin. Pompey turned his attention to the kingdom of Numidia. Domitius' ally king Hiarbas had fallen foul of Bogud, king of Mauretania, and was in flight, looking for refuge. Pompey lost no time and caught him up, put him to death and installed the previous ruler Hiempsal, all of which implies that Pompey had already made contact with the Numidians and had made his decision as to what to do once Hiarbas was found. Pompey now had useful allies in Sicily and Africa. Sthenius of Himera and Hiempsal of Numidia were bound to him personally, and alliances such as these would compensate for the lack of a political following in Rome. He had also gained experience of co-operation with native kings on the periphery of the Empire, of the judgement necessary to choose between rivals, and of the power of Rome in making that judgement. He had his first taste of independent action outside Rome, without reference to the Senate, and the fortunate experience of winning wars and making administrative and diplomatic decisions, which on this occasion do not seem to have been challenged.[20]

He also had the most telling experience of all, in that the soldiers were indubitably loyal to him, and could be manipulated for his own good if he so wished. He cannot have underestimated his own talents in this connection, nor the undoubted power that could accrue from the association of victorious general and loyal armies. As well as hailing him Imperator, the soldiers called him Magnus, the Great, a name that he carried to his death. The occasion may not have been totally unprompted, since Pompey liked to flaunt his physical resemblance to Alexander the Great, and the addition of the name could only enhance this affinity.[21]

Pompey was shrewd enough to realise that once the campaign in Africa was over he would be redundant, unless he could find another command to exercise his military talents. He cannot have imagined that he was strong enough to challenge Sulla in an attempt to take over the state, despite the loyalty of his soldiers. That was not his aim, either on this occasion or any other. But nor was it his intention to disappear into obscurity. He was perhaps quite prepared for his recall when it came. Sulla ordered him to send back to Italy his five or six legions and to remain in Africa with one legion until a replacement could be sent out as governor. The implication was that when his successor arrived Pompey would return to Rome alone, leaving his one legion behind as garrison troops. By the time he arrived in Rome the rest of his army would have been disbanded or sent elsewhere. His command would be a dead letter and he would not be able to hold a triumph. He imparted this news to his troops, whose protests reached riotous proportions. The soldiers said that they would go to Italy only with Pompey at their head.[22]

Pompey put on a display of emotion, the value of which he had learned when he prevented the mutiny in Strabo's camp. He shed tears, and retired to his quarters, only to be brought back out again; the soldiers begged him to lead them to Rome, he in turn begged them not to lead him into open rebellion. So it went on all day, until Pompey threatened to commit suicide rather than be induced to rebel. When he retired to bed that night, Pompey was probably highly pleased with the scenario that had just been enacted. It was a demonstration to Sulla, to whom it would be reported, of what he could do if he so desired, and that he had complete control of his troops, which was a two-edged sword. It meant 'I can stop them, or I can start them, whichever I choose'. The main effect of the riotous behaviour was an even stronger demonstration that Pompey was not foolish enough to try anything against the state, or against Sulla.[23]

The demonstration paid off: Pompey was allowed to return home to Italy with his army. When Sulla met him, he hailed him as the troops in Africa had done, as Magnus, thereby giving his approval and contributing to the perpetuity of the name. His splendid reception may have encouraged Pompey to insist upon holding a triumph. It cannot have been the first time that he thought of it; without it, his achievements would remain unacknowledged by the multitude, and that much more easily forgotten. Sulla countered with the obvious objection: Pompey was an equestrian, not a senator, and was six years short of the required age to become a senator. Triumphs were reserved for senators, and then not just for any senators; they had to be men of praetorian or consular rank, and though Pompey had been appointed with propraetorian powers, he was not eligible to hold a triumph. It was no doubt galling to be reminded that although he was eligible to command several legions and fight battles for Rome at personal risk, he was not eligible to celebrate his victories in public, or to allow his soldiers to celebrate with him. His famous reply to Sulla was probably fuelled by frustration and anger, though some would construe it as petulance. At first Sulla did not hear what he said, but the amazement on the faces of his associates alerted him to the fact that Pompey had just overstepped the mark. Sulla asked him to repeat what he had said, and once again Pompey reminded him that more people worshipped the rising than the setting sun. There was a silence. Then Sulla burst out 'Let him triumph! Let him triumph!' He had probably mentally run through the responses open to him. Punishment would seem churlish and only tarnish his own reputation, and would possibly stir up trouble among Pompey's troops; indulgence would simply mean that Pompey would parade through the streets in a chariot with his face painted red, followed by his soldiers as he approached the Capitol and dedicated his spoils of war to the gods. It would not mean that Pompey's next move would be to take over the state or usurp Sulla's own position. Sulla judged the young man correctly, in that he wanted glory and recognition, but not supreme power.[24]

There were two disappointments to deal with before Pompey held his triumph. The first was that he had arranged for his chariot to be drawn by elephants, but in a practice run he found that they were too big to pass through the city gates. Allegedly he tried on two separate occasions, perhaps after he had ordered smaller elephants. In the end he had to accept that he would have to appear in a horse drawn chariot, like ordinary men. Perhaps it is just as well, since he would have looked ridiculously minuscule behind two such large beasts. The second problem was a near mutiny of his troops, at least among the disruptive elements among them. The men had been stirred up to demand more pay. They had two main bargaining tools, if their demands were not met; firstly they refused to march in the parade, and secondly they threatened to seize the booty from the wars and divide it up between them. They miscalculated if they thought that vanity would force Pompey to capitulate on this issue. He made it plain that he would forego the triumph rather than submit to coercion. Frontinus reports that he flung the *fasces* wreathed in laurel to the soldiers and told them to begin their theft of the booty by stealing those. This mistreatment of the revered symbols of authority made the soldiers ashamed of what they had done, and they backed down. By his determined, common-sense action Pompey earned considerable credit from both friends and enemies alike. The triumph may have been held in 81, though no one can be sure of the year, since the ancient authors (none of them exact contemporaries) cannot agree on Pompey's age. According to the various sources he was anywhere between 23 and 26, which sets the date for the triumph between 82 and 79. The latter date has been ruled out, but the choice between the others is not so clear. All that is known for sure is that it was held in March.[25]

In the marriage stakes, Pompey was probably the most eligible young man in Rome. No one could imagine that after his triumph he was going to retire to his estates and fade into obscurity. On his part a good marriage alliance with the right clans would help him in his future career; his association with the Metelli, that had ended when the unfortunate Aemilia died, was now renewed by his marriage to Mucia, whose half brothers were Quintus Caecilius Metellus Celer, and Quintus Caecilius Metellus Nepos. The marriage may have been happy, in so far as these political associations went. Mucia produced three children for Pompey, a daughter and two sons, who were to carry on the war against Caesar after their father's death.[26]

Pompey's main problem after his triumph was to identify where his career was to take him. He had begun as an anomaly and was to remain anomalous all his life. He was too young to hold any meaningful office, and could not contemplate the transition from the commander of armies to an administrative post concerned with routine tasks. Sulla was prepared to let him bend the rules up to a point, so with his blessing Pompey had become the youngest ever and the only equestrian *triumphator*; but when it came to political influence Pompey was not to be the exception to the rule. The strict regulations as to age restrictions for each magistracy, and the concomitant stipulation that there should be a specific number of years between tenure of posts, had been reinforced when Sulla executed Ofella because he intended to stand as a consular candidate while still under age and without having held any prior office. Deprived of any hope of reaching the consulship himself for many years, in 79 Pompey supported a candidate for the consulship for the following year. This was Marcus Aemilius Lepidus, eminently unsuitable as far as Sulla was concerned, except in so far as he was of the correct age and fulfilled all the required criteria. He had held the requisite offices, in line with Sulla's dictate that the quaestorship and the praetorship should precede the consulship. Sulla could not oppose his candidacy on any of these counts, and would therefore have to oppose it simply because he did not approve of Lepidus' ideals and character – and that would have made him the tyrant that his detractors said he was. Sulla's legislation could ensure that no one reached the consulship without the necessary experience and maturity, but no amount of laws could guard the Republic against character and intentions. As for Pompey, there is no clear reason why he supported Lepidus, who had made no secret of his anti-Sullan stance. It is not recorded that there was already a serious breach between Pompey and Sulla, and there is no evidence that Pompey ever wished to turn against his benefactor. Seager suggests that Pompey's motives were purely personal, and characteristically devious, in that he saw the election of Lepidus and the implementation of his policies as a potential flashpoint that would necessitate the restoration of order by someone in command of troops, a role that he had earmarked for himself. It is possible that Pompey had begun to think that Lepidus as consul could offer more than Sulla as Dictator, because he could find no means of circumventing the limitations on his political career with regard to the holding of offices in the correct succession, with the relevant number of years between them. The age restrictions alone would exclude him from any prestigious or influential position for some considerable time, and though Sulla's insistence on upholding his own laws even with regard to his friends is understandable and even necessary, Pompey's situation was in stasis unless he could find employment or a post of some kind. Since none of Lepidus' dealings with Pompey has been preserved, this conjecture remains incapable of proof. The implication is that Pompey was duped by Lepidus, or that he had seriously misjudged his character, especially since he soon found after the elections that association with the new consul was hazardous. But it is quite possible that Pompey was looking for something simpler than revolution, in that he imagined that Lepidus would be able to further his career in some way. Sulla had tried to warn Pompey before the elections, and afterwards he castigated him in public. If he had originally included Pompey in his will, he now removed all trace of his name from it, so that of all Sulla's associates Pompey was the only one who was thus excluded. When he met Pompey in the Forum, Sulla warned him to look out for himself, because he had just helped to raise a man who was really an enemy to a more powerful position than himself.[27]

Lepidus' colleague in the consulship was the staunchly conservative Quintus Lutatius Catulus, but he was not strong enough to curb Lepidus' proposals. Sulla himself did not take any action against Lepidus, either before or after his election. If he exerted the undoubted power that he held while Dictator, and could still call upon when he had resigned, Lepidus would be elevated to martyrdom, and then there would be more men like him to step into his place. Sulla would not always be there to guard against such disruptive elements, or to select and reject suitable consular candidates. The government that he had set up and fortified would have to take its chance with such circumstances in the future. For the time being, Sulla contented himself with a sort of gentleman's agreement, persuading the two consuls to swear on oath that they would not settle any quarrels by violent means.[28]

Sulla was approaching his voluntary retirement, probably not undertaken on a sudden whim. In his public speeches Lepidus reminded the people of Sulla's crimes, wondering if retirement as a private citizen would be wise for a former Dictator who had been responsible for so many deaths. But Sulla proved him wrong. At some unknown date, before the middle of 79, or possibly even earlier, he abdicated and contrary to Lepidus' predictions he survived, presumably because his real power lay in his great following of his discharged soldiers and a large number of freedmen called the Cornelii who owed everything to him. Killing Sulla for revenge would have to be the act of a suicidal aspirant for martyrdom. In any case it was obvious in 78 that those who wished for Sulla's death would not have to wait long. He went to live at one of his villas on the coast, where his demise was prolonged and horrific. He developed ulcers that would not heal, perhaps from an internal abcess, possibly as a result of syphilis; he had led a debauched life that exceeded the bounds of anything that most Romans could dream of. Whatever it was that killed him it was relentless, merciless and undignified.[29]

The proposal for a state funeral for Sulla was nearly defeated by Lepidus; if he had carried the day there would have been no honours and no cremation in the Campus Martius. Lepidus' colleague Catulus opposed him, and with the assistance and determination of Pompey a funeral was arranged. It was all the more noble, since Pompey had received nothing from Sulla's will, but despite this snub, Pompey took charge of the proceedings, with his flare for organisation and administration. The funeral was a memorable occasion, attended by virtually everyone in Rome, because no one dared to reveal his dissent. Sulla's veterans paraded through the streets to conduct the bier through the Forum, where speeches were made, and then to the

Campus Martius. It is to Pompey's credit that the soldiers did not riot, nor did he stir them up to make any demonstration on his own behalf. By backing Catulus over the funeral, Pompey had nicely detached himself from Lepidus. But if he was not attached to Lepidus he was still no more firmly attached to the Senate, and without Sulla to utilise his talents and secure his advancement, he badly needed a special project to keep him in the public eye, rising ever upwards in dignity and status. Even though Sulla was no longer there to enforce his laws, it would be difficult for Pompey to persuade the senators to take him seriously as a politician, especially since the recently strengthened Senate owed its pre-eminence to the Dictator. A young man in his twenties with a penchant for military command could be utilised, but only if circumstances required military action, and since he had little chance of starting out on a political career unless he began at the beginning, it was only through military action that Pompey could hope to rise to a position of importance, preferably in a command that was bestowed on him via the approved legal process.[30]

Fortunately, Lepidus played into his hands quite soon, so soon in fact that it supports the accusation that Pompey backed Lepidus for the sole reason that he could foresee that he would be guaranteed to cause trouble that would require suppression; but this is perhaps stretching the young man's perception too far. Lepidus' track record up to now had been one of twists and turns, never consistently adopting either a Marian or a Sullan stance, but opportunely following in whichever direction the prevailing winds blew. After Sulla's death he came into his own, as an avowed anti-Sullan, still not fully committed to the Marian cause, but wholly dedicated to the furtherance of his own interests. He perhaps had not planned his career in minute detail until opportunity presented itself, for there were many causes for him to champion. Even while Sulla still lived, there were issues that could have been fought for, but after his death it was no doubt easier for the discontented and the disinherited to convince themselves that reckoning and recompense were within reach. Lepidus took up the challenge. There were exiles from the Marian party to be recalled, the families of the proscribed men to be restored to their original status, and corn doles for the people to be reinstated. There was also the promise of the restoration of tribunician power, guaranteed to bring popularity to the man who achieved it.[31]

The most threatening source of discontent came from outside Rome. Sulla had settled his veterans on lands, in Etruria and elsewhere, which were wrested by force from the original inhabitants, who now saw the removal of Sulla as an opportunity to regain their farms without the risk of co-ordinated punishment. The situation was serious, verging on civil war, so the Senate despatched both consuls to deal with the problem. Both Lepidus and Catulus recruited armies, and since they were not noted for their sympathetic attitudes to each other, the Senate forbade them to use these forces against each other. Lepidus attracted many Marian sympathisers because it seemed that he was dedicated to the suppression of Sulla's governmental machinery; to the rebels who were trying to regain their lands, it seemed that Lepidus was their saviour, especially when he sent his legate Junius Brutus to recruit troops among the Gauls on both sides of the Alps, as he was legally entitled to do because he had been allocated Transalpine and Cisalpine Gaul as his proconsular province in 77, after his consulship ended.[32]

No one can be certain of the exact point in the proceedings at which Lepidus decided upon armed insurrection. As the events unfolded it might have seemed to onlookers that he had been intent upon it all along, but it may simply be the case that he seized his opportunity because he saw that there would never be a better one. Whilst Catulus was also in the field at the head of troops there was some check on Lepidus' activity; however, when the time came to hold the consular elections for the following year and both consuls were summoned back to Rome to oversee them, Catulus obeyed, but Lepidus remained with his army. It is questionable whether he was committed to the cause of the dispossessed farmers or whether he merely used the rebellion as a vehicle to put himself at the head of an army with which to threaten Rome – for that is the course he took, marching on the city and demanding a second consulship. Lepidus may have intended to initiate many high-minded projects for which he needed the sort of continuity of power that Sulla had acquired, but if so, then these ideas have escaped the record. Without benefit of any knowledge of his plans or his mindset, his schemes seem to be somewhat hysterical and harebrained, and his demand was preposterous. The Senate was hardly likely to succumb without at least an attempt at opposition. It was L. Marcius Philippus who was the driving force behind the Senate, urging that the *senatus consultum ultimum* (literally meaning the last decree) should be passed, to empower Catulus to move against his consular colleague. As consul already in possession of an army, Catulus was the obvious choice of commander to lead an expedition against Lepidus; but since he was not especially gifted in the military sphere, and since there were two enemies to deal with, the one near Rome and the other in the north of Italy, Pompey was the obvious choice to lead another army against the Gallic troops under Junius Brutus. The Senate acquiesced to Pompey's appointment, but it is not elucidated precisely what his rank and power were to be. Most likely he was to assume praetorian rank as he had in the Sicilian and African commands; but neither this nor his relationship to Catulus is stated, with the result that it is possible to argue on the one hand that he was to operate independently, or on the other that he was subordinate to Catulus.[33]

While Catulus faced Lepidus who was marching on Rome, Pompey soon had Brutus under siege at Mutina (modern Modena). Allegedly he negotiated a surrender on the grounds that he would write to the Senate and accept the terms imposed on him with regard to his adversary. Brutus was imprisoned, awaiting the verdict, and Pompey did in fact write to the Senate; but the next day either something happened that caused him to change his mind, or he treacherously went back on his word. He had Brutus assassinated, supposedly while trying to escape, as he reported in a second letter to the Senate. It may have been true that Brutus attempted to flee, but the execution did nothing to enhance the reputation of the boy butcher, and probably most people received the escape story as modern readers would take in the phrase 'slipped on a bar of soap'.[34]

The chronology of the battles in the north and the fighting for possession of Rome is variously interpreted; it may be that Pompey's news of his success reached Rome before Catulus met Lepidus in combat. Lepidus' troops forced Catulus back from the Milvian bridge, but once he had penetrated as far as the Campus Martius he was overwhelmed. He fled from Rome and then from Italy, a declared enemy of the people and the Senate, though this official declaration did not take place until late in the proceedings when he was approaching the city. His life came to an end in Sardinia. He was a disappointed man; the final straw was said to be the news that his wife had been unfaithful to him. Perperna rounded up the remaining soldiers and headed for Spain, where he joined Sertorius.[35]

Now that the danger had been averted, Pompey's troops were no longer necessary, so he ought to have disbanded his army and returned to Rome. There he could have been the hero of the moment, lauded, celebrated and feasted, and then made redundant. But he had his sights set on something more, so he kept his troops together, despite the request, or possibly the orders, of Catulus to pay them off. He kept making excuses, while his friends worked on the Senate on his behalf. It could be considered that he intended to seize power and therefore represented a real threat to Rome, but this is unlikely. He was bluffing, and if his bluff had been called, or even if he did not obtain what he wanted quite quickly, he would have been compromised for no real gains. He had just relieved Rome from the threat of armed insurrection, and yet seemingly he now posed the same threat himself; but total domination was not his style, now or ever, and especially at this juncture he was not prepared for it. What Pompey wanted was another military command, and there was a ready-made need for one in Spain, where Metellus Pius had made little headway against the rebel Sertorius. It is not certain whether Metellus had asked for help; some authorities think that he may have done so, and if that is the case, then Pompey would probably have had his complete support as the best general to go to Spain and fight at his side, though there is no evidence that Metellus had actually asked the Senate to send him.[36]

Once again the proposal that bestowed on Pompey his next command originated with L. Marcius Philippus. It was the third time that support and encouragement had arisen from the same source, starting at the time of the lawsuit against Pompey just after the death of Strabo. Philippus was a survivor, who had begun by opposing Sulla. When Sulla came to power, he joined the regime seamlessly, but after Sulla's death he was not noted as a staunch follower of Sullan policies. He can be censured for lack of principle and loyalty, acting purely in his own interests; or on the other hand he can be seen as a man of common sense acting on behalf of Rome. Gelzer calls him a realist. Philippus would have agreed with the sentiments of Talleyrand, who survived the French Revolution, the Napoleonic regime, and the restoration of the kings; in his opinion there was and is nothing wrong with accepting positions in times of crisis and revolution, when the absolute good is impossible to achieve, because one must move on, considering not only the present but also what will be. Philippus may have been in communication with Pompey for some time before his proposal to send the young general to Spain was presented to the Senate. Otherwise the events must be attributed to spontaneity and opportunism on the part of Pompey in refusing to disband his troops, and on the part of Philippus in suddenly thinking how suitable Pompey would be as an adversary of Sertorius, especially since neither of the two consuls nor any of the other magistrates or ex-magistrates showed any inclination to go to war. The reluctance was so marked that Philippus honed his reputation as a wit from the circumstances; when he was challenged about sending Pompey to Spain with proconsular power, *pro consule*, he replied that no, he was not proposing to send him *pro consule*, but *pro consulibus*, on behalf of the consuls, underlining the fact that neither of them wanted to take on the task, nor indeed was suited for it.[37]

Pompey set out as soon as possible for Spain, but spent his first campaigning season carving his way through the Alps and into Gaul. The only source for his activities in this first year derive from Sallust, in his version of the letter that Pompey wrote to the Senate at the end of the operations of 75. In asking for supplies and for reinforcements, Pompey reminded the Senate of his past services, including his passage through the mountains, the establishment of a new road and the conquest of the tribes controlling the passes into Gaul and in Gaul itself. He claimed to have conquered Gaul and overcome many strongholds; even with allowances for gross exaggeration it seems that there were serious problems that took a long time to overcome. There are few details besides the information contained in this letter, but the Romans never gained complete control of the Alps until the reign of Augustus, so Pompey's account is probably not too exaggerated. [38]

Once he arrived in Spain, Pompey found a position of stalemate. Sertorius had embedded himself securely in the country, recruiting Roman settlers and native Spaniards from the various tribes. He set up a school for the sons of the tribal chiefs, so that they could be educated as Romans. Though he was a rebel as far as Rome was concerned, his regime in Spain was thoroughly Roman, with a Senate and Roman magistrates. Though he utilised the country and its inhabitants he did so within a Roman framework, but it was his own charismatic leadership that enabled him to maintain his strength for so long. He had fought hard to gain a foothold, initially having been driven out by Sullan forces sent across the Pyrenees. He made an abortive attempt to establish himself in Africa, but finally settled upon Spain as his theatre of operations. When he returned there from Africa he took up the cause of the Lusitanians, who had long been engaged in a struggle against the Roman governors who oppressed them: in other words they were indirectly opposed to the regime of Sulla. It may seem odd that the Lusitanians would shrug off Roman control only to accept another Roman as their leader, but Sertorius was careful to avoid the oppressive methods of the previous governors. He ended the exploitation of resources and the vicious taxation, and came to a successful understanding with the ruling classes. In this way he was able to win over most of the tribes and cities of northern Spain, but he was implacable against those that opposed him. For the Spanish tribes and townsmen there was little choice in the struggle between the two opposing Roman forces. If they embraced the cause of one side then they automatically incurred the enmity of the other. Neutrality was not an option, because while the Romans chased each other over wide ranging areas of the country, using up food supplies and other resources, a refusal to assist or to give up supplies invited immediate retribution, and also the loss of the supplies taken by force; but on the other hand, ready co-operation signified partisan activities and invited punishment by the opposing force.[39]

5 *Map of Spain, where Pompey and Metellus fought Sertorius.* Drawn by Jan Shearsmith

Metellus Pius had not been able to defeat Sertorius, and though it is said that Pompey probably underestimated his adversary, it seems likely that he did not underestimate the country. If he realised how difficult the campaigns would prove to be, he did not impart this opinion to his troops or even to his friends, since pessimism at the start of a war is not very helpful. His officers could work out for themselves that Spain was a difficult country in which to seek and find an enemy, especially one who knows the terrain and has the support of the natives. The campaigns hinged, as all campaigns do, and certainly as they would in the civil wars in Greece, on supplies. Henri IV of France pointed out that Spain is a country where large armies starve and small ones are defeated; it was equally true of Spain in Pompey's day. His first concern was to secure the coastal towns so that he could be supplied by sea; but at a later stage in the war he would be severely hindered by the pirate fleets, in alliance with Sertorius, which blocked access to the ports.[40]

By the end of 76, the first year in Spain, Pompey had achieved even less than Metellus. His attention to the coastal cities drew Sertorius down to the plains around Valencia, where the two armies faced each other without engaging in pitched battle. The war centred on winning over tribes and cities and reducing resistance in those that could not be won over. Thus the Spanish peoples were brought into a war that was not of their making and not fought for their benefit. Pompey met with defeat at Lauron, one of the cities that had refused to declare for Sertorius and was consequently besieged by him. Pompey came to the rescue to try to trap Sertorius between the city and his own troops, but he seems to have failed to gather information, or at least he did not know that there were more Sertorian troops to his rear. Foraging became a problem; there was an area where Sertorius' men never seemed to patrol, so the Pompeian troops began to forage there, just as Sertorius had planned. The Pompeians were pinned down and surrounded, and when Pompey sent a general of his own to extricate them, he too was overwhelmed, while Pompey himself was prevented from moving by the Sertorian troops in his rear. He was helpless while his men were butchered, and to add the final insult to injury, Lauron capitulated. It was a hard lesson to learn, and his credibility was much reduced, since this was a bad example to other cities that may have resisted Sertorius if only there had been a Pompeian victory at Lauron.[41]

In 75 Pompey had better success. He defeated Sertorius' generals, Perperna and Herennius, and captured and destroyed Valencia, but then departed from the plan, which was to wait for Metellus' troops to join him. He attacked Sertorius on the line of the river Sucro, thinking he had the advantage, but he was soon disillusioned and nearly lost his life. He rode a white horse with golden trappings, commensurate with his rank and importance, and no doubt with the intention of emulating Alexander the Great, but mostly in order to be recognised after he had nearly been killed by one of his own men in a previous battle where his helmet disguised him. The trouble was that Pompey was now far too recognisable, and an easy target for the enemy. He fought leading his right wing, which succeeded in pushing Sertorius' left wing back, and it seemed that he would bring about a victory. Sertorius was in command of his own right wing, but once he knew that Pompey was winning the battle on the left he rushed there himself with reserves. His Libyan bodyguard charged up to the enemy general on the white horse. Almost surrounded, Pompey had to dismount and get away on foot, abandoning his horse and leaving the enemy squabbling over the possession of the animal and its magnificent harness. Though he did not enjoy much success that day, Lucius Afranius on his left wing had done very well. At first, facing Sertorius himself, the men had begun to falter, but then when Sertorius transferred to the other wing, Afranius surged forwards, driving the Sertorians back into and beyond their own camp; but while his men were looting, Sertorius himself came up and routed them. Another battle on the following day was averted by the arrival of Metellus, so Sertorius withdrew. He said that he would have thrashed the boy, if the old woman had not turned up.[42]

The opposing forces did not engage again for some time, but employed harassing tactics, preventing each other from foraging. Supplies were hard to find because the area was already devastated, and now that Pompey's army was joined by that of Metellus the problem was compounded by the number of mouths to feed. The next battle was fought on the river Turia near Saguntum. Pompey's scouts reported that Sertorius and Perperna were approaching with their whole army, so Pompey and Metellus braced themselves for a fight. Metellus faced Perperna, and Pompey faced Sertorius. The battle was hard fought; Pompey's brother-in-law Memmius was killed, and Metellus after an initial success suddenly found himself opposed by both Perperna and Sertorius, gradually driven back and eventually fighting for his life. His men rallied, formed the tortoise with their shields all around and over him, and rescued him. It was not a victory for either side, except in so far as Sertorius marched away into the mountains, to the headwaters of the river Douro, finally taking refuge in the city of Clunia. Pompey and Metellus followed him and began to besiege the city, but the Spanish natives turned out in support of Sertorius and made life very difficult for his enemies. Since the season was already late and soon the weather too would make their lives even harder, Metellus and Pompey gave up and went into winter quarters.[43]

Pompey remained near to Sertorius, setting up quarters in the Douro valley, while Metellus crossed the Pyrenees and wintered in Gaul. Pompey wrote to the Senate to ask for supplies and reinforcements. This was not the first such letter that he had written but the early ones have not been preserved, so it has been assumed that the Senate was deliberately neglecting him by refusing to acknowledge his requests. Seager refutes the idea that there was a corporate senatorial policy behind the neglect, but some authors concede that Pompey had not received as much help as Metellus, and the support that did come was dilatory at best. Sallust preserves and perhaps elaborates upon the letter that Pompey wrote after the campaigning season of 75. The salient points that Pompey made in this communication were that he had supported his army from his own resources and had received hardly enough to cover his expenses for one year, even though he had been at war for three years. During this three years he had used up all his own wealth and had even exhausted his credit, and now the soldiers had not been paid for some time. The most contentious part of the letter concerns the threat that if he received no support from the Senate, then the war could be brought into Italy. Some scholars have seen in this a form of blackmail, with Pompey hinting at the possibility of joining with Sertorius and marching on Rome together, a concept which has no foundation whatsoever. What Pompey implied was that if he was too weak to win the war, then there would be no barrier except two ranges of mountains between Sertorius and Rome. The name of Hannibal need not be invoked; even though modern authors dismiss the possibility that Sertorius would have left Spain to follow Pompey, to contemporaries the fear was probably real enough for Pompey's words to strike home.[44]

The outgoing consuls for 75 were not interested in Pompey's situation, but the consuls for the following year were more concerned. These were Lucius Licinius Lucullus and Marcus Aurelius Cotta. They had been appointed to a military command against Mithridates, whose Empire-building activities had begun to impinge once more on Roman territory in the east. It was in their interests to see Pompey well supplied and supported in order to avoid a full-scale disaster in Spain that might require resources that would have to be diverted from the eastern war effort. If Pompey were defeated and the whole province fell prey to Sertorius, the preoccupation of the Senate would be with the loss of revenue and the proximity of a hostile army in the west. The situation was further complicated by the fact that at some point, possibly now when he learned of the planned expedition of Lucullus and Cotta, Mithridates sent envoys to Sertorius offering him an alliance. The date is disputed, but it is most likely that the offer of an alliance did not take place until after the death of Nicomedes of Bithynia and the annexation of the kingdom by Rome, which in the eyes of Mithridates was highly disagreeable, not least because it would bring Rome to his doorstep and provide bases from which to attack him, quite apart from the fact that he had designs on the territory himself. Preparing for war with Rome, Mithridates asked Sertorius for Roman officers to train his troops to fight like Romans, and for recognition of his conquests. Sertorius called his Senate, and granted the first of these requests but not the second, refusing to acknowledge that Mithridates had any rights to Asia Minor. In return for his co-operation in sending Roman officers, Mithridates despatched money and ships to Sertorius. As Greenhalgh points out, Mithridates preferred to see Metellus and Pompey and their hundreds of troops tied down at the opposite end of the world. So did Lucullus, but on the other hand he did not want them to be annihilated either, so he exerted himself strenuously on Pompey's behalf, with the happy result that supplies and two legions were sent to Spain. This sudden activity on Pompey's behalf, and the hints in his letter that this was only one of a series of letters, have been taken to indicate that the Senate had until now followed a deliberate policy of starving Pompey; but this is perhaps to overstate the case somewhat. It is more likely that though supplies and resources were voted to him and Metellus, the organisation and administration had not been as efficient as it ought to have been.[45]

For the military activities of 74 there is little information, and for 73 there is even less, but the themes running through all the campaigns of Pompey and Metellus are the avoidance of pitched battles and the reduction and capture of Spanish cities that were loyal to Sertorius. On this basis, the war in Spain was likely to be very slow and very hard. In 74 Pompey took Cauca by a ruse, asking for quarters for his wounded, who once inside miraculously recovered and captured the city. But he failed at Pallantia and Callagurris, driven off by Sertorius. In 73, Appian says that both Metellus and Pompey redoubled their efforts against the Sertorian strongholds.[46]

The whole war was beginning to go sour, for both sides. The country was already exhausted two years before when Pompey had written to the Senate, explaining the situation in both Spain and Gaul, where supplies had dried up because both countries were devastated. Sertorius was no less affected by the supply problem, and he faced another more serious dilemma. Pompey and Metellus had not yet succeeded in decisively defeating Sertorius, but they were still there in Spain with their armies intact, so it was also true that Sertorius had not yet succeeded in decisively destroying them or driving them out. It was clear that even if he did, there would be another army sent from Rome, and so it would go on for ever, while the Spanish cities and tribesmen bore the brunt of the fighting. Their loyalty did not crumble, but dissensions grew between them and the Romans among the Sertorian army. Basically the elements of the Sertorian forces were fighting for different ideals. Sertorius was carrying on a protracted civil war with whatever support he could find against a specific Roman government, that of Sulla. The Romans who fought with him were less and less convinced of the need to continue this war, especially since he seemed to favour the Spanish troops over them, because he had to rely upon their numbers in the absence of loyal Romans. The Spanish tribes and city dwellers had different aims; they did not care about the civil war, but were opposed to government by Rome, and if they had to fight under a Roman to keep Rome out of their affairs they could resign themselves to the anomaly by equating Sertorius with Rome's arch-enemy Hannibal, by which name they had already labelled him. What they did not see was that if the government changed in Rome to one to which Sertorius could be reconciled, he would probably go home, because Rome was where he really wanted to be. Without this insight the Spanish allies defined Sertorius as one of their own, and began to turn against even the Romans who fought by their side. Desertions began from the Roman contingents, especially when it was discovered that Metellus was ready to pardon everyone who came over to him.[47]

In most circumstances when dissatisfaction begins to show among the followers of a particular leader, someone among the followers will begin to imagine that he or she can lead rather better than the current chief. Perperna considered his own pedigree superior to that of Sertorius, but perhaps had never recognised that his skill in conducting war was inferior. Apart from his faith in himself and his lack of faith in his master, his motives when he arranged to have Sertorius assassinated remain obscure. Invited to a banquet, Sertorius attended, unsuspecting, and was killed. When this news reached Metellus and Pompey, it was decided that with Sertorius deleted, the campaign could be safely left in Pompey's hands. Perperna then did what Sertorius had been careful to avoid, except when he had a clear advantage: he offered battle to Pompey, who presumably could not believe his eyes and then seized the opportunity with glee. Perperna allowed himself to be led into a trap, and was defeated and captured. He offered all Sertorius' correspondence to Pompey, possibly hoping to bribe his way into the young general's confidence by allowing him the opportunity to find out who in Rome had been sympathetic to the cause; but it was a shabby trick and was treated with disdain by Pompey, who earned a great deal of credit by promptly burning the whole lot without reading any of it. When this news reached Rome there will have been sighs of relief among the closet Sertorians, and then afterwards a growing suspicion that maybe Pompey only said that he had burned all of the letters, whilst keeping a few for his own private designs. The sense of unease will have persisted until Pompey had been back in Rome for some time, and still no blackmail notes had arrived by special messenger; only then would everyone accept that Pompey was not interested in that kind of hold on power.[48]

The war was over, after five years for Pompey and more for Metellus. Two cities still held out, Uxama and Calagurris, but were reduced eventually. At Calagurris, there were tales of cannibalism as the siege came to a bitter and inglorious end. Spain had now to be brought back to Roman control, pacified, and reorganised. This sort of administration was one of Pompey's talents, which he combined with the recruitment of adherents to swell the ranks of his clients. The most famous of these is Lucius Cornelius Balbus of Gades, who received citizenship in 72 from Pompey. He became one of Caesar's most trusted associates, going on after the death of Caesar to become consul in 40, the first non-native Roman to reach the office. Metellus too recruited friends and clients, and bestowed citizenship on individuals; possibly at Pompey's request, a law was passed in Rome by the consuls of 72, Lucius Gellius Poplicola and Cn. Cornelius Lentulus Clodianus, to ratify the grants of citizenship made by him and by Pompey in Spain.[49]

Pompey chose to mark his achievements in Spain by setting up a monument in the Pyrenees, not far from the Mediterranean coast at Col de la Perche. There was no mention of Sertorius on the monument, because victories over other Romans were not widely advertised, and in triumphal processions the fiction was usually maintained that the war had been fought against an external enemy. The monument was in any case a glorification of Pompey and his troops. It was adorned with his statue and an inscription proclaiming that he had conquered 876 cities between the Alps and the borders of Further Spain. The term city is presumably loosely applied to anything that happened to be fortified, including individual towers. Nonetheless, even with the hyperbole toned down, it denotes considerable achievement. The soldiers who saw it being erected or heard of it afterwards could share in this proud achievement, brought about through the talents and genius of their commander, Pompey the Great. Self-advertisement came naturally to Romans of the upper class, but Pompey turned it into an art form. This early example of his sense of his own importance would be superseded when he campaigned in the east, founding cities in his own name and accepting the worship of the people; but all that lay in the future. In the meantime, the usual problem for Pompey at the end of a war, that of what to do next, was neatly avoided at the end of 72, when he was recalled to Rome, not to disband his army and lay down his command, but to fight another battle against the slave army of Spartacus.[50]

6 *Head of Pompey with the characteristic hair style, deliberately emulating Alexander the Great.* Courtesy Ny Carlsberg Glyptotek, Copenhagen

3 Consul and Imperator

The war with the slaves under their leader Spartacus had begun in 73, when the gladiators of the school at Capua killed their guards and escaped to set up their refuge on the slopes of Vesuvius. The news of their rebellion spread quickly to the slaves of the nearby farms and villas, and the numbers swelled; what should have been a little fracas, easily policed and put down, turned into a war. The first troops that Rome sent after the slaves were defeated and killed. Three Roman officers with three more armies were sent against them and met the same fate; the first was Claudius Glabrus, a praetor, whose strategy ought to have finished the slaves in their own refuge on Mount Vesuvius. He dug siege lines cutting off the route into the mountain fastness, but Spartacus got behind him and attacked from the rear. The Romans would not face him, and Glabrus was left without troops. This success alerted Rome to the fact that Spartacus and the slaves posed more of a serious threat than might have been supposed, and it also alerted more slaves and many discontented poor to the possibility of freedom bought with armed force. Two more armies under the praetors Varinius and Cossinius fared no better than Glabrus. Next, the consuls took the field and were also defeated. Spartacus was marching northwards, intent on reaching the Alps, so that the various peoples in his army could return home, to Gaul, Germany and Thrace; but having battled his way into Cisalpine Gaul and defeated the governor, he turned back, and it was said that he was about to attack Rome. This is where Crassus enters the scene. His military exploits had been negligible since his success in the civil war when he defended Rome from the Samnites, but he knew that he could raise another army, because he was wealthy enough and there were veterans of Sulla's ready and waiting to sign up. So he offered to raise six legions, in return for which he wanted proconsular power to command them. Since there was no one else immediately to hand, the Senate agreed. Crassus tackled part of Spartacus' army and won; it was the first Roman victory, but the end of the war was still a long way off, and the farms and villas of the Italian countryside were still vulnerable to devastation.[1]

While Crassus fought the slaves with his six new legions, the concern of the people and the Senate for their own safety and that of the city prompted them to pay more overt attention to the successful Pompey in Spain. There is controversy over Pompey's recall to Italy, and some have doubted that he was formally asked to return. Plutarch presents conflicting information. With regard to Pompey, he simply says that the general brought his army back to Italy and almost by chance he encountered the remnants of the slave army of Spartacus, while the servile war was at its height. Concerning Crassus, Plutarch describes how he had cornered the slaves in Bruttium, as they headed for the coast to look for pirate ships to take them to a safe haven, probably in the east. Blockading them, Crassus dug lines across the peninsula, 35 miles from coast to coast across the toe of Italy. According to Plutarch, it was at this point that he wrote to the Senate recommending the recall of Lucullus from the war with Mithradates, and Pompey from Spain. Later, he regretted his action, and worked frantically to defeat Spartacus before receiving any help from Pompey and therefore sharing the glory. Greenhalgh suggests that he proposed recalling Lucullus and Pompey only because the Senate would have turned to their other generals anyway, and by pre-empting this decision Crassus was spared the embarrassment of being considered incapable of holding his own against the slaves. The Senate did in fact vote for the recall of both Pompey and Lucullus, and although both generals arrived in Italy blocking Spartacus from the north and the east, it was Pompey who claimed all the glory.[2]

The same divisive quarrels that had affected the army of Sertorius, and helped Pompey to defeat him, now came to the aid of Crassus. Spartacus escaped from the blockade with many of his men, but failed to maintain the cohesion that had held them all together during their first victories, thus enabling Crassus to defeat individual sections that broke away from Spartacus. He cut them down in a series of skirmishes and won the final battle, but did not kill or capture all the slaves. About 5000 of them, just about the strength of one legion, escaped northwards and ran into Pompey, who commanded several legions. It was not a difficult battle, but on winning it, Pompey said that though Crassus had won pitched battles, he himself had finished off the war, cutting it out by the roots.[3]

Hyperbole was one of the main tools of self-advertisement, and Pompey was popular enough to get away with it. Crowds of people came from Rome to meet him and his army as he approached the city, which he could not legally enter at the head of troops. The number of people who turned out was not simply a measure of his popularity, it was a political declaration that had almost formal sanction, a deeply significant event for returning generals. His family and friends would naturally go to meet him, with all his clients and anyone with an interest in him, or who wanted something from him, so the larger the numbers the more important the returning general. Pompey did not suffer from lack of confidence, nor did he have a diminished sense of self-worth, but perhaps because of his atypical rise to fame and power, he was conscious that perception of him as a successful military commander was not equalled by the senatorial and perhaps even the popular estimation of him in the political arena. His experience of politics was from the outside looking in, as an observer, none of which qualified him for the obvious next step that he needed, to become consul.[4]

With his army at his back, still enthusiastic and loyal, Pompey could have demanded the consulship, just as Lepidus had tried to coerce the Senate; but there is no evidence that he did anything of the kind. He did not disband his troops, but that was because he wished to hold a triumph, in which his soldiers would play the significant part, so to disband them and then collect them together again would be slow and impractical. Besides, he said that he was waiting for Metellus to return. Some authorities have seen in this delaying tactic an overt threat of force, but there is probably no need to interpret his actions in such a derogatory fashion. He promised to disband as soon as he had held his triumph, and perhaps the majority believed him. Pompey in his youth managed to project an appearance of innocence, even if that were not his true inner feeling, but now as in the future when he returned from the wars in the east, he displayed no ambition to take over the state. The concessions that he did demand were to be allowed to stand for the consulship while still under age and without having held any of the requisite offices, as outlined in Sulla's restructured constitution, and also to stand *in absentia* because he could not cross the city boundaries while still in command of troops. The senators who were friendly to him readily cleared the passage for him by waiving the regulations as to age and previous magistracies.[5]

Plutarch tells the tale of Crassus suggesting to Pompey that they should stand for the consulship together. He says that Crassus did not have the courage to seek the consulship until he had secured the support of Pompey, which is difficult to accept at face value, unless Crassus really thought that he must ride on the back of Pompey's popularity to achieve the office. It is more likely that they both realised that they would do better by singing from the same song sheet than by working against each other. Crassus would not have been human if he had not felt some disappointment that he had been voted the lesser form of triumph, the *ovatio*, for his success against Spartacus, while Pompey celebrated his victories in a full triumph. This was in accordance with established custom, and not prejudice against Crassus or favouritism to Pompey, since Crassus' victory over the slave army was not rated as highly as Pompey's victories in Spain. But even though Crassus may have held a long-standing grudge against the younger and more flamboyant Pompey ever since they both turned out to fight for Sulla, his animosity could be subsumed in the run up to the elections, while the prized consulship was at stake. There may have been bribery and corruption, but the elections were held without resort to armed force, possibly because no one else was foolhardy enough to stand against the two of them; no other candidates are recorded. Thus Pompey and Crassus were duly elected consuls for 70, both of them *in absentia*. It was merely a formality in this case, but in the not too distant future a great deal would hinge upon the request to stand for the consulship *in absentia*. When Pompey concluded his eastern campaigns and returned once more as conquering hero, the Senate voted against allowing him the same privilege, and he did not pursue the matter, preferring instead to hold his triumph and then try to influence the political developments not as consul himself, but through deputies. In 60, Caesar asked for the same favour, returning from his conquest of the Lusitanians in Spain, but he too was refused, and decided to forego his triumph so as to be able to cross the city boundary as a private individual and present himself at Rome for the elections. By the time that Caesar was ready to return from his conquest of Gaul, the whole question of being elected *in absentia*, and therefore stepping directly from military command to consulship, had become extremely fraught. [6]

Pompey's triumph, his second whilst still only an equestrian, was held at the end of December 71. On the following day he formally took up his office as consul. Presumably, he had by then read and digested the contents of a little manual on senatorial procedure, written for him by his friend Varro. Since he had not yet become a senator, despite his long years of military experience, he had no idea of how business was conducted in the Senate. His father had been consul, but Strabo's year of office had been spent at the head of his troops while he fought the last battles of the Social War, so there was little to pass down to his son in the way of political conduct and management of business during his consulship. Most young men would enter the Senate without knowing everything about the formalities, but they would have the advantage that Pompey had never had, namely that of starting at the bottom and picking up the necessary details by observation for several years, before they ever had to participate in the business of the day. Pompey was starting out in the highest office, responsible for conducting business with the added ability to shape policy and make laws, with only a handbook to guide him on how it was done. No stories of disasters or of any faux pas have been handed down about his first appearances in the Senate, so perhaps everything passed off without problems.[7]

While still consul designate he had made a speech to the people, assembled outside the city to hear him. He had already been elected so it was not a pre-election manifesto, but an outline of what he intended to do when he became consul. He promised to restore tribunician power, reform the courts, and improve provincial government. The last two features were closely bound together. The first promise, to restore the office of tribune to its former status, was not as sweeping as it sounds, since inroads had already been made in this direction by determined politicians, some of whom were defeated in the first attempts. In 75 Caius Aurelius Cotta had succeeded in removing the ban on holding further offices after the tribunate, so that it did not cripple men's careers to become tribunes. From 76 to 73 various proposals to restore the full power to the tribunes were squashed. Pompey's name was already associated with the tribunate before he returned from Spain, when the tribune Caius Licinius Macer made a speech in 73, implying that he had Pompey's ear on this subject. According to Sallust, Macer accused the die-hards in the Senate of delaying any action on the tribunate, implying that they were hiding behind Pompey, waiting for his pronouncements. Seager dismisses this as the garbled rubbish it is. Macer went on to say that when Pompey came home, he was certain to throw his weight into the struggle to restore the legislative powers of the tribunes. No one knows if he was acting on Pompey's instructions, leaking information that had been discussed privately by letter or previous conversation, or simply blurting out Pompey's name as though he enjoyed the full support of the general, when in fact he did not. It did not compromise Pompey, because as it turned out it was not something to which he was opposed. In 71 when Pompey made his speech to the people, he combined forces with Marcus Lollius Palicanus, who was tribune that year. It is significant that Palicanus hailed from Picenum, and was probably already closely associated with Pompey; he was also the father-in-law of Aulus Gabinius, another of Pompey's adherents, and he was active in the reform of the jury courts during Pompey's consulship. Palicanus probably did much of the donkey work in drafting the bill regarding the tribunate. The act to restore the legislative powers of the tribunes was a product of the joint consulship of Pompey and Crassus, and as Seager points out, it was the only instance where they co-operated during the entire year. They did not have to fight tooth and nail to pass the law, since there was an inevitability about it that the Senate recognised. Gruen points out that it was preferable to put tribunes back into operation so as to go through the proper channels than to have demagogues stirring up the people directly.[8]

The matter of the jury courts was left ultimately in the hands of Lucius Aurelius Cotta, and though Pompey may have discussed the issues with his associates and principally with Palicanus, he was not especially active in the Senate or in making speeches to people when the time came to push the legislation through. Presumably he was satisfied with the way in which Cotta handled the bill, and with its outcome. Before it was passed, there were wild rumours that the courts were to be wrested from the control of the senators to be placed firmly in the hands of the equites again, as had been the case before Sulla's reforms; but this was not what the bill proposed. The juries were to be made up of three groups of men drawn from senators, equites, and the *tribuni aerarii*. The significance of this last group is not known. The original *tribuni aerarii* were officials of the treasury, responsible for military pay and collecting tribute, but the office had gone out of use long before the title was revived in Cotta's law. They were probably of equestrian status; but it is not clear why they should be enumerated separately, and some scholars think that they were exactly the same as other equites. Whatever they were, they were short lived, since Caesar eventually removed them from the composition of the courts and the title is not heard of again. It may seem that with two thirds of the jurors drawn from the equestrian classes and only one third from the senatorial class, the courts had in effect been returned to the control of the equites, but as Gruen points out, the amount of judicial business had vastly increased and senators had complained of the insupportable burdens that it imposed, so the new make-up of the courts served to dilute the labour by broadening the base of those responsible for carrying it out.[9]

After the restoration of tribunician power and the reform of the courts, in which last case he was not particularly active, Pompey did not produce any further legislation or put into operation any more policies. His talents were turned to the entertainment of the people, in splendid games which he had vowed to the gods if he defeated Sertorius, and in the *transvectio* or parade of the equites, a pageant which was arranged for him by the censors, as part of their duties. Sulla had abolished the post of censor, but one of the achievements of the consulship of Pompey and Crassus was its reconstitution, once again on the rotating five-yearly basis. The men appointed to this office were the consuls of 72, Lucius Gellius Poplicola and Cornelius Lentulus Clodianus, who had passed the laws to ratify the grants of citizenship made by Pompey and Metellus in Spain. The census of citizens was taken in the year of Pompey's consulship, together with the revision of the membership of the Senate, and the review of the equites. This consisted of a parade of all the young men of equestrian status, leading their horses in a line to pass before the two censors and to be questioned in public on their military service record, enumerating the campaigns in which they had fought. Included in this particular review was the young consul, marching behind the twelve lictors, each carrying the *fasces*, that signified his *imperium* or power. All Roman magistrates with *imperium* were preceded by lictors who cleared the way for him through the crowds; a praetor was entitled to six lictors and consuls to twelve. The sight of the lictors and then the consul himself constituted a strange anomaly in a parade of the equites, as no doubt Pompey intended it should. When it came to his turn to give an account of himself, the censors asked him, as they asked all the participants, if he had fulfilled all his legal obligations by serving in military campaigns. The people roared approval when Pompey replied that he had indeed served in military campaigns, and in all of them he acted under his own command as Imperator. There was a sense of festival as the censors accompanied him to his house; he was at the absolute zenith of his career. He would go on to greater conquests, but never again would he enjoy such undiluted popularity as he knew that day.[10]

After his triumph, he scarcely needed to remind anyone of his military exploits, and his gate-crashing and upstaging of the parade of the equites is the act of a young man, not a hardened general or an experienced politician, who would not have been able to carry it off with any credibility. Pompey was not naive or innocent, but liked to project an image of straightforward goodwill as a front for his more devious ambitions. He cashed in on his youth and good looks while it was appropriate to do so, and intended to put his undoubted military and organisational skills to use as soon as he could. But for that he would have to wait, because there was no immediate command available for him, so he had to work in the wings to create one. In the meantime, Crassus was busily entertaining the populace in far more lavish form than Pompey, and building up his network of clients. The two men were not the best of friends, and their joint consulship had not made them so; in fact it could be said that their constant quarrelling had prevented them from doing anything spectacular while they were in office. When the day came to step down in favour of the incoming consuls, their rivalry was temporarily brought to an end. During the speech making, a man called Aurelius asked permission to address the people, and on being given leave, he said that Jupiter had appeared to him in a dream and told him that the consuls should not be allowed to vacate their office while still unreconciled. Aurelius went on his way, and the two consuls sat momentarily motionless, until Crassus stood up to take Pompey by the hand, proclaiming that it was not unworthy of him to yield to his colleague, who had been called Magnus while still only a youth, and who had been voted two triumphs before he became a senator. It is a curious little scenario, probably orchestrated according to a prearranged script, but whose script and for what purpose is not elucidated. If Pompey saw any barbed comment behind Crassus' speech, he did not show it, professing himself always willing to please his colleague.[11]

Neither of the retiring consuls of 70 went on to a proconsular command to govern a province or take charge of any specific task. Crassus had already made a name for himself in the courts, and was also a business magnate in his own right; he returned to the life in the city that best suited him. Pompey almost disappeared for three years or so. He did not appear in public very often, but whenever he went out he made certain that he was accompanied by crowds of his clients and friends. He seems to have kept out of politics, but his re-emergence in the fraught legislation to bestow upon him the command against the Mediterranean pirates, and the speed with which he carried out the tasks, could be taken to indicate that he was not idle during this fallow period of his career. He probably spent much of his time thinking and planning his next objective, combining opportunism with intelligence reports, monitoring the situations all round the Roman world. Spain and Gaul were relatively quiet at the moment, but had there been any trouble it is certain that Pompey would have watched closely for an opening to employ his particular talents. As it was, the action was all in the east, with Lucullus fighting against Mithridates, and the pirates menacing the seas. Both could be turned to advantage, but not until there was a demand, and that would have to be created.[12]

Meanwhile, Pompey at home, as husband, parent, landowner and landlord, is not easy to see. Such details did not interest the historians, except perhaps in the form of anecdotal incidents recorded for the amusement of readers. In Pompey's case, little of that survives, and generally does not concern his private life. If there is a lack of detail, then there is also a corresponding lack of what modern journalists would call the dirt. Scandal never attached itself to Pompey's personal life. He and his wife Mucia had a young son, Gnaeus, born in 79, who would by now be about ten years old. Their second son, Sextus, was born *c*.67, and was therefore a product of Pompey's years of comparative inactivity. There was also a daughter Pompeia, who may also have been born during this period. She was betrothed to Faustus, the son of Sulla, in 59, but that gives no real clue as to her age and the date of her birth, since betrothals could take place between young children if their families wished to cement an alliance in that way. However, since Pompey went away from Rome in 66 and did not return until 62, when he sent a bill of divorce to Mucia immediately upon his arrival without seeing her, their daughter was presumably born at some time between 70 and 66.[13]

It is usual to compare Pompey unfavourably with Crassus with regard to his wealth and influence. The assumption is that he did not have access to anything like the same resources as Crassus; but without an inspection of the balance sheets of both men it is impossible to support or reject this assumption. The proscriptions authorised by Sulla had made some of his associates very rich, and Crassus had probably been one of those who had been able to buy up estates at cheap prices. One advantage that Crassus did have over Pompey was a few extra years spent in Rome enabling him to adopt each and every means available to him to augment his fortune. Stories are told of his famous fire brigade chasing round Rome in search of the ubiquitous conflagrations that broke out from time to time. It was said that Crassus offered to buy the burning buildings, and if his bid was successful his slaves put the fires out; if not, then the building burned and the owner lost his property just the same. Senators were forbidden to engage in any form of work, which was considered degrading; but their business interests were none the less widespread for all that, closely bound up with their middle class agents drawn from the equestrian classes. These men looked after the business interests of senators and made their own fortunes out of doing so; Crassus was no doubt as active a landowner, entrepreneur, and businessman as any of his colleagues. His legal activity in the courts was also potentially lucrative, and he made a point of extending patronage to aspiring young men, by lending money and supporting them politically. It was generally assumed that Caesar owed him a fortune before he went off to govern Spain. But Crassus was not alone in being able to make loans. When Pompey was in the east in 64, he lent significant sums of money, allegedly 40 million sesterces, to Ariobarzanes of Cappadocia, whose kingdom had been devastated in the Mithridatic wars. There is no doubt that Pompey profited hugely from the eastern wars, but to be able to lend so much money only two years into the campaign implies that he had already amassed considerable wealth while in Rome.[14]

Against Crassus' financial wizardry, Pompey is usually portrayed as a non-starter, or at least a slow learner. Much of this could possibly derive from the projected images that Pompey and Crassus chose to exercise. Pompey made a show of being youthful, fresh and untainted with greed or vices, open, honest and just. Crassus, according to what has come down to us, liked to make great play of his wealth; no one could call himself wealthy unless he could equip and pay an army, he said, the implication being that he could do so several times over if he so wished. Perhaps he was of the same ilk as those moderns who like to proclaim 'I could buy and sell you all'. Pompey would perhaps not choose to express himself in such a fashion, but there is no need to suppose that despite his reputation for honesty and fair dealing he had neglected to make his fortune under Sulla's wholesale removal of wealthy men and the sale of their estates, or that he had turned a blind eye to the possibilities on offer from his exploits in Sicily, Africa and Spain. This is not to say that he was an accomplished criminal who could afford to be hypocritical because he was simply never caught. After his death, Cicero's judgement of him was that he was a highly principled man of good character, but notwithstanding that Pompey was as nearly as possible squeaky-clean, it should be remembered that it was not always necessary to resort to extortion to make money in the Roman world. Pompey also had his estates in Picenum to draw upon, and through his mother he may have inherited the estates of the poet Gaius Lucilius, near Tarentum. Land ownership was lucrative; according to Cato the censor, who lived from 234-149 and wrote a book on farming, the three best methods of making a fortune were firstly to own an agricultural estate, secondly to own an agricultural estate, and thirdly to own an agricultural estate. It is probably erroneous to say that Pompey lagged far behind Crassus as regards his wealth; they perhaps made money in different ways and used it for different purposes, and if he was relatively the poorer in 70, then Pompey had far outstripped Crassus by the time he returned from his campaigns in the east a decade later.[15]

In the political arena, Pompey's influence was less strong than he could have wished. It is not recorded that he tried to set up numerous candidates of his own for the chief magistracies, but he did try to establish as consul for 66 (significantly the year when Manilius introduced the bill concerning the eastern command) his associate Marcus Lollius Palicanus, who had worked for the restoration of the tribunate and the reform of the jury courts. In this endeavour he was defeated, because C. Piso, one of the consuls of 67 and therefore one of the presiding officers over the elections, refused to accept him as a candidate, and said that even if he were elected, he would not reveal the result. Seager examines this case and also that of C. Cornelius, a tribune of 67 who tried to introduce legislation to control the rampant bribery at the elections, a measure that Pompey probably supported. This too was defeated by Piso, and Seager concludes that the senators who opposed Pompey had closed ranks and resorted to bribery to prevent any of his associates from reaching political power.[16]

Pompey himself did not seek political power during his semi-retirement. The only office open to him would have been a second consulship, which according to Sulla's legislation was closed to him for ten years. He did not attempt to flout the regulations by standing for office again, nor did he take a firm stand on provision of land for his discharged veterans, and those of Metellus Pius. The necessary law (*lex Plotia*) had been passed to allocate lands to them, but it was not put into effect, perhaps because the commission appointed to do so met with problems over finance. There is no recorded serious disturbance about it on the part of the veterans themselves, though Clodius tried to stir up trouble within the ranks of Lucullus' army by claiming that Pompey's soldiers were living a life of luxury on their allocated lands, while Lucullus' men had been in the east for years, with victory still not in sight, and the rest that came after it was even further away. The fact that he was lying does not seem to have weighed with anyone. Pompey did not succeed in installing his own adherents in offices where they could have facilitated the land settlements for his men. Nor did he express any interest in the court cases that scandalised the city. It has been said that he was engaged in a dispute with the Metelli over the infamous Verres, the governor of Sicily from 73-1, who was successfully prosecuted by Cicero for extortion in 70. The Metelli supported Verres, insofar as they were able in view of his too obvious guilt, and Pompey had a personal interest in seeing him condemned because Verres' rapacity had extended as far as Sthenius of Himera, Pompey's client from the time of his command against Carbo. But it need not be construed as a battle between Pompey and the Metelli, nor does it constitute a pivotal case for the reform of the courts, though it was closely bound up with that issue. Similarly Pompey seems to have distanced himself from Cicero's defence of Marcus Fonteius, who had been governor of Transalpine Gaul while Pompey was in Spain, and had helped to supply the army. Cicero name-dropped during the trial, but this does not mean that he had Pompey at his back directing operations. Pompey's ambitions lay in an altogether different direction, outside Rome. There were two potential areas where he could operate to good effect, one in the Mediterranean to clear the seas of the pirates, and the other in the east, where Lucullus had started well but was finishing badly.[17]

The tribunician laws of 67 and 66 bestowing these two commands on Pompey cannot have been spontaneous gestures on the part of Gabinius and Manilius, with no previous considerations behind them and no prior contact with Pompey himself. The problems in the east and the Mediterranean escalated simultaneously. Pompey took up his whirlwind command against the pirates before he progressed to take over in the east, but the machinations that culminated in both commands took place in parallel. It will be more convenient to deal with them one at a time, in the order in which Pompey conducted them.

The pirates in the Mediterranean had become such a nuisance that not only was travel by sea hazardous, but also the corn supply of Rome was disrupted. Eminent Romans had been captured and ransomed, including the young Julius Caesar when he was on his way to Rhodes in 75. Caesar lived with the pirates for a month while the money was raised to pay for his release, cordially promising to crucify them all, and just as cordially carrying out his promise once he was free. Clodius Pulcher was also captured, and professed to be outraged that the pirates accepted such a low figure for his ransom payment. He said he was worth much more.[18]

There had been several attempts to eradicate the pirates, with very limited success. The shortage of corn from 104 onwards, caused by the disruption in supply from Sicily and north Africa, was addressed by the appointment of Marcus Antonius in 102, but he did not achieve significant results. A fragmentary *lex de piratis* of about 100 survives, and though much of the text is missing it seems that this was an attempt to make sweeping laws against the menace of the pirates. In 77 Publius Servilius Vatia attacked the pirate strongholds of Cilicia, but in depriving the culprits of their lands he reduced their capacity for self-sufficiency and gave them no choice except to return to piracy for a living. This was a point that Pompey perhaps considered seriously his plans for how to deal with the problem when his turn came.[19]

The scourge of the seaways increased when Mithridates came to power, and began to advance into Roman territory. He saw that encouragement of the pirates was one way of harassing Rome and protecting himself, so he gave them money and ships, exacerbating a problem that was already severe. Pirate activity had closed the Spanish ports to Pompey and made it difficult to bring in supplies while he fought Sertorius, and when Spartacus was bottled up in southern Italy, he tried to ally with the pirates to persuade them to carry the slave army out of Italy. On their part the pirates kept their eyes and ears open for what was happening in Rome and the Roman world, looking for and exploiting opportunities when the Romans were compromised.[20]

The next attempt to defeat the pirates was nothing short of disastrous. The praetor Marcus Antonius, the son of the commander of 102, was assigned the task in 74, but was soundly beaten and lost his ships to the Cretan pirates, with whom he made a shameful treaty and claimed the victory title Creticus. Before he could do more harm, he died in office in 71, leaving three young sons, the eldest being better known as Mark Antony. Quintus Metellus took over in Crete in 68 and won back some of the prestige that Antonius had lost, but his successes extended only to the harbours and inlets of the island and did not affect the rest of the Mediterranean. In 67 a pirate fleet appeared in the mouth of the Tiber, defeated a consular commander and attacked the harbour at Ostia. Whether this outrage occurred before or during the activity of the tribune Gabinius, it made his bill to appoint a supreme commander against the pirates all the more pertinent.[21]

When Gabinius introduced the bill, no specific person was named as potential commander, but the powers and resources that this hypothetical commander would need had been discussed, most probably with Pompey himself after he had given the matter considerable thought. It stretches credibility too far to suggest that Gabinius and Pompey had not collaborated before the bill was introduced. The problem was seen in its entirety, in that it concerned the whole of the Mediterranean, and therefore the answer was to think big. A little squadron of ships on a seek and destroy mission could succeed only in wearing itself out chasing some of the pirates while the ones who were still free could plunder where they liked. In order to eradicate the problem huge resources and unprecedented power would be required, so it was perhaps only after the scare of the attack on Ostia that the need for all this could be impressed on the Romans. The people were sure that they wanted the bill to be made law, and were also sure that they wanted Pompey to be the commander. The Senate as a corporate body was sure that something must be done about the problem, but almost to a man the senators were unsure about the enormous power that Gabinius urged them to put into the hands of one man. Pompey pretended that he was tired, and had already done enough for Rome in all his battles in Sicily, Africa and Spain. He did not wish to appear too interested in the appointment, but his attempts to deflect popular demand did not ring true. He said that there were plenty of other commanders who could do the job just as well, and that the people must choose someone else. This would be one way of ascertaining that in fact there were no other contenders and that the people really wanted him.[22]

The original bill stipulated that there should be a fleet of 200 ships, divided into squadrons under 15 legates of praetorian rank, subordinate to the supreme commander who would be a consular. He should have the right to levy troops as and when he required them, and to finance the entire enterprise he should have access to the funds of the main treasury in Rome and also the tax resources of the provinces. The territorial extent of his power was to be vast; he should control the whole of the Mediterranean, and in addition, his authority should extend up to a distance of 50 miles inland in all the provinces bordering upon the Mediterranean, and all the islands within it. Debate centres on the nature of this *imperium*, as to whether it was to be equal to (*aequum*), or greater than (*maius*), that of the provincial governors. The ancient written sources are of no help in clarifying this issue, since according to Velleius Paterculus, Pompey held *imperium aequum*, which placed him on exactly the same footing as all the provincial governors, but Tacitus contradicts this, when he compares the *imperium maius* of Corbulo in the reign of Nero with that of Pompey during the Mediterranean command. Whatever the true nature of the proposed and actual *imperium* bestowed on Pompey, the most worrying factor for the Senate was that very little of the Roman world would be exempt from this tremendous command. It was a dangerous precedent to set, and was open to the wildest abuse. The command was not to be permanent; it was to last only for three years, but what if the man who was appointed should decide after the terminal date not to lay down his powers and disband his troops?[23]

Not surprisingly there was violent opposition to the terms of this bill. The chronology of the riotous proceedings is not absolutely clear, but it was probably as a result of the speeches of C. Piso, the consul, that the senators were whipped up into a fury and attacked Gabinius, who just about escaped with his life, and it was probably as a result of Gabinius' speech to the people that they in turn almost killed Piso, who could be portrayed as an opponent not only of the bill but also of any improvement in the corn supply and provision of food for the populace. Ironically, Piso was rescued by Gabinius, who calmed everyone down; the action would probably not have been reciprocated if Gabinius had been threatened again. A voice of reason was found in Hortensius, Cicero's rival in the law courts. He suggested that if such a supreme command were ever to be created, then indeed Pompey was the very person to take it up; but no such post with so much weight should be created, because it would jeopardise the state. One senator spoke in favour of the bill, but his political standing was not so great that his opinion could sway the Senate; this was Gaius Julius Caesar, lately returned from Further Spain, where he had been governor in 69. It has been pointed out that the ancient sources attest that he spoke in favour of one of the bills conferring great powers on Pompey, that of Gabinius in 67 or that of Manilius in 66, so it is not absolutely certain that he supported Gabinius' law; but as Seager points out it is likely that he was consistent and supported both of them. Having been a victim of the pirates himself in his early career, and having executed some of them when he was ransomed, Caesar may have supported Gabinius because he understood the problems and saw the need for a wide-ranging command with control of the whole Mediterranean. Later, when he had attained supremacy over the state, it was said that Caesar supported the bill simply because he thought that one day he might need such sweeping powers for himself.[24]

Legitimate means of thwarting Gabinius were now sought by the Senate. Any of the other tribunes could veto his proposals, so two of them, Lucius Trebellius and Lucius Roscius Otho, were recruited to oppose the bill. Trebellius prepared to make a speech, but he was not permitted to utter a word because the mob cried him down, so he had to content himself with interposing his veto. It is probable that Pompey and Gabinius had thought of this possibility and decided upon what to do if the circumstance should arise. Only once before, in the troubled times of Tiberius Gracchus, had a tribune been deposed by a vote of the people. Gabinius proposed the measure and the voting began to remove Trebellius from office. This extreme action, the removal of a tribune from office, came only a very short time after Pompey and Crassus had passed the necessary laws to restore full tribunician power; but the grim irony of the circumstance was probably submerged in the violence of the proceedings. Trebellius was stubborn; he held out until it was clear that there was no hope of remaining in office, and then he withdrew his veto. Roscius was cried down as Trebellius had been. The Senate had been defeated.

The elder statesman Catulus was invited to speak. He agreed with Hortensius that the proposed command would endanger the state. He thought that no single person could control the entire area of such a wide-ranging post, an opinion that Pompey probably found slightly pathetic; he could be forgiven for exclaiming the Roman equivalent of 'Watch me!' at such a notion. Catulus tried to modify Gabinius' bill by suggesting that the legates should not be subordinate to a supreme authority, but that there should be a few independent commanders. He did not explain the most difficult aspect of his suggestion, which was how the activities and efforts of these independent commanders could be co-ordinated, an essential element if they were to be effective. He rounded off his speech by asking what would happen to the command if Pompey should be killed. Who would replace him? he asked, and the mob quickly responded 'You, Catulus!'. So opposition collapsed and Gabinius' law was passed.[25]

After further legislation, the original bill was augmented. A second law was necessary to appoint Pompey as the commander, and the final version of his powers increased the number of his ships to 500, and there were to be not 15, but 24 legates (25 legates in some sources). All that remained now was to assemble the fleet, appoint the legates, recruit the soldiers, the sailors and the rowers, go to sea, and sweep the pirates off the face of it. It was a daunting task, but popular confidence in Pompey was total and unquestioning. Before he had lifted a finger, the price of corn fell as soon as his command was made law.[26]

This extraordinary command combining control of naval and land-based operations represented the first corporate assault on the pirates. The usual pattern had been to endow a single commander with limited powers and resources, in an attempt to eradicate the pirates from one particular area, without co-ordinating attacks over the whole of the Mediterranean. As the last few commands had revealed, even successes against the pirates could be overturned in a few months. The Romans were almost congenitally wary of granting the kind of powers that were demanded in this case to one man; but they had on occasion found it necessary to override the governmental system to deal with recurrent or serious problems where a supreme commander was necessary to take control of large armies or wide territorial areas. The most recent precedents for Pompey's command were those of Marius in two wars, against Jugurtha in north Africa and then to stem the serious invasions of the Celtic tribes of the Cimbri and Teutones that threatened northern Italy. During prolonged wars like these continuity of command and singleness of purpose were necessary, a factor that would have been wrecked by the appointment of a series of individual commanders, no matter whether they were proconsuls with military experience behind them. Not all men had the talent for leadership that Marius and Pompey possessed, and the charisma that is an important part of it. This last was a quality that Pompey, consciously emulating Alexander, knew how to exploit. He assembled his forces with remarkable rapidity, and was ready to sail by early spring. It was not an ideal time for venturing to sea; thc Mediterranean was as unpredictable as any other maritime region, and storms could arise without warning.[27]

Thus began the most startlingly brief campaign to round up the pirates. Pompey divided the whole of the Mediterranean and the coasts into 13 regions, with a legate in command of each one. The names of these legates have survived in two separate lists, in the accounts of Appian and Florus, but unfortunately they do not agree with each other on all counts. Only nine of the names in Florus' list agree with those of Appian, and it is the latter whose account is considered the most reliable. A remarkable feature is the high status of the legates appointed by Pompey; two of them, in command of the seas on either side of Italy, were the consuls of 72, Lucius Gellius Publicola and Cn. Cornelius Lentulus Clodianus. These men rose to the censorship, restored by Pompey and Crassus in 70. Their support for Pompey is self-evident in their willingness to serve under him in the naval campaign. Epigraphic evidence suggests that at least one of these legates, Cn. Cornelius Lentulus Marcellinus who was assigned to patrol the Mediterranean off the coast of Egypt, was directly responsible to Pompey and not the Senate, which illustrates the unprecedented nature of Pompey's command, foreshadowing the way in which Augustus controlled many of the provinces through legates responsible to him alone. Though the commanders of the 13 regions of the Mediterranean are known, the remaining 11 or 12 legates are not named in the ancient sources, and it is not certain where or how they operated. Since Pompey's command extended 50 miles inland in the territories around the Mediterranean, some of the legates would have been land-based, and possibly some would have commanded native levies whose knowledge of the areas would have contributed greatly to the round up of the pirates from their strongholds.[28]

Pompey's first concern was to drive the pirates from the western half of the Mediterranean, enabling him to clear the seaways to and from the corn-producing areas of Sardinia, Sicily and north Africa. This task was accomplished in 40 days, according to the ancient sources. Whilst hyperbole may have entered the accounts to give a hackneyed time span, there is no need to doubt that Pompey exceeded all expectation in sweeping the harbours, inlets, secret landing places and seaborne traffic of the western Mediterranean. His determined actions persuaded some of the pirates to surrender, and those that did not capitulate were driven eastwards towards their traditional strongholds in Cilicia. Before Pompey could turn his full attention to the second half of his campaign, he had to return to Rome to deal with an adversary of a different kind: the consul Piso who had so strongly opposed him when Gabinius' bill was being debated. Piso had been assigned to Transalpine Gaul as his proconsular province, and there he stopped all recruiting by Pompey's agents. Worse still, he was alleged to have discharged troops already recruited, trying in a pusillanimous way to disrupt Pompey's campaign. The tribune Gabinius had prepared various measures to use against Piso, the most serious of which was a bill to depose him; but when Pompey arrived he would not allow Gabinius to present any of the bills. Perhaps he was content to allow information to leak about the retaliatory measures that he could have adopted, so that Piso and everyone else would know that he chose not to endorse such a procedure. Pompey had the power and influence, and if he had stirred up the people sufficiently, it is fairly certain that Piso would have been deposed; however he declined to use this influence, much as he demonstrated to Sulla years before that his troops would obey him if he chose to mutiny, but in fact he controlled them and opted for peaceful methods instead. No extant ancient source documents precisely how he dealt with Piso, which is unfortunate, since an interview between the two of them would have made an interesting scenario. It is not even known for sure if they held a meeting. Whatever happened, Piso stopped his anti-Pompeian activity. As Greenhalgh points out, it is difficult to understand how Piso thought he could achieve anything against Pompey when popular support for the project and the commander was running so high.[29]

After this unwelcome interlude, Pompey returned to his fleet. He had ordered part of it to assemble off Brundisium, and the rest to patrol the eastern Mediterranean coasts, flushing out the pirates from every hiding place, except from the coasts of Cilicia, which had been deliberately left open, neither blockaded from the sea nor harassed by land. It was hoped that this policy would encourage the surviving pirates to gather there, and the strategy worked. The pirates who had already surrendered were able to inform the Romans of many hiding places, which were reduced one by one as Pompey prepared for the final assault. He built up armed forces and a siege train on land, and concentrated the ships not engaged in patrols into attacking squadrons, finally coming to grips with the last of the pirates at Coracaesium (modern Alanya). If he had expected to conduct a long blockade and siege, he was probably pleasantly surprised at how quickly the surrender was brought about. The eastern Mediterranean campaign was over in 49 days, and the pirate menace was eradicated. The ancient sources rightly eulogise the achievement, but some of them lapse into hyperbole, declaring that pirates were never seen again in the Mediterranean. As Seager points out, in one of his speeches Cicero acknowledges that a few years later it was still necessary to guard against pirate activity; and during Gabinius' governorship of Syria, there was a pirate menace on the coasts. It is highly unlikely that Pompey managed to eradicate piracy entirely, and he can hardly be held responsible for any misdemeanours of resurgent or novice pirates after his campaigns. The greatest irony of all is that after Pompey's death his younger son Sextus took to the seas and became one of the most successful naval commanders that the Romans had ever faced, harassing the corn ships and disrupting supplies so thoroughly that there were food riots in Rome.[30]

Those pirates who had survived the rapid onslaught were settled on the land far from the sea, in cities that were revived and in one case renamed. This was the Cilician city of Soli, from which place the original inhabitants had been forcibly removed by Tigranes to populate his capital of Tigranocerta. Pompey refounded and renamed the city Pompeiopolis, a successful exercise in self-advertisement, and a successful enterprise as far as the settlement was concerned. It is not recorded how the original inhabitants fared when they returned home after Lucullus liberated them from Tigranocerta, but perhaps there was sufficient room for both them and the pirates. The other pirate settlements named in the sources are Dyme in Achaea, and Mallus, Epiphaneia and Adana in Asia Minor. These towns had suffered destruction and depopulation during the wars of Mithridates, so there was room for new settlers without disrupting the lives and the livelihood of existing inhabitants.[31]

The only blot on Pompey's justly lauded campaign was the fracas with Metellus and the struggle for control of the island of Crete. There could have been civil war, but the escalation was stopped before matters reached that stage. The background to the situation was that Metellus had been specifically appointed in 68 to deal with the Cretan pirates, with whom Antonius had made his shameful alliance in 74. By the time that Pompey took up his command, Metellus had still not finished the task, and because the Cretan pirates heard that Pompey was more lenient than Metellus, they offered to surrender to him. Pompey was probably delighted, and sent envoys to receive the surrender. But Metellus was not the sort to submit easily to Pompey's demands, even though the latter was supposedly given powers over the whole sea and coastal areas up to 50 miles inland. This gave Pompey effective control over the entire island; but since it is not known whether Pompey's *imperium* was *aequum* or *maius*, scholars have argued for two opposite views, either that Metellus' refusal to obey must mean that Pompey had only equal authority, or on the other hand that Pompey's readiness to give orders must mean that his powers were greater than those of Metellus. Neither argument is founded on anything more than guesswork and opinion. Likewise, opinion is divided as to who was more at fault in the Cretan incident, Pompey for high-handed action in interfering, or Metellus for opposing his wishes. At any rate, Metellus refused to recognise Pompey's authority and carried on his actions against the pirates, who were now even more hard pressed by the relentless and unforgiving assaults of Metellus. When Pompey's legate Lucius Octavius arrived to organise the capitulation of the pirates, Metellus ignored him, escalating his attacks on the cities that wished to surrender to Pompey. At one stage Octavius was trapped inside a besieged city, and though he was prepared to fight against Metellus, in the end he was forced to flee from Crete.

This challenge to Pompey could not be ignored. The general himself was in Cilicia, organising the settlement of the pirates on the land and in the cities, and he now prepared to sail to Crete to deal with Metellus. Had he done so there would probably have been another civil war, setting one general with his supporters against another from a powerful clan. Fortunately, the dreadful scenario did not develop, because it was at this point that Pompey heard that the tribune Manilius had managed to pass his bill in Rome, awarding the command against Mithridates and Tigranes to him, instead of Lucullus. Crete was now a side show, and could be left to the tender ministrations of Metellus, who rounded off his conquest of Crete in his own particular bloody manner, going on to take the title Creticus and hold a triumph for his achievements in 62. Pompey took some slight revenge by removing the two principal pirate ringleaders who were reserved for Metellus' triumphal procession. These men had surrendered not to Metellus, but to Pompey, so the latter stood his ground on this formality.[32]

The eastern command is generally assumed to be the one that Pompey really wanted, before he embarked on clearing the seaways. Manilius had been a willing tool in arranging for the appointment, but he received no reward for his work. He was prosecuted in the following year, and despite popular demonstrations on his behalf, he was condemned. Pompey sacrificed him, partly because he was not in a position to help him, and partly because Manilius was belligerent and unpredictable; Seager calls him a dubious asset. In 66, Manilius had served his purpose, and Pompey had been given the coveted eastern command. When he heard that he had been appointed to it, the story goes that he lapsed into histrionics and melodrama, bewailing his fate that kept him permanently fighting for Rome, never enjoying peace and quiet with his family. Those who knew him well probably assumed that this was all play acting to be taken with a pinch of salt, and perhaps even joined in the joke. Those who did not know him well would perceive a total contradiction in the professed reluctance to take on the command and the alacrity and eagerness with which he started to prepare for it.[33]

Agitation to deprive Lucullus of his command and to replace him had begun at least as early as 69, in parallel with the build up to Gabinius' bill to deal with the activities of the pirates, which had been increasing since the first Mithridatic war, and was hardly likely to cease while Mithridates was actively encouraging and supporting the pirates with the purpose of compromising Roman energy and manpower. Pompey probably viewed the two problems as a whole, calculating that he could deal with the pirates first and hope that the situation regarding Lucullus would conveniently worsen sufficiently to render the appointment of another commander an absolute necessity. It would not be possible to bring about events in the east that could cause Lucullus' downfall, but it was possible to monitor developments closely and take immediate advantage of any opportunity to discredit him. Appointed in 74 to stop the expansion of the newly energetic Mithridates, Lucullus had enjoyed enormous successes in the first three years. By 71 when Pompey returned from Spain, Lucullus had thrown Mithridates out of the Roman province of Asia, recovered Bithynia and invaded and captured Mithridates' own territory of Pontus. The one significant failure was that he had not captured Mithridates himself. The king had escaped to Armenia, where he took refuge with

7 *Map of the eastern provinces*

Tigranes, who was married to one of Mithridates' daughters. The war would still go on, and now there would be two enemies to fight, backed by the resources of the kingdom of Armenia. Lucullus was not daunted by the task, and initially he did well. He invaded Armenia, defeated Tigranes' army even though it greatly outnumbered his own, then defeated the combined forces of both Mithridates and Tigranes, and prepared to press on to the Armenian capital at Artaxata. But he had lost the confidence of his troops. The soldiers had been fighting for a long time, and though they had won battles, somehow the end of the war was never in sight, and now winter was approaching – and in Armenia that meant extreme hardship. The army would not go on, so Lucullus turned back and contented himself with taking the city of Nisibis further south. At this point at the turn of the year 69/68 the tables were turned on him, with Mithridates back in control of Pontus and Tigranes threatening Cappadocia. At Rome, Aulus Gabinius started agitating to deprive Lucullus of his command. The province of Asia was detached from Lucullus, most likely because he had damaged Roman business interests there. This so-called damage to Roman business interests actually resulted from Lucullus' fair and even-handed administration in Asia, so unusual and so benevolent that it caused citizens to erect statues to him and celebrate festivals called Lucullea. The respected Lucullus had corrected the many Roman abuses, and restored the prosperity of the communities which had been strangled both by Roman indemnity payments imposed after the last Mithridatic war, and by the raising of exorbitant loans from Roman money lenders in order to meet the indemnity payments.[34]

The next loss from Lucullus' command was Cilicia, given to the consul Marcius Rex, who did precisely nothing to help when Lucullus asked him for assistance just as Mithridates and Tigranes descended on Asia and Cappadocia. In 67, the tribune Gabinius detached Bithynia and Pontus from Lucullus, assigning them to M'. Acilius Glabrio. The dismantling of the whole eastern command had been achieved. The troops who were already disaffected now went on strike, and Lucullus could do nothing with them. He had sent to Rome for commissioners to organise the Mithridatic kingdom of Pontus as a Roman province, but by the time they arrived, Rome had no control over the territory and Mithridates was back in command. Lucullus was not only back where he started, but in an even worse situation, because now he had no keen army willing to follow him wherever he led. In one way it was perhaps a relief to be relieved of his burden, but he took it badly, and remained resentful of Pompey for the rest of his blighted career.[35]

Manilius' law had not had an easy passage in Rome. It was opposed by the same senators who had opposed Gabinius' bill, and for the same reason – that it bestowed too much power on one man. But this time several consulars spoke for the Manilian bill. These included Publius Servilius Vatia, Caius Curio, and Caius Cassius Longinus. It is recorded that Julius Caesar also supported the Manilian proposals, as he had supported those of Gabinius. Another voice was heard in favour of the bill, that of the praetor Marcus Tullius Cicero, who spoke at considerable length if the whole of his published speech was actually delivered. Cicero's motives may have been purely altruistic, centred on the fortunes of Rome; but there is the slight suspicion that he desired to gain some standing with Pompey, or even that he had been asked to deliver the speech. Pompey's personal involvement in promoting Manilius' bill is not known, but his long-standing interest in the command is assumed, and if he did not frame the proposals himself for others to put before the Senate and People of Rome, he had probably outlined what he wanted and left his agents to watch and wait upon events, ready to exploit the slightest chink in Lucullus' campaign to suggest a new arrangement. The danger to Roman territory posed by the resurgence of Mithridates and Tigranes may have been exaggerated in order to enhance Pompey's reputation as saviour of the Roman state, but at the very least there would be much to do to extricate the Romans armies from their current situation and stabilise it. In fact Pompey went much further, and the end result after four years was a thorough and sensible reorganisation of the eastern kingdoms, allied states, and Roman provinces.[36]

On setting out to take over from Lucullus, Pompey would need to consolidate what he had achieved so far. Though it is not recorded in detail, the fleet would still be operative, naval patrols would ensure that there was no revival of pirate activity, and would keep the Mediterranean as safe as possible for travel, trade and more important for the transport of troops and supplies if necessary. Pompey used the fleet to blockade the coasts of Asia Minor, to safeguard his rear and to stop any movements that might be favourable to Mithridates. The settlement programme for the pirates who had surrendered would require supervision, and officials would be left in place to organise it. For the eastern campaign, Pompey was authorised to take over from the governors of the Asian provinces, to appoint his own legates, to make war or peace according to his needs, and to conclude treaties with anyone he wished. This effectively put into the hands of one man the direction of the whole of Rome's foreign policy in the east.[37]

One of Pompey's first arrangements was the appointment of additional legates. He chose Lucius Afranius who had served him in Spain; his relative by marriage Quintus Metellus Celer; and Aulus Gabinius, whose term as tribune had ended, and who now probably needed to put distance between himself and the enemies he had made during his office. Pompey also appointed Lucius Valerius Flaccus, who had served under Metellus in Crete. The army that Pompey had at his disposal consisted of the troops he had levied for the pirate war and the allies he had raised from local communities. These he increased, summoning allied kings with their armies to meet him for the eastern campaign. In addition there would be the main body of Lucullus' army, once Pompey had taken over from him, and whatever troops Acilius Glabrio and Marcius Rex had at their disposal. These two governors were ordered to hand over their provinces to Pompey and withdraw; it may have afforded some slight consolation to Lucullus to see the men who had so recently taken over parts of his command now unceremoniously ousted from their own provinces. Pompey had made it clear that he had no desire for their assistance, thus setting the seal on his opinion of their military capacities.[38]

Before he made any move, Pompey arranged as many of the diplomatic settlements and safeguards as he could from his headquarters in Cilicia, which became a hive of activity as messengers came and went. Dio says that Pompey sent an envoy called Metrophanes to Mithridates, to make friendly overtures to the king. Greenhalgh accepts this account, but not at face value; suspicious of Pompey's motives, he suggests that the mission was one of information gathering, and not a bona fide attempt to reach a settlement. Seager dismisses the expedition of Metrophanes altogether, pointing out that the tale is told only by Dio, and that Pompey probably did not want to end the war so rapidly and so easily. On the other hand Sherwin-White opts for diplomatic missions as a normal practice at the outset of a war, to allow the enemy to agree to terms; it was not an attempt to stall for time, or purely to gather information.[39]

The sources for the whole of the eastern campaign are not necessarily wholly reliable, and they certainly vary as to chronology. Dio's approach was annalistic, keeping as far as possible to a consecutive narrative; but since he wrote in the early third century AD, the intervening two and a half centuries, laden with Imperial propaganda, could have greatly distorted the chronology and thereby altered later perception of cause and effect. The tendency of some ancient authors to group their information into themed sections sometimes makes it seem as though certain events happened simultaneously or consecutively, when in fact they may have been quite different in date. For instance, in his account of the events of 64, after Mithridates was defeated but not fully subdued, Appian describes embassies to Pompey from 12 kings, and in his narrative he also mentions that Mithridates sent messengers to try to make a settlement with the Romans by offering to govern his kingdom as an independent state but paying tribute to Rome. The date of this embassy from the defeated king is not established and may not have been simultaneous with those of the other 12 kings. Unfortunately there is no surviving contemporary account of Pompey's eastern campaigns, although it is likely that such accounts were written, perhaps by several of the men who accompanied his expedition. Just as General Bonaparte's expedition to Egypt included military men and an equally large body of scientists and artists, Pompey took with him the equivalent philosophers and writers. Of these, Theophanes and Posidonius probably wrote of their own experiences, if not of the army and of Pompey, but nothing has come down to us directly. Strabo, Nicolaus of Damascus, and Josephus preserve and regurgitate some of Theophanes' work when dealing with the campaign of 63. Plutarch, Appian and Dio may also have had access to contemporary material about Pompey's eastern achievements, but if they did, they interpreted it differently, and their accounts diverge and even contradict each other. This makes it more difficult for modern historians to produce a structured narrative, especially as in some sources everything seems to happen twice: there are two attempts to sue for peace, two pursuits of Mithridates, two ambushes by Pompey's troops, and two or more attacks on Gordyene, a disputed realm between Parthia and Armenia. Another factor, as Leach points out, is that while Pompey himself was achieving great things, his legates were also engaged in their allotted tasks, so there were simultaneous Roman operations in several parts of the east.[40]

The balance of power between the eastern kingdoms was a constant problem for Rome from the moment her Empire began to expand in that direction, bringing her into contact with both friendly and hostile regimes. The rivalry and hatred that kept many of these kingdoms from uniting with each other generally worked to Rome's advantage, but it could also draw her into subsidiary wars that had to be fought alongside the main operation, and that could escalate out of all proportion to the initial objective. Alliances shifted without warning, and sometimes there were internal dissensions within the ruling family that could be exploited by one opponent or the other. The war that Pompey had just entered already involved more than the king of Pontus. Tigranes, king of Armenia, had been brought into the arena because Mithridates was his father-in-law and had taken refuge with him. Quite apart from this family alliance, Tigranes probably discerned an opportunity to expand his own territory. After his initial success against the two kings Lucullus had failed to capture or contain them, and eventually they had won back all that they had lost, and more. Pompey left the troops that had been commanded by Marcius Rex to watch over Cappadocia in case Tigranes invaded. In order to keep Tigranes tied down on his borders, Pompey sent a diplomatic mission to Phraates, the king of Parthia. If he could arrange friendly terms with Phraates, encouraging him to take predatory action against his neighbouring rival kingdom of Armenia, this would enable him to divide his enemies and attack them one at a time, counting on a holding action against Tigranes while he concentrated on Mithridates. Pompey's understanding with Phraates, even if he merely intended it to be temporary, would inform Mithridates that there would be no hope of assistance or a diversionary attack on the Romans from that quarter, much less an alliance with Parthia.[41]

It is alleged that Mithridates sent an envoy to Pompey when he knew of the pro-Roman activity of Parthia, to negotiate a truce with a view to making peace. Pompey replied in high-handed terms, demanding the surrender of the king and the return of all the Roman deserters in his army, perhaps similar to the demands he had made at the outset of the war when he sent Metrophanes, unless the two events have been conflated. It was clear that Mithridates could not agree to these terms, and no doubt the king understood that the Romans would never end the war until they had effected his capture or his death. All the successes of Lucullus were negated because he had failed to achieve either of these aims, and Pompey was not disposed to achieve anything less. His terms were deliberately personal, and he would have been very surprised if the old king had accepted them. Before he made a move he was concerned to isolate Mithridates from his former allies and from potential new ones. Not yet ready to fight it out, Mithridates withdrew into the mountains, hoping to draw Pompey after him, cut his supply lines, and starve him to death.[42]

At some point very early on in the proceedings, Pompey met with Lucullus at Danala in Galatia. The encounter began reasonably well but ended acrimoniously. From the start, it was noted that the laurels of the lictors who marched before Pompey were fresh and green, whereas those of Lucullus' lictors were past their best and turning brown. After a few polite remarks the meeting degenerated and insults were hurled. Lucullus accused Pompey of always turning up like a carrion crow to pick over the remains of other people's wars, and Pompey charged Lucullus with greed and incompetence. He said that Lucullus had delayed victory in a war that should have been speedily wound up, but since it had been going on for such a long time, the advantage had passed to the enemy because they had been granted time to observe how the Romans fought and had reorganised their armies on Roman lines. The two men parted as enemies. Lucullus was left with 1600 men with which to return to Rome and hold his triumph; the rest of his troops were absorbed into Pompey's army. It might be expected that Lucullus would be glad to withdraw after this humiliating interview, but he lingered on, trying to organise Mithridates' kingdom as a new Roman province. Pompey monitored and cancelled all his pronouncements, no doubt heaving a sigh of relief when Lucullus packed and left to return to Rome.[43]

The chase after Mithridates hinged, as most campaigns did then and still do now, on supplies. Mithridates himself was hard-pressed to find food in the western parts of his kingdom because Lucullus had devastated the area, but as Pompey followed him into the mountains it was the Romans who were short. Mithridates camped on an impregnable hill, but had to abandon it because of lack of water, then made another camp at Dasteira in the Lycus valley. Unable to bring Mithridates to a final pitched battle, Pompey turned off the trail and began to forage in Lesser Armenia, hoping to bring Mithridates to attack him in response. He was able to lure some of the king's troops into an ambush, but still could not defeat Mithridates himself, who used the old trick of leaving the campfires burning and slipped out from his hilltop camp through the Roman siege lines at dead of night. Pompey gave chase, and finally managed to overtake the king without being observed, posting some of his troops on the heights on both sides of the pass through which Mithridates was about to march. In the ambush, many of the king's troops, possibly a third of his army, were killed. Once again Mithridates himself escaped, with a few comrades and not many soldiers. He decided to throw himself upon the mercy of Tigranes for the second time, but was firmly rebuffed. Tigranes made himself abundantly clear by offering a reward for his father-in-law's head. Mithridates had no choice but to continue his flight northwards, pursued for some time by Pompey, who eventually gave up and turned his attention to Armenia.[44]

The royal house of Armenia was at war with itself. The younger Tigranes had turned against his father and was besieging the capital of Artaxata with the help of the Parthian king, Phraates. The situation was quite delicate, given that Pompey had an understanding with Phraates, who now backed down and kept a low profile. One of the reasons why Tigranes refused to assist Mithridates was his suspicion that his father-in-law had encouraged the revolt of Tigranes junior. Pompey utilised the situation to his own advantage, listening sympathetically to the claims of the younger Tigranes as he approached Artaxata. The end result was less bloody than it might have been. The elder Tigranes submitted to Pompey, making as much of an elaborate show as he could, prostrating himself before the victorious Roman, who could afford to be magnanimous, ceremonially handing back to Tigranes his crown. In addition, he returned the kingdom of Armenia, for an indemnity of 6000 talents. Tigranes was also stripped of the territories that he had taken over during the wars, including Cappadocia, Syria, Cilicia, Phoenicia and Sophene. This last small kingdom was given to the younger Tigranes, and though he perhaps did not turn his full attention to Syria at this time, Pompey dated his possession of it from the time when Tigranes relinquished it.[45]

Sophene was not long under the hand of the younger Tigranes. When Pompey needed money, he refused the Romans access to the royal treasury, and for this and probably other misdemeanours he was removed and imprisoned. Sophene was handed back to Tigranes senior. The kingdom of Armenia, under the watchful eye of Lucius Afranius, would serve as a protection against Parthian ambitions. Phraates was worried, and sent an embassy to Pompey to ask if the frontier was to be the Euphrates, and Pompey replied that it would be drawn wherever he considered most suitable. Parthian ambitions were not diminished, and at some point, perhaps during Pompey's next campaigns against the Albanians and the Iberians, Phraates invaded Gordyene, but he was driven out and Afranius was sent to take over the territory. It was handed back to the elder Tigranes, and for the time being relations between Rome, Armenia and Parthia were tranquil, if not friendly.[46]

The Albanians and the Iberians had been allies of Mithridates. Pompey may not have planned to wage war on them during the campaigning season of 65, but the Albanians attacked him while his forces were split into three divisions in winter quarters in the Cyrnus valley. The Albanian king Oroeses allegedly took on the task of rescuing the imprisoned younger Tigranes, which suggests that the disinherited Armenian may have encouraged the attack on Pompey's camps. Oroeses may have suspected that he would be next to be absorbed into the sphere of domination by Pompey and tried to strike first, but all three of his co-ordinated attacks failed. His warriors faced Pompey himself, Metellus Celer, and Valerius Flaccus, each of whom led their separate divisions to victory. If Pompey had not originally entertained plans to campaign against the Albanians, he now had good reason to change his mind, and spent much of the next season fighting them. Although after this initial defeat Oroeses came to terms, he later rebelled, while Pompey was otherwise engaged.[47]

The kingdoms and tribes of the east were as wary of Pompey as Oroeses had been, and accordingly sent envoys to him. The chronology of his dealings with the smaller kingdoms is not elucidated, but the underlying principles remain the same. Mutual distrust and suspicion meant that intentions and clandestine movements required careful monitoring, and Pompey's agents worked well enough to inform him that while Artoces the king of the Iberians offered to come to terms, he was also preparing for war, probably hoping that protracted negotiations would give him time to manoeuvre into position. Instead Pompey struck first, taking control of the route into Iberia. At the river Pelorus, which was in flood, the Romans slaughtered the Iberians in a pitched battle, but the floods saved the remaining Iberians who escaped, including the king, because the Romans could not chase them and cut them down. There were no further battles, since Artoces accepted terms and sent his children to the Romans as hostages.

Unlike the Iberian king, Oroeses of the Albanians had not yet given up hope of victory; but when Pompey heard of his rebellion, he marched back over the ground already fought over and consequently low on supplies, to bring about the final battle at the river Abas. He used techniques learned from his adversary Sertorius, in that he disguised the numbers of men in his army by ordering the infantry to kneel down out of sight behind the cavalry. When the enemy charged, the Roman cavalry fell back, and then the infantry rose up, letting their own horsemen through and closing again as the Albanians reached them. The cavalry then turned, and came round from behind the Roman lines on either side of the enemy, securely hemming them in at front and rear.[48]

This battle was the last of the campaigning season, but the army was still active. Afranius was in Armenia, and Gabinius had been sent to Mesopotamia. Pompey's troops were still patrolling the coasts to reduce the chances of renewed activity of the pirates. Others will have been assigned to guarding routes and strategic points, to organising supplies, to police work and intelligence gathering. The troops that could be spared accompanied Pompey on an expedition to the Caspian Sea. This was not primarily a military exercise, but an exploration; some of the geographical and scientific information that was gathered still survives in the works of Strabo and Pliny. Unfortunately the expedition was aborted before the shores of the Caspian were reached, and Pompey turned back. One of the reasons for not going on was the presence of numbers of poisonous snakes and tarantulas; the fatal bite of the spiders sent people giddy and made them literally die laughing. The troops were only a short distance from the Caspian shores, but probably no one wished to continue the journey. If it was wanderlust and emulation of Alexander that drove him on, at least Pompey knew when to call a halt. There were several problems to attend to, not the least of which was the fact that Mithridates was still alive and potentially dangerous (despite his great age), and his kingdom had not yet been reorganised on lines acceptable to Rome.[49]

Instead of relentlessly pursuing the old king, who was out of the way and relatively harmless, in 64 Pompey set up his headquarters at Amisus. Mindful of maintaining his standing in Rome, he allowed, or perhaps sent, Metellus Celer and Valerius Flaccus home to stand in 64 for the praetorship of 63; both were elected, as were Titus Ampius Balbus and Titus Labienus to the tribunate for 64/3. It is possible that Servilius Rullus, also elected tribune for the same year, was one of Pompey's officers. None of these men achieved anything significant for Pompey in Rome.

With his remaining legates Pompey turned his attention to the south, first to Syria, and then to Judaea, and to Nabataea and its king Aretas. The three kingdoms were inextricably bound together, continually interacting with each other, making it impossible for Pompey to deal with just one of them in isolation. The ruler of Syria, Antiochus XIII, the last of the Seleucids, was harassed by incursions of Jews and Arabs, and had once been kidnapped and held prisoner by Sampsiceramus of Emesa, who installed another ruler, Philip II, in his place. Pompey dated his possession of Syria from the time when Tigranes surrendered his conquests, ignoring the claims of the Seleucids to govern the territory. He had sent Lucius Lollius, Metellus Nepos and Gabinius to Syria ahead of him, and Lollius and Metellus had captured Damascus, probably in 65, although the chronology and the exact dates are not established beyond doubt. Another of Pompey's legates, Marcus Aemilius Scaurus, was sent to Judaea. He arrived at Damascus shortly after it was captured, and continued on his way to Jerusalem. When Antiochus presented his case in an effort to maintain his position, Pompey referred to his continued lack of success in defending his borders. He wasted no time on diplomacy, insisting on the Roman annexation of Syria in order to protect it against the Jews and Arabs. There was probably never any question of allowing Antiochus to retain power, even though the king had enjoyed good relations with Lucullus.[50]

When Pompey arrived in Syria, Ptolemy XII Auletes, ruler of Egypt, sent him a convoy of gifts, consisting of money, soldiers, and clothing for his army. There were strings attached – Ptolemy needed help to quell riots among his own subjects in Alexandria; but Pompey had enough to do and his remit did not extend as far as Egypt.

In addition, he might have heard that Crassus had urged the Senate to annexe Egypt in 65, proposing that the young Julius Caesar should be sent out to supervise the process. Crassus' suggestion was crushed by Catulus, but there may have been further complex undercurrents that Pompey wished to avoid at this time. It may also have been at this point, or a little later when he was already embroiled in the thorny problems of Judaea and Nabataea, that Pompey heard that Phraates had once again invaded Gordyene, which provoked an appeal for help from Tigranes. Effectively this meant going to war. Pompey was not ready for that at the moment, and presumably never would be. He said that the law that granted his power to wage war on Mithridates did not authorise him to make war on the Parthians, and instead he sent three of his officers to negotiate between the kings of Armenia and Parthia. A potential flashpoint became a damp squib, and both Tigranes and Phraates accepted the arrangement. Fortunately they disliked each other and did not attempt to unite and turn on the Romans.[51]

The Judaean and Nabataean problems had arisen after the death of the queen, Salome Alexandra, whose two sons quarrelled over the possession of the throne. These were Aristobulus and Hyrcanus, each of whom had a following urging them on. Initially Hyrcanus stepped down in favour of Aristobulus; but he then teamed up with his so-called friend Antipater, who encouraged him to think again, especially since he seems to have considered that he could use Hyrcanus as a front man while the real power fell to him. It was Antipater who persuaded Hyrcanus to appeal to Aretas of Nabataea to support his claim to the throne, with the result that Aristobulus was put under siege in Jerusalem. At this juncture Aemilius Scaurus arrived and forced Aretas to withdraw, or be declared an enemy of Rome. Aristobulus installed himself as king, and so the position remained for a while. Pompey would not make a hasty or immediate judgement, and told both Hyrcanus and Aristobulus to meet him at Damascus in the spring of 63. He kept his word, and listened to both sides of the story but still made no pronouncement, explaining that he would first deal with Aretas. Perhaps he wished to make one or other of the two rivals show his hand, and if so, he succeeded, since Aristobulus left Damascus determined to fight the Romans. He installed himself first in the hill fort of Alexandreion not far from the Judaean border, and then, pursued by Pompey, in Jerusalem. Hastening after him, Pompey reached the ancient city of Jericho. There he received the news that Mithridates was dead, and announced it to the troops. Some sources place the arrival of this welcome news after the siege of Jerusalem, but the precise timing is not as important as the result, principally that the final settlement of the east could now begin in earnest, and soon the command against Mithridates would be at an end. The soldiers could expect to receive rewards and respite, in that order.[52]

Aristobulus did not fare very well in Jerusalem. His resolve gave way, and he tried to enter into negotiation with Pompey by turning up in the Roman camp, but was instead taken prisoner. This did not put an immediate end to the war, because his supporters who were still in the city refused to surrender, dragging out the siege for three months. When it fell, the loss of life was high. In so far as he understood them, Pompey respected most Jewish customs, and did not rob the temple treasury; but he insisted upon entering the inner sanctuary, a gross and unforgivable sacrilegious act in the eyes of the Jews, and one that Pompey may have found somewhat disappointing, because the sanctuary was empty. After satisfying his curiosity, he made arrangements for Hyrcanus to take over, but refused to acknowledge him as king. Instead Hyrcanus was to be High Priest. Maintenance of the balance of power between rival states was crucial, and it suited Pompey to create a relatively weak Judaea on the frontiers of his new province of Syria. Likewise he needed to reduce the strength of the Nabataeans, perhaps planning to conduct the campaign against Aretas himself; but now that Mithridates was dead, he delegated the task to Aemilius Scaurus, and returned to his headquarters at Amisus.[53]

The son of Mithridates sent his father's body to Sinope. Pompey refused to look at the corpse, and since he had nothing to gain by refusing his adversary all proper burial rites, he allowed the funeral to take place. He read the letter or letters that Pharnaces sent him, learning of the pathetic end of the once great Mithridates, who had caused so much trouble with his empire-building activities to the other – now supreme – empire builder, Rome. The sons of Mithridates were not necessarily of like mind, and after putting an end to the rebellion of one of his offspring called Machares, Mithridates had begun to build up another army; but his troops had lost confidence in him. He was an old man, advanced in years but not diminished in ambition; however his dreams were impossible of realisation, because he lacked the funds that might have attracted mercenaries to his army. It became clear that all hopes of peace with Rome were useless, and that the main obstacle to peace was the presence of Mithridates himself. Pharnaces confronted that reality by turning against his father, converting many of the king's troops to his cause. When Mithridates knew that all was lost, so the story goes, he tried to kill himself by taking poison, but all his life he had inured himself to all kinds of poisons, allegedly by ingesting small amounts until his system became accustomed to them. He had ensured that no one would ever assassinate him by poisoning his food, and so now when he sought death that method was denied him. He tried to stab himself but failed, and was finally despatched by a faithful servant. Some authors have suspected that Pharnaces was the one who actually killed Mithridates, but no one will ever know the truth. Whether he had killed him or not, Pharnaces had certainly precipitated the death of Mithridates, thus relieving Pompey of a burden that he had not been able to put off himself. Expecting to be rewarded Pharnaces asked Pompey's permission to retain the old kingdom within its original boundaries, or if that should prove impossible, that he should be allowed to keep control of the Bosporus. This Pompey granted, with the exception of the city of Phanagoria, governed by the pro-Roman Castor. Pharnaces was also recognised as a friend and ally of the Roman people.[54]

The winter of 63-2 was spent in organising the east to the satisfaction of Rome, but with consideration for the welfare of the natives as well. Lucullus, too, would have been as lenient as Pompey, but having lost the confidence of the troops, he would never have reached the stage of making any settlement, and he had already angered the businessmen in Rome – in particular the equestrians who controlled the tax contracts, and saw the east as a vast extent of exploitable territories providing unlimited wealth. The arrangements that Pompey made seem to have stepped carefully as possible between all the pitfalls on both the Roman and the native sides. Many of the petty kingdoms and states had welcomed Mithridates as a better option than being governed by Rome, and to punish them too severely would only underline the point that they had been correct to choose the eastern king rather than the Romans, who cared for nothing except extracting booty. In general, without bleeding the east dry, Pompey took over what was governable and profitable, either in the sense of monetary profit or defensive capacities. The territories further away were placed under friendly rulers whose abilities and pro-Roman sympathies he had discerned. Pompey established Roman provinces around the coast of Asia Minor and along the southern shore of the Euxine: Pontus, Bithynia, Asia, Cilicia and Syria. Roman legions were to garrison them, one in Bithynia and two each in Cilicia and Syria. The territorial boundaries are not precisely known, but some of the provinces such as Cilicia and Bithynia were augmented by the addition of parts of the adjoining territories, not purely for the sake of enlarging them but to rationalise the government of the provinces and their relations with the surrounding kingdoms. In those provinces where there had been a long history of Greek settlement, there were established cities which provided the infrastructures that readily supported Roman provincial administration; but in territories like Pontus, this substructure had largely to be created. Pompey divided the latter province into 11 districts with an administrative centre in each, but he did not set in motion an ambitious programme of public and private building; in many cases throughout her early empire-building and even into Imperial times, Rome was content to set the example and then let local initiative develop as it would. The mode of government in each province would probably have been outlined in a law, purposely drawn up on standard Roman lines but also incorporating local customs and traditions as far as possible. Only the law concerning Bithynia is known, and as Seager points out the greatest tribute that can be made to Pompey's forethought and planning is the fact that in the early third century, when Dio describes the province, no one had discovered any need to alter or annul his administrative arrangements.[55]

Bithynia was ringed by small client states, whose rulers were installed or confirmed in their possession by Pompey. Deiotarus of Galatia had his kingdom enlarged by the addition of some lands formerly in Pontus. He also received the kingdom of Lesser Armenia; some sources say this was directly from Pompey, and others that it was a gift of the Senate, but it has been suggested that this confusion arose from a conflation of the grant by Pompey and the confirmation of it by the Senate. Another king, Ariobarzanes of Cappadocia, received some parts of Cilicia when the boundaries were rationalised. Aristarchus was to rule in Colchis, and Attalus was given parts of Paphlagonia. Not all the names of the client kings are known, but the principle holds good for all of them, in that the territories that Rome was not prepared to administer directly were governed by rulers who would protect their own and Roman territory against initial attacks from enemies further away, especially from Parthia, perhaps the only large state that could rival Rome in organisation, manpower and wealth.[56]

There remained the distribution of rewards to the soldiers, amounting to 384 million sesterces. The financial benefits to Rome and to Pompey and his senior officers far outweighed this enormous expenditure, but it cannot be said that Pompey exploited the eastern provinces and kingdoms in order to secure his own fortune. He had exacted tribute from many sources during the war, and made arrangements for continued payments into Rome's deep coffers; but he had also brought peace and a secure and well-planned administration, so the eastern kings and princes perhaps did not consider it an expensive exercise.[57]

It was a leisurely trip back to Rome. Pompey took time to visit the city of Mytilene on the island of Lesbos, the home of his friend Theophanes. The city had supported Mithridates, and consequently had lost its freedom, but Pompey restored it, and remained there to listen to poets reciting their works, all describing his campaigns and achievements. He took careful note of the theatre where the poets recited, and since Rome did not possess a permanent theatre, he formed the idea that one day he would build one, and had several drawings of the building made for future reference. After his short stay in Mytilene he went to Ephesus, Rhodes and Athens, distributing gifts and donations of cash. He probably felt a great personal satisfaction and a sense of real achievement as he made his way back to Rome, where he looked forward to holding his justly-deserved triumph, and to setting before the Senate his administrative arrangements for the east, so they could be formally ratified and firmly established. Then perhaps he would secure a second consulship, and wait upon events for another chance to take up a military command.

There were two flies in the ointment, which perhaps would not be overwhelmingly troublesome. There was the overweening confidence of Pompey's friend Marcus Tullius Cicero, whose consulship in 63 culminated in the arrest and execution of the conspirators who had joined Catiline. He sent two letters, the first lauding his own achievements and the second rebuking Pompey for not taking him seriously enough, but at the same time proposing that they should be allies, working closely together, the great statesman advising the great general. Pompey did not feel that he needed help from Cicero, so he probably dismissed the letters as trivial. Then there was the failure of his legate Metellus Nepos as tribune for 63/2. Nepos had introduced a bill advocating that Pompey should stand for election as consul *in absentia*, and that he should be immediately recalled from the east to deal with the remnants of the Catilinarian conspiracy, since Catiline was still free, armed and dangerous. There was scarcely any need for such hysterical action and it is said that Pompey's wife Mucia tried to moderate the behaviour of her kinsman, for the purpose of which she allied herself temporarily with Cicero. The tribune's strong-arm tactics did Pompey more harm than good, but when Nepos fled Rome to return to the army early in 62, Pompey received him at headquarters, seemingly without rancour. Nor did he take immediate action in defence of his supposedly-wronged tribune, by wading into politics backed by his troops. He already had enemies enough in Rome, and it was clear that the numbers had increased; but Pompey had survived among enemies before, and now he had stupendous victories, loyal soldiers, and unimaginable quantities of money. He was in the same position as Sulla had been in, when he returned from the east to face his enemies in Rome. As Pompey landed at Brundisium at the end of 62, many Romans probably held their breath.[58]

4 Tarnished triumph

It was a magnificent journey from Brundisium to Rome. Just after he landed and everyone disembarked, Pompey made a speech thanking his soldiers for their loyal service, and then dismissed them, asking them to come to Rome when he held his triumph. After this deliberately publicised ceremony, Pompey and his retinue began their slow march to the city, received as heroes in every town they passed through; and when they neared Rome itself, thousands of people were there to meet the great man and escort him home. The sense of relief was tangible, just as Pompey had intended. The dismissal of his troops was calculated to show that he had no designs on seizing power, as much to reassure the wary, as to assert himself and make it plain to those who may have hoped to rise to prominence via a civil upheaval that this was not an option.[1]

On the way home Pompey may have reflected on the contrast between the eager reception and the avid hero-worship on the one hand, and on the other his lack of success in the last few years in the political arena. The world of Rome had moved on since he left to deal with the pirate menace, and Pompey had no strong home-based party in the political sense to direct legislation that would be favourable to him when he came home. From far away in the east, he had tried to influence events, in so far as he was able, by sending various officers home to stand for election as tribunes and praetors; but it cannot be said that they had shaped political policies in any way. The principal opponents of the Pompeian cause were Catulus, Hortensius, Lucius Lucullus and Quintus Metellus, and now Marcus Porcius Cato. Metellus and Lucullus had been forced to wait for a long time before they could celebrate their triumphs, after their exploits respectively in Crete and in the east. Lucullus in particular was embittered because he had achieved a great deal in the struggle against Mithridates, and Pompey had taken over before he had been afforded an opportunity to rally his men and win back all that he had lost.[2]

The new and aspiring politician Cato was a powerful and persuasive orator, and it was clear that he could sway the opposition and perhaps take the lead. But since he was relatively new on the scene, he could perhaps be won over to Pompey, and so create a small power block to stand against the other intransigents in the Senate. This is not to suggest that there was a Catonian power block already formed in the Senate, or that Cato enjoyed supreme power and influence on his own account; but an alliance of some kind with him might possibly neutralise him and make one less determined enemy. This is presumably what Pompey had in mind when he broke off relations with his wife Mucia by sending her a note while he was on his way home, requesting a divorce and giving her notice to quit his house. The charge was adultery,

8 *Bust of Marcus Porcius Cato, from the Roman city of Volubilis (modern Oubili) in North Africa, and now in Rabat Museum. It was Cato's intransigence that threw Pompey into the arms of Caesar, and set in motion the coalition which ultimately caused the destruction of the Republic that Cato tried to uphold.* Photo David Brearley but it probably did not cause any grief to Pompey whether or not it was true. It was time to realign himself politically. The Metelli had not been especially loyal or useful to him, and he had two sons and a daughter by Mucia, so the question of heirs and spares did not arise. Almost immediately on his arrival, Pompey requested a marriage alliance between his house and that of Cato, the proposal being that he should marry one of Cato's nieces, and his eldest son Gnaeus should marry her sister. Cato refused, although the two sisters were by no means pleased with him for doing so. But Cato was never one to be compromised. At least Pompey now knew where he stood.[3]

When Pompey arrived in Rome there were still raw memories of the disturbances of the last two or three years that overshadowed his achievements in the east, because they were more immediate and affected people's lives more closely than distant wars in lands that were only vaguely known and probably hard to pronounce. The big scandal of 63 was the so-called Catilinarian conspiracy, discovered and defeated by Cicero in his finest hour as consul. Catiline was said to have considered raising revolt when he failed to be elected to the consulship in 66 and had been prevented from standing in 65 and 64. The stories about him were probably fabricated, and applied retrospectively to his previous career. In order to bolster up the theory that he was about to take over the state in 63, there had to be a suspicion that he had been scheming for some time. The truth is now so shrouded in mystery that it can never be known, and does not seem to have been fully elucidated at the time. In his eagerness to save the state, Cicero rounded up the ringleaders, one of whom was Lentulus Sura, stepfather of Mark Antony. On Cicero's command, they were executed without benefit of a fair trial, and for this he was to pay heavily at a later date. Catiline was not among the men who were executed but he was eventually hounded to death. He may not have posed such a terrible danger to the state, but Cicero firmly believed that Catiline was guilty of all the crimes and conspiracies of which he accused him, and wrote a pamphlet about the affair (although it was not published until after his death).[4]

Cicero was piqued because Pompey had not been effusive enough in praise of his achievements. Pompey's lack of enthusiasm may or may not have derived from the fact that Cicero had wittingly or unwittingly wrecked what could have been a forward-thinking plan for land settlements for the urban poor and for Pompey's veterans. The built-in checks and balances in the Roman political system were admirably designed to ensure that no single individual assumed and retained supreme power, but the down side was that the same checks and balances enabled politicians to thwart other politicians with monotonous regularity, with no clearer motive sometimes than the satisfaction of seeing opponents flounder and fail. The result was that even well thought-out plans designed to benefit of one or more sections of the community could be arbitrarily squashed, and there was no central authority directing state programmes and policies with long-term aims in view. The question of land settlements for time-served veteran troops was a constant theme in Roman politics, and the proposals for the settlement of soldiers who had served with Pompey and Metellus Pius in Spain had never been fully implemented. It may have been with this in mind that the tribunes of 63, led by Servilius Rullus, tried to pass a law designed to solve the veteran problem and that of the landless urban masses.[5]

The extent to which Rullus was involved with Pompey, and whether or not the latter was wholly behind these proposals, is not known; but Rullus had been one of Pompey's commanders, taking charge of the Black Sea fleet two years before he became tribune. The care with which Rullus drafted the bill to exclude any possibility that Pompey might be one of the directing forces suggests that if Pompey was behind it, then he did not wish to be prominently involved with it, perhaps to avoid suspicion of undue bias. Rullus proposed that there should be an elected commission of ten men in charge of the land settlements, with praetorian power extending over the whole Roman world. He was concerned that the urban poor should be included in any land allocations so that the emphasis was not wholly on veteran soldiers, and he proposed that state lands should be used as far as possible to create new plots for the chosen men to establish their farms. Rullus' land bill was never put into operation, but if it had been passed it would have alleviated several problems at once. The theory behind the agrarian bill was clear; the population pressures in Rome would be lessened if the poor could be settled on their own farms, and the food shortages that sometimes erupted into rioting would be reduced. Rullus was aware of the problems caused when Sulla uprooted people to make way for his veterans, and planned to avoid forced sales or arbitrary seizures of land. With this in mind he stipulated that the veterans already settled by Sulla were to be left alone, unless they expressed an interest in selling up and moving. He also hoped to ensure that sufficient lands would be provided and there would be no shortfall which would disappoint people, by making arrangements for the purchase of other lands if there was not enough acreage under public ownership in Italy. In order to raise the money for this it was suggested that state-owned property in the provinces should be sold, and that any booty from foreign wars should be dedicated to the same purpose. This may be Pompey's contribution to the proceedings – that war should pay for war, at least in arrears: and he was in a position to know exactly how much could be raised from the four years of war that he had just fought in the east. There was a clause that commanders of successful military expeditions should dedicate their personal booty to the land commissioners as well as the general spoils of war that they brought to Rome. Pompey, however, was to be exempted from this ruling. No one can tell whether this clause was instigated by Pompey himself in a blatant and shameless attempt to protect his own assets, or whether Rullus inserted it to divert suspicion that he was trying to compromise Pompey.[6]

Despite this favourable clause aimed at leaving the great commander's wealth intact, Cicero took the line that this bill would be harmful to Pompey. Why he assumed this stance is not known; it is much more likely that the bill was intended to assist Pompey, and may have been drawn up with his approval or under his direction. At least one scholar, in a recent examination of Rullus' proposals, concludes that it was very similar to the land bill put forward by the tribune Flavius in 60, and also to the bill that Caesar forced through as consul in 59. In that case, since Pompey was known to be associated with these bills, his interest in what Rullus proposed was probably more than just perfunctory. He may have intended to create a ready-made agrarian law, preparing for his return home so that there should be a smooth transition for his veterans from newly-discharged soldiers to peaceful farmers, without disrupting anyone in the process, and so pre-empting the criticism that he had filled the countryside with dangerous footloose and idle soldiers. If this is what he intended, presumably he had failed to mention it to Cicero. It is hard to believe that Cicero would deliberately set out to destroy Pompey's plans if he had been forewarned of them.

Another of the several possible options borders on the tragi-comic: perhaps Cicero genuinely thought that he was rendering good service to his friend. He may have sincerely believed what he was saying, or perhaps he had other motives, too deep to be discerned at a remove of 2000 years. Cicero's main arguments against Rullus' land bill related to the fact that Pompey would not be a member of the ten man commission to organise the settlements, and that the proposed sale of lands in the territories that Pompey had fought over was a little premature, because these territories had not yet been organised, so it seemed that the commission would be interfering with Pompey's arrangements before he had any chance to ratify them. As far as the allotments were concerned, Cicero said that they would be worthless, because they would consist of unproductive marshes, and he further contended that the sale of public lands would entail a damaging loss of revenue.[7]

Rullus backed down as soon as Cicero had stirred up the populace against the bill. Rumours started to circulate that Crassus and Caesar were involved in this affair, and that they were planning to use the bill to harm Pompey, depriving him of lands to settle his veterans, and at the same time building up their own power base to enable them to stand against him when he returned home. Crassus' dislike of and rivalry with Pompey was already legendary, so anything that added to the fable was accepted with few questions asked. Crassus had persuaded the Senate to appoint Calpurnius Piso as governor of Nearer Spain in 65, which was seen by some as an attempt to undo Pompey's work in the province and to undermine his client base there. In the same year, he had tried to arrange for the annexation of Egypt, proposing to send Caesar, who was not yet of praetorian rank, to oversee the proceedings. Even though Pompey himself considered that Egypt lay outside his remit, and despite the fact that he had most of the remaining eastern territories to draw upon, this action on the part of Crassus was interpreted as an attempt to build up a command and a client base to rival Pompey, and the motion was defeated by Catulus, using this excuse. Caesar's alleged intention to thwart Pompey at this stage is without foundation. Since Caesar had supported various measures connected with Pompey, probably voting in favour of Gabinius' bills and definitely voting for the Manilian bill, the suggestion that he planned to take a hostile stance against him is not tenable. Whilst Caesar was not a confirmed or slavishly-consistent Pompeian and could obviously think for himself, it was clear that when the great man returned there would probably be more mileage to be gained in co-operating with him than in opposing him. It was said that in 63 Caesar supported the motion put forward by the tribunes Labienus and Ampius Balbus, that Pompey should be allowed to wear triumphal dress at the games, and a gold crown at the theatre. Such distinguishing marks of high status could be considered meaningless baubles, but their significance to the Romans should not be underestimated, and

Caesar's support for them probably did not conceal a hidden agenda. He had concerns of his own to occupy him, since he was heavily in debt and required a legitimate means of making his fortune, in both the political and monetary sense.[8]

Whether or not Pompey had instigated Rullus' bill, in 63 he lost irrevocably the opportunity to effect a settlement for his veterans before he returned home. Now he would have to start the laborious process of arranging for veteran settlement after his arrival, in the teeth of opposition. If he entertained hopes that one of his officers, Metellus Nepos, could accomplish anything as tribune in 62, he was again disappointed, for Nepos did more harm than good. He prevented Cicero from making a speech at the end of his consulship, and in this he was supported by Caesar who had strongly objected to the execution of the Catiline so-called conspirators without trial. Caesar, who was praetor in 62, also co-operated with Nepos in an attack on Catulus, who had been awarded the honourable task of restoring the temple of Jupiter. The two of them proposed that the task should be wrested from Catulus and bestowed on Pompey. Whether or not Pompey heard of this action on the part of Caesar is only conjectural. He will have heard that Caesar had been appointed as Pontifex Maximus in 63, in place of Metellus Pius who died in 64. Catulus also desired the office, and was likely to be elected if the Senate had its way. It was Labienus who proposed that the voting should be returned to the people, and so by popular consent Caesar won the office, which was bestowed for life, and held great political potential. Other than hearing news of each other in an informal way it is unlikely that Caesar and Pompey were in direct correspondence at this time, and even if they had contacted each other, Caesar could do nothing more for Pompey after 62, because he left Rome as Pompey returned, to take up his post as propraetorian governor of Further Spain for 61: he did not wait for the end of the year before setting out. It was said that Crassus paid all his creditors off as he was leaving.[9]

Military commands for Pompey were not out of the question, as far as Nepos was concerned. Since Catiline had not yet been brought to book in 62, Nepos proposed that Pompey should be recalled to deal with the situation. The similarity with the end of the war against Spartacus is obvious, but it is not certain whether Nepos was acting alone or whether Pompey wanted to come home to another series of battles to save the state, more spectacular than Cicero's political victory. He had upstaged Crassus, so it was not beyond the bounds of possibility that he wished to upstage Cicero. It was said that Nepos also proposed that Pompey should be elected consul *in absentia*, though this assertion is not found in all sources. In trying to overcome all opposition, Nepos brought armed men into the Senate, but the only result was his own defeat and disgrace, and he fled to Pompey, who was still in the east. To what extent Pompey had engineered this fiasco is not known. It is unlikely that he could have communicated with Nepos while he was in office, and he could not have guaranteed that there would be any excuse for his recall to deal with an alleged rebellion. It is more likely, as Seager suggests, that Pompey laid down a very loose agenda for Nepos and then let him act upon it according to whatever circumstances he met with in Rome. The only result was that Pompey probably beseeched the gods to protect him from his friends.[10]

Having failed to install successful candidates in office in 63 and 62, Pompey backed his friend Marcus Pupius Piso for the consulship of 61. At Pompey's request, the Senate delayed the elections in 62 to allow Piso enough time to travel to Rome. There is some confusion over this request, in that it seemed that Pompey wanted to hold up the elections until he arrived home himself, either to canvass for Piso or even to stand for election in person. It is possible that he asked for postponement of the elections twice, but only one of his requests was granted, or that he intended to cover both himself and Piso in the one request but the Senate co-operated only in the case of Piso. However, given that Pompey did not stand for the consulship even when it became obvious that he was not going to find it easy to have the necessary legislation passed to round off his eastern campaigns, it is perhaps unlikely that he wished to stand for election in 62. Whatever it was that the Senate blocked, the prime motivator for the blocking was Cato. In any case, being held up in Judaea and unable to return home as early as he originally thought, Pompey perhaps sent Piso on alone to prepare the way for the return of the army. Piso was duly elected, with Marcus Valerius Messalla as his colleague.[11]

Whatever expectations Pompey had entertained of Piso, they were not to be gratified. The year 61 was one of stalemate as far as Pompey's political aims were concerned. There was a great scandal in full swing when he arrived home, and everyone's head was full of it, with little time to spare for the conquering hero. The culprit who had caused all the trouble was Publius Clodius Pulcher, of ill repute, who had disguised himself as a woman to infiltrate the festival of the Bona Dea, which only women were allowed to attend. The celebration was held in the house of Caesar, and Clodius was discovered, ejected and reported, in that order, by Aurelia, Caesar's mother. No one knows what on earth Clodius intended to do; it was suggested that he was having an affair with Caesar's wife Pompeia (no relation to Pompey, but the grandaughter of Sulla). Caesar promptly divorced her, saying that Caesar's wife must be above suspicion. He fully intended to bring Clodius to justice for his sacrilegious actions, and when Pompey arrived home the trial of Clodius was in progress. The fact that he was acquitted did not lessen Clodius' anger and hatred of Cicero, who had systematically demolished his alibi and underlined his obvious guilt. From the days of the trial, Clodius and Cicero were enemies. Pompey's enemies used the opportunity to extract opinions from him about the affair, which Pompey hedged and sidestepped by anodyne remarks designed to keep him out of trouble. He said that he had the greatest respect for the actions of the Senate, but would not comment on anything else, much like modern politicians sweeping tight-lipped past reporters to the sanctuary of their cars. He made a speech to the people, but failed to hit the right notes. He had been absent for four years, and as the modern phrase has it, a week is a long time in politics, making it difficult for him to slot back into the heady pace of change.[12]

Pompey could not win over the support of the Senate, nor did he win over the people, except by entertaining them magnificently when he held his triumph in September 61. This was a stunning display lasting for two days, though no one really knows exactly how it was organised. There may have been two parades through Rome, or only one procession and feasting and entertainments on the other day. The second day of the triumphal celebrations was 29 September, Pompey's forty-fifth birthday, and perhaps the day on which he processed through the city and dedicated the spoils of war to the gods. The parade included captives from all the nations that Pompey claimed to have conquered. There were 14 defeated nations named on placards carried before the procession, and an enumeration of all the cities and strongholds that he had taken, including 800 pirate ships. Pompey was concerned to list the revenues accrued for the benefit of the state as a result of his campaigns, which he demonstrated by the cartloads of booty paraded through the streets. Where he could not put on show illustrious prisoners, he substituted statues; the deceased Mithridates was portrayed in this way, and although Tigranes was now an ally of Rome, a statue also represented him, since Pompey had in fact subdued him before setting him back on the throne of Armenia. Then there were the spoils, numerous pieces of jewellery, priceless ornaments and cups, and enough gold to pay off the national debt of any modern fully-developed western country.

People talked of Pompey's third triumph for many years after the event. Not only had he celebrated three triumphs, which was enough to make him the foremost man in Rome, but he had triumphed over Europe, Africa, and Asia, in fact over three continents. This made him unique in his own lifetime. He had reached the zenith of his career, and as Plutarch comments, it would have been better if he had died then, and never experienced the later political turmoil and his final defeat in the civil wars.[13]

He may have found some solace in his architectural projects, which included the building of a house on the Pincian Hill in the city, and a sumptuous villa at Albano outside Rome. This villa was taken over in the late first century AD by the Emperor Domitian, who lived in the older house that Pompey built while his own architects created a vast complex of buildings, sweeping away in the process several smaller residences that were eventually swallowed up by the Domitianic palace. The site is now occupied by Castel Gandolfo, one of the summer residences of the Pope. Pompey's plans for the theatre, the first permanent one in Rome, may have been put into operation about this time. He had seen the theatre at Mytilene and had drawings made, so at some time after his arrival in Rome, he presumably contacted an architect and started proceedings to clear the land in the Campus Martius, outside the city limits. Until Pompey's theatre was built, when the citizens of Rome attended performances of plays they had always been accommodated in temporary structures with seating built for the purpose, and then removed. Since theatre performances were bawdy affairs, the upright Romans of the day, probably encouraged if not led by Cato, objected to Pompey's ideas, until he surrounded the theatre with religious precincts and made it respectable. The dedication of the whole complex was carried out in 55, and since no one knows the precise date when construction started it cannot be said how long the building work took. There is nothing to see in modern Rome of this theatre, but an aerial view of the city shows the outline immediately, since the later buildings kept within the confines of the theatre and temple walls, even so far as tracing the curved end of the theatre itself. A carved marble plan of the theatre, partly damaged so that only one side of the temple precincts can be seen, survives from Severan times, when a complete and very detailed map of the city was created in stone.[14]

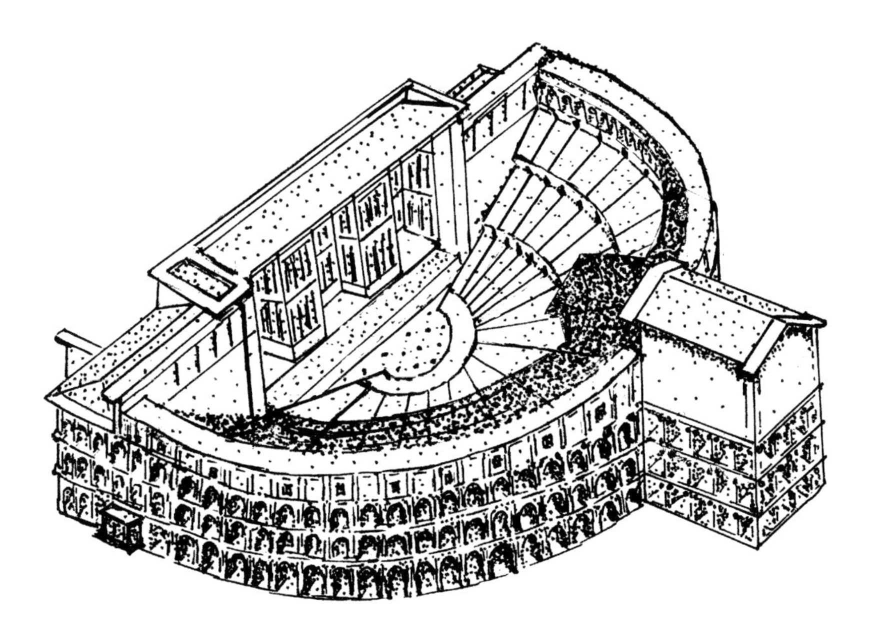

9 *Reconstruction drawing of Pompey's theatre. This was the first permanent theatre in Rome, based on the examples that Pompey had seen in Greece, in particular that of Mytilene, where he had drawings made with a view to erecting a theatre in Rome. The whole complex consisted of colonnaded walks and several temples. The building was planned to run east to west in the Campus Martius, behind a series of earlier Republican temples, and incorporated some shrines and small temples into the main structure. The main temple was dedicated to Venus Victrix, the goddess with whom Pompey felt a personal affinity.* Drawn by Jacqui Taylor

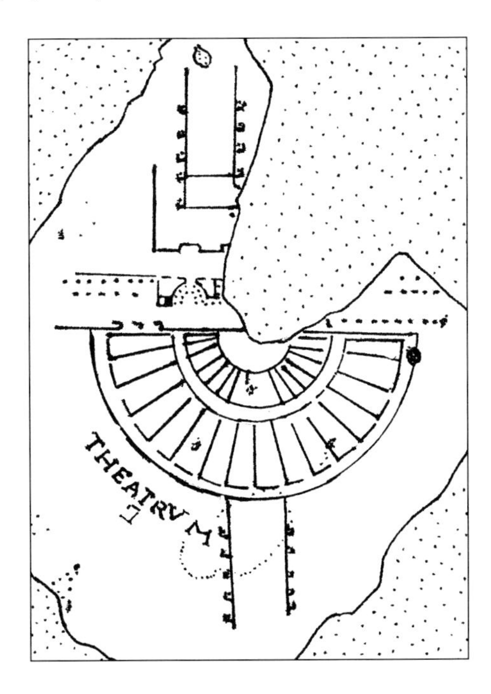

10 *The theatre depicted on a fragment of the marble plan of Rome, the Forma Urbis, that was drawn up in Severan times. The theatre was at the western end of the complex, and the huge colonnaded portico, part of which is just visible on this fragment, ran towards the east, into the modern Largo Argentina. A glance at a detailed street map of modern Rome reveals that the road layout preserves the curved end of the theatre, marked by the Via di Grotta Pinta. There are no remains of the theatre to be seen, except for some of the concrete vaulting inside restaurants in the Piazza del Biscione and the Piazza del Paradiso.* Drawn by Jacqui Taylor

Pompey's consular candidate for the year 60 was Lucius Afranius, who was elected along with Metellus Celer. Though Pompey had continued to support Celer, the latter had by now decided that he need not tie himself securely to his old commander, so he was able to oppose Afranius successfully. There can be no doubt of Afranius' loyalty, but like Pompey himself he had insufficient political experience to be able to compete with the phalanx of Pompey's opponents. The tribune Flavius did no better with his land bill. He proposed that land should be purchased by using the tribute payments from the east for the next five years, and the proposal for settlement was designed, like that of Rullus, to include the urban plebs. Principally it was aimed at securing land for Pompey's veterans, who by now would probably have spent all the money from their war gains and from the gratuities paid to them when they were disbanded. Cicero tried to suggest some modifications to the bill, perhaps showing a willingness to vote in favour of it, but Metellus Celer opposed Flavius, who lost his temper and his head and marched Celer off to prison. Unrepentant, Celer invited the senators to meet at the prison. Flavius, in his sacrosanct personage as tribune, sat down before the prison door, but Celer encouraged the senators to break the walls down, circumventing Flavius. The scenario descended into farce, and Pompey called Flavius off. Thus in 61 and in 60, he was no further on with his promised land settlements, and his eastern arrangements were being endlessly debated clause by clause in the Senate. Lucullus had come out of retirement to enjoy this prolonged scrutiny of Pompey's administrative schemes.[15]

Pompey had nowhere to turn, except to call up his soldiers and take what he needed by force – and that was not at all what he wanted to do. If he went down that route then he would have to fight for the rest of his life to stay in power, or even to stay alive. His speciality was saving the state from dangers, not in creating them. The fact that he backed Afranius for the consulship of 60 suggests that he had no contacts he could set up in office who would be powerful enough to push through the necessary legislation to achieve his two goals, the ratification of the eastern provinces and client kingdoms, and the settlement of his veterans. He needed allies who were accustomed to the political scene, bold enough to counter opposition without crumbling or making mistakes. In 60, Gaius Julius Caesar returned from Further Spain. He had been voted a triumph for his exploits in subduing the Lusitanians, but he faced a dilemma, since he also wanted to stand for election to the consulship for 59. Accordingly Caesar asked permission to stand *in absentia*, because he could not enter the city until he had laid down his command and held his triumph. The Senate refused. Caesar spent no time in agonising over his priorities. He abandoned the triumph and entered Rome to stand for election in person.[16]

His election was not highly contested, except that Cato spent lavish sums of money on bribing the electorate in support of his kinsman Marcus Calpurnius Bibulus, who became Caesar's colleague for the second time; the first time they had met was when they served as aediles together, and it had not been a pleasant experience for Bibulus. The consulship was to be even less pleasant for him, and engendered in him an extreme hatred for Caesar that kept him at his post as a sick man during the civil war, guarding the sea lanes until his untimely death. Syme comments that Cato should have made sure of the other consul as well. It was clear that Bibulus and Cato would oppose

Caesar's measures as consul, no matter what these measures concerned or how they were drafted, because they were against not just the proposals but Caesar himself. Even so, at the outset of his consulship, Caesar tried to do everything according to the rules, presenting bills to the Senate with ample opportunity for debate. Only after it had become obvious that there was no hope of success in this way did he bypass the Senate and turn directly to the people to pass his legislation.[17]

Caesar's consulship is notable for many things, but principally, as far as Pompey was concerned, for the formation of an alliance that modern historians have misleadingly called the first triumvirate, because of the vague resemblance to the official triumvirate formed some years later when Caesar's heir Octavian, Mark Antony, and Lepidus seized power and then had it legalised and rationalised by the Senate. The so-called first triumvirate had none of this official legality or permanence. It is generally assumed that Crassus was the third member of the unofficial alliance, perhaps not as active politically as Caesar and Pompey, but working in the background, mostly doling out cash. This view has been largely moderated in the reaction against the whole hypothesis of the first triumvirate, an invented title that imbues the alliance of 59 with an authentic official existence that it never had. The theory that there was an alliance is strengthened by the contemporary opinion among the Romans that Caesar was deeply and inextricably involved with Crassus; the two of them were accused of various dastardly schemes whenever there was a hint of disturbance on the political scene, and it was known that Crassus had paid all Caesar's debts when he went to govern Spain. The rivalry between Pompey and Crassus might seem to preclude any co-operation between them, but both Plutarch and Suetonius suggest that Caesar was determined to persuade them to work together. Cicero reported to his friend Atticus that reconciliation between Pompey and Crassus was on the cards; he had received a visit from Cornelius Balbus, who benefited from the patronage of Pompey in Spain and was also latterly very closely associated with Caesar. Balbus told Cicero that Caesar would be glad of his advice, and that he would try to bring Pompey and Crassus together. This does not necessarily mean that their co-operation was to be anything more than skin-deep, and provides no proof of any long lasting agreement between the three men; but the ancient sources do infer that there was an unofficial liaison, and it was said that it had been sealed by an oath. Another implication that there was or had been a mutual agreement of some kind in 59 derives from the fact that in 56 all of the so-called partners met with Caesar at Lucca, though it has been doubted whether all three of them were present at the same time. But a mutually acceptable agreement was reached somehow, and in the following year both Pompey and Crassus became consuls, while Caesar's command in Gaul was extended, all of which suggests that there was a close co-operation if not an alliance.

In 59, Crassus may not have played a significantly large part in the proceedings, except in so far as he too had been thwarted in the Senate and Caesar pushed through legislation that solved some of his problems. Crassus formed networks of his own via the loans and financial help he gave freely to young and aspiring politicians. Plutarch says that he did not charge interest on these, because his aims in lending

11 *Idealised portrait bust of Julius Caesar.* Courtesy Vatican Museums

money were not to make profit but to gain whatever political advantage he could derive from the arrangements. He also pursued a successful career in the law courts as an advocate, another activity that placed people in his debt in more than just the financial sense. As for Crassus being the financier of the wheeling and dealing of the first triumvirate, this is probably just a myth, accepted because Crassus was rich and loaned money. The other two members of the group were not exactly in penurious circumstances. Caesar was once in Crassus' debt, but he had ample opportunity to accrue considerable wealth from his term as governor of Spain, and Pompey was probably wealthier than either Crassus or Caesar, or even the two of them put together. Nonetheless, Crassus had a part to play in the events of 59 and after.

To the ancient authors who wrote about the period retrospectively it seemed clear that Pompey, Crassus and Caesar worked together at least in 59, to achieve their own ends. It was Caesar who linked the other two; he always called upon Crassus to speak first in the Senate, and only after the betrothal of his daughter Julia to Pompey did he began to ask Pompey to speak first instead. Crassus was present at the riotous scenes accompanying the passage of the agrarian law that at last enabled Pompey to settle his veterans, and he may have been one of the leading members of the commission of 20 that was set up to put the settlement into effect. Apart from the term 'first triumvirate', which should be avoided like the plague, it is only the depth of Crassus' involvement that is in doubt.[18]

It is not known how Pompey and Caesar began to work together. One presumably contacted the other with an agenda for a business deal; on balance it was probably Caesar who made the first move. A mutual friend may have had some small input in the matter: Lucius Lucceius, who was a friend of Pompey, and very wealthy. He was a candidate for office himself, but being persuaded by Caesar that they should campaign together, and combine Lucceius' money with Caesar's popularity, he helped Caesar financially in his election campaign. The fact that Lucceius was not elected himself was due to the large-scale bribery that Cato condoned in order to secure the election of Marcus Calpurnius Bibulus. One interpretation of the failure of Lucceius is that he had been duped by Caesar, who had set out deliberately to mislead him; but in fact there may have been no subterfuge. The combination of Caesar and Lucceius as consuls, working together in agreement, would have caused tremendous problems for the Senate, so the hardliners led by Cato worked diligently to set up their rival candidate. The theory that Lucceius was simply being used by Caesar leads to the supposition that neither he nor anyone else had any inkling of the fact that Pompey and Crassus also featured in Caesar's agenda. It is possible that Lucceius may have been well-informed, but others were not; the secrecy that surrounded the so-called first triumvirate was a prudent measure, since it would probably not be too long before observers worked it out for themselves.[19]

It was well known that since Pompey's return to Rome the two themes that concerned him most, the settlement of his veterans and the ratification of his eastern administration, had been consistently opposed by the Senate, and that anyone who could produce a scheme for effecting a secure passage for the necessary legislation would probably gain a ready hearing from Pompey. This is not to suggest that after the rebuffs he had suffered from the Senate Pompey retired into the background and did absolutely nothing. He would have devoted much thought to each and every clause of Rullus' and Flavius' bills to find a way round the objections to them, and sought likely people to put a new bill to the Senate. The agrarian bill that Caesar promulgated in the early part of his consulship was complex and very carefully considered, not the sort of document that could be drawn up in an evening or two, which presupposes that the drafting of it was carried out in anticipation of Caesar's consulship. In December 60 it was already known that Caesar intended to put forward such a bill, and he may already have been in collusion with the tribune Vatinius, who was perhaps the author of it. The bill was drawn up with extreme care, taking into account the pitfalls that previous attempts had encountered, like those of Rullus and Flavius. It is pure speculation, but it may be that when Caesar considered that he had a bill that would offend no one, or as few people as possible, that would satisfy most if not all demands, and that above all was workable, he and Pompey colluded and agreed that he should try to put the law into effect, and so start the process of settling the veterans of the eastern campaigns. No one knows whether contact between the two preceded the consulship; Suetonius says that it was only after his election that Caesar approached Pompey and reconciled him to Crassus.[20]

When Caesar presented his land bill to the Senate, he had thought of all the loopholes. The money to buy lands was to come from the tributes flowing in from the east after Pompey's conquests, and any acreage thus purchased was to be rated at the last census evaluations, and not at an inflated new price. There were to be no compulsory purchases, and therefore no disgruntled evicted farmers whose cause could be taken up by inflammatory politicians in an effort to stir up trouble or make a name for themselves. A commission of 20 with a steering committee of five was to oversee the settlements, which included the urban poor as well as the ex-soldiers.

There was nothing in this bill with which the opposition could legitimately argue, so they decided on another tactic, that of debating it endlessly. Cato took the lead. On the first day he talked until sunset, and at that point business would have to cease until the next day, and still Caesar had not been able to pass the bill. Impatient and by now very angry, he arrested Cato and sent him to prison, just as the tribune Flavius had arrested Metellus Celer. Pompey must have had a sense of déja vu, especially as the senators decided to accompany Cato. This was probably a low point for Pompey, since even one or two of his own men disagreed with Caesar's methods, if not with the terms of the agrarian bill. Significantly, it was Marcus Petreius, one of Pompey's adherents, who said that he felt more comfortable in prison with Cato than in the Senate with Caesar. The action of Petreius may signify that he knew nothing about the fact that Caesar was working in collusion with Pompey; but even if he did, he was at liberty to agree with the proposals wholeheartedly, but at the same time to disagree strongly with Caesar's methods.[21]

The next stage was violent. Pompey may have anticipated this, and reconciled himself to it, because after more than two years of frustration and delays, and the recent demonstration by Cato that the bill would never be passed by the Senate, there was no other method left except to take the bill to the popular assembly. At a public meeting prior to the voting assembly, Caesar gave Bibulus and Cato another chance to outline their objections to the bill. This could have led to fruitful discussion, reconciliation and the easy passage of the bill, but Caesar knew that this would not happen; his purpose was to reveal to the public how intransigent and unreasonable the opposition really were. Bibulus did not disappoint him, shouting to the assembled onlookers that they would not get the bill passed that year, not even if they all wanted it. Caesar then asked Pompey to speak. Reminding people that the land settlements for the veterans of the Spanish war had been agreed but never put into operation, Pompey turned attention to the revenues that he had brought in from the eastern campaigns. Lack of money had prevented the settlement of the soldiers of the Spanish war, but now there was no excuse. Pompey rounded off his speech with the martial promise that if anyone raised his sword against this bill, then he would raise his shield. Crassus spoke next, in the same vein. When the day for voting arrived, Caesar had already posted his own men at night to secure the area, and Pompey's veterans, summoned to Rome, surrounded the assembly. Bibulus was attacked before he was able to speak. A bucket of manure was thrown over him, and he and Cato were lucky to get away with their lives. Thus was the agrarian bill passed. Pompey may have regretted the event, and more so the obstruction that made the event necessary, but perhaps by now he did not care, as long as the bill was passed somehow. The fragility of legislation was clear to both Pompey and Caesar; there had been a law to enable Pompey to settle his veterans from the Spanish war, but law did not automatically guarantee the outcome, and the settlements had never come about. Another, more serious problem was that in the next consular year, legislation could be annulled. Caesar decided to set the seal on his success by making every senator swear an oath to observe the terms of the new law, a precedent set by Appuleius Saturninus 41 years earlier. Cato, Metellus Celer and others would not take the oath at first, but were finally persuaded to do so by Cicero. Bibulus eventually retired to his house to watch the heavens for omens, a device which normally put an end to all public business, but Caesar ignored him and carried on as normal, as though there was no consular colleague. Men began to rename the year; henceforth it was not known as the consulship of Caesar and Bibulus, but the consulship of Julius and Caesar.[22]

There remained the question of the eastern settlements, that the Senate had delayed for so long. After the strong-arm tactics of Caesar's previous legislative activity, there was little opposition. Lucullus tried to speak out, but Caesar threatened him with punishment for his own failures, whereupon Lucullus fell to his knees to beg for mercy – not a craven act of cowardice, but to demonstrate that everyone was now under Caesar's thumb. The long-awaited ratification of the administrative arrangements that Pompey had made in 62 could now be finalised. It is generally agreed that the tribune Vatinius did all the hard clerical work on this matter, presumably with the help of notes or personal advice from Pompey or his secretaries. Several separate treaties with client kings had to be drawn up, and each of the new provinces settled. Pompey could breathe a sigh of relief.[23]

The next two projects may have been connected to the eastern settlements, though the chronology is not definitely attested. The Egyptian affair had been rumbling on for some time, and Crassus had already had a hand in it, but to little avail, because he was blocked by the usual opponents. Now Caesar took control of the situation. Ptolemy XII Auletes was shored up as ruler of Egypt with Roman backing, as a friend and ally of the Roman people. The price was high, but Ptolemy could draw upon the legendary wealth of Egypt to pay the reputed 6000 talents or 150 million sesterces to Caesar and Pompey. Apparently these sums were never paid in full, and Ptolemy did not remain stable on his throne; but Pompey could hardly lose in this project, and later on in 55, his adherent Gabinius mounted an expedition from Syria to replace Ptolemy Auletes. After the battle of Pharsalus, Pompey reasoned that the ruling house of Egypt owed him something.[24]

Caesar had now dealt with the two most pressing problems that had tormented Pompey for the last two years and more. Crassus had also experienced difficulties in his various projects, opposed by the same men who opposed Pompey. One of these projects concerned the tax contracts for Asia. The *publicani*, or the groups of equites who put in bids for tax collection in the provinces, had overestimated the sums that they could expect to raise from the province of Asia, and had consequently incurred great losses. Crassus had already attempted to rationalise the situation, but had met with failure. Caesar had more success, arranging for a remission of some of the debt, and warning the tax farmers not to bid too high next time. This was not without profit to himself, because he was able to reward Vatinius with shares in the tax contracts.[25]

The Senate and people did not succumb willingly to Caesar's lawmaking. It is not clear how and when the coalition between Pompey, Caesar and Crassus became generally known, nor if much more was made of it than was really necessary. The three of them did not stand firmly together presenting a united front, so the alliance could not have been viewed in the same way as the later coalition between Antony, Octavian and Lepidus. According to Cicero, Crassus rejoiced whenever Pompey was put into an awkward position, as he was when colleagues asked him what he thought of Caesar's legislation, and he replied that Caesar must answer for it. He refused to be drawn into condoning or condemning the consul, and was accordingly damned anyway.

In March, Cicero spoke out in public against Caesar's methods, using the vehicle of the trial of Gaius Antonius Hybrida, his colleague in the consulship of 63. Antonius was an unsavoury character, and Cicero did not really want to defend him, but he felt that he owed him a debt because of his support during the struggle against Catiline. If he had confined himself to the defence, all would have been well, but he chose to speak his mind on the current political situation. By the afternoon of the same day, his arch enemy from the Bona Dea scandal, Publius Clodius Pulcher, had been adopted into a plebeian family, renouncing his patrician status, a move that he had tried to make in the previous year. Plebeian status gave him the right to stand for the tribunate, to which he was denied access as a patrician. The adoption had been arranged by Caesar and Pompey, who officiated at the farcical ceremony where a man younger than Clodius adopted him as his son, and then immediately emancipated him afterwards. For the time being, all was quiet; Clodius was biding his time. In April, it was proposed that Clodius should lead an embassy to Tigranes of Armenia, but he refused to go, probably because he needed to be back in Rome for the tribunician elections that were traditionally held in the summer, in July or August.[26]

Another agrarian law was passed by Caesar concerning the state-owned Campanian lands, which were to be divided up into 20,000 allotments for the urban poor, with preference being given to those families with three or more children. Cato went to prison briefly over this bill, but Caesar employed a tribune to use his veto against the imprisonment so that he would not have to back down himself. Despite Cato's objections, the bill was passed. The first land law had dealt with Pompey's veterans, and also some of the landless men from Rome, but this law was not an additional measure for the veterans; it was aimed at reducing the population pressures of the city. Like the first law, it was protected by an oath.[27]

May 59 was an eventful month for Pompey, with highs and lows following each other in exhausting succession. On 13 May, Bibulus informed Pompey that there was a plot to assassinate him, and Pompey thanked him for the information. What happened about it is not known at this stage, but later on during the late summer or early autumn this or another plot was reported to the Senate and an investigation began. Modern scholars point out that Pompey was highly susceptible to suspicion when plots on his life were mentioned, which is perhaps not surprising for a young man who grew up in Strabo's camp and narrowly averted assassination at the age of nineteen. Such events tend to make a lasting and somewhat vivid impression. Nothing is known of how Pompey reacted to Bibulus' news, but he probably increased his household minders and set in motion some investigations of his own.

On a happier note, the alliance between Pompey and Caesar was sealed in that month, when Pompey, the most eligible bachelor in Rome, married Caesar's daughter Julia. She had been betrothed to Quintus Servilius Caepio, but this arrangement was broken off in favour of the dynastic marriage. It may have been arranged as a political expedient to ensure that the alliance was not broken off. Pompey was very uneasy about the violent methods that Caesar had used in order to pass the necessary legislation to satisfy his two demands of veteran settlement and establishing his eastern conquests on a firm footing. Though Pompey was a pupil of Sulla, he did not necessarily condone all Sulla's programmes, and had been at pains to demonstrate that he wished to achieve all his aims by peaceful means. If he had not met with such opponents as Cato, he would never have needed Caesar and his determined politics; it is assumed that he regretted the stormy months of Caesar's consulship and wished to distance himself from the whole affair. Unadulterated popularity was a high priority for Pompey, and the events of the first months of 59 had sullied his reputation. Caesar's motives in arranging for the marriage of Pompey and Julia are interpreted by modern scholars as an attempt to keep Pompey bound to him more closely. If Julia was to be used as a pawn, then at least she found an attentive and kind husband, who was allegedly besotted with her for the few years of their married life, and devastated when she died in childbirth. This undoubted affection may have been a fortunate by-product as far as Caesar was concerned, but Julia was his only legitimate child, and perhaps he would not have condemned her to a difficult match with someone she loathed but whom he needed as an ally in the political arena. Definite marks of Caesar's favour to

Pompey after the marriage can be discerned in the fact that while Crassus had always been asked to give his opinion before anyone else, now Caesar asked Pompey to speak first. At some point, Caesar made Pompey his heir; Seager suggests that it may have been at this time, just after the marriage. Since Caesar had no son, it would make sense to write a will in favour of his son-in-law.[28]

It was also in May that Caesar began to make arrangements for his proconsulship. The provinces that had originally been assigned to the retiring consuls of 59 were not territorial, but concerned the administration of woodlands and paths. Originally the word province denoted any tour of duty usually taken up after holding a magistracy. When Rome was young and did not yet directly control half of the ancient world, there were no territorial provinces to administer, but various administrative tasks had to be performed under the title province. Gradually as Rome acquired an Empire, the territorial governorship was also included under the same title, until the word became synonymous with specific territories. The administration of woodlands was not the normal task for a proconsular command, and the assignation has been seen as a deliberate ploy to block Caesar's rise to power via the more normal territorial province, especially if it involved the command of an army. Seager disagrees with this theory, in that when the decision was made Caesar had not actually been elected, and the administration of woodlands would also have inhibited the other consul. He suggests that since there was obvious unrest among the tribes to the north of Italy, and because trouble was brewing in Gaul due to the threatened migration of the Helvetii from the Alpine regions, the Senate wished to hold consuls in reserve in case there was sudden need for them, as had been the situation with Marius several decades earlier. The prolonged struggle against the Cimbri and Teutones had not diminished in Roman collective memory. Cicero reported to Atticus in March 60 that the Aedui had fought a great battle, and the Helvetii had begun to take up arms and were raiding Roman territory. The two provinces of Cisalpine and Transalpine Gaul were assigned by lot to the consuls of 60, Lucius Afranius and Metellus Celer, before they had retired from their office. Celer died in the spring of 59, and the praetor Pomptinus was left to fight a battle against the Allobroges in Gallia Narbonensis. The danger of invasion could be magnified to the benefit of Caesar, and soon after the news of Pomptinus' victory arrived, the tribune Vatinius presented a bill to the popular assembly that gave Caesar the command in Cisalpine Gaul and Illyricum with three legions. Unconventionally the command was to take effect immediately, while Caesar was still consul, and it was to last until 1 March 54. There was to be no discussion of the command before this date, so Caesar was protected from early recall or interference in his operations. Pompey and Lucius Piso supported the bill. It was passed by the people; the Senate was once again circumvented and ignored.

The dual territorial command of Cisalpine Gaul and Illyricum has been interpreted as an attempt by Caesar to hedge his bets, so that he could be certain of a war to fight in either one or the other of his commands. It may have been a matter of recruitment opportunities as well, to draw on the tribes of both Cisalpine Gaul and Illyricum. Sometime later, Pompey proposed that Caesar should also be given the command in Transalpine Gaul, with another legion; this command was renewable annually. If trouble came from either side of the Alps then Caesar would be authorised to deal with it. The conquest of the rest of Gaul could be carried out from these bases, though it is questionable if anyone, including Pompey, could foresee at this stage that Caesar would engineer and achieve this goal. It was clear enough that there was going to be a war, but the Gauls were not united into a single nation, and wars would be fought against single tribes or federations of tribes; in 59 conquest of all of Gaul was not necessarily even on Caesar's agenda.[29]

Pompey spent some part of the summer in June and July overseeing the land settlements in Campania. His popularity had reached a low ebb, so he was probably glad of an excuse to leave the city and begin the administrative work in which he could display his talents. He probably heard that during the performance of a play put on as part of the *ludi Apollinares*, the principal actor had earned tremendous applause with the line *nostra miseria tu es magnus*, in which no one in the audience failed to see the reference attributing Pompey's greatness to the misery of the people. When Pompey returned to Rome, he found that Bibulus had been able to use his influence to postpone the consular elections. Annoyed that he would not be able to secure the election of Aulus Gabinius, Pompey protested, but to no avail. He made a public speech at the end of July, but it would have been better if he had stayed at home and not tried to speak to the people. Cicero reports that he made a sorry spectacle, and even when the hyperbole and wishful thinking are subtracted from Cicero's letter, there remains a definite note of failure. There was probably another low moment for Pompey when the tribuncian elections were held and Clodius was returned as tribune for 58. He had already threatened to annul all Caesar's legislation, and it was anyone's guess how he would take his revenge on Cicero. In order to pre-empt this Caesar and Pompey tried to provide a safe haven for Cicero, either on an embassy to Egypt to reassure Ptolemy XII Auletes, or as a legate with Caesar's army in Gaul. Cicero chose to stay in Rome. At this stage Pompey perhaps thought that he could still help him.[30]

The autumn saw a reversal of the unpopularity that had dogged Pompey since the beginning of the year. The proceedings started when the younger Curio, one of Caesar and Pompey's most virulent opponents, reported to his father that Lucius Vettius had tried to involve him in a plot to murder Pompey. It is usually suggested that this is the same plot that had been reported to Pompey by Bibulus in May. The chronology of the Vettius case is by no means clear, and the reasons and the circumstances are even more murky. During the investigation Vettius named Curio as the ringleader, and said that Bibulus was party to the conspiracy. On the following day he was brought before the public by Caesar and Vatinius, and named more suspects, among them Cicero's son-in-law, Piso Frugi. He did not name Cicero himself, but by implication Cicero was involved in some way. Before the investigation could go further, Vettius was found strangled in prison. Various motives have been suggested on the part of many of the possible candidates who may have been responsible for this strange intrigue. Cicero told Atticus that Caesar was the culprit in an attempt to frame the young Curio, but modern authors do not believe that this could be so. Leach suggests that Pompey put Vettius up to investigating the plot as an undercover man, when he heard from Bibulus in May that something was afoot. Greenhalgh prefers to see Vettius as a lone and probably unhinged conspirator. Seager sees the hand of Clodius behind the plot, which was designed to pry Pompey from Cicero in an atmosphere of distrust, and to dissuade him from attempting to ally with his opponents in the Senate. Thus isolated, Pompey could probably be disregarded, and the way would be clear for Clodius to deal with Cicero.[31]

When the consular elections were held at last in October, Gabinius and Caesar's father-in-law Lucius Calpurnius Piso were returned. In an attempt to oust Gabinius, Gaius Cato announced his intention of prosecuting him, but could not proceed because the praetors blocked him. Frustrated, he denounced Pompey at a public meeting, and since he considered that it must have been Pompey who instructed the praetors to thwart him, he labelled him a dictator. The result was unexpected. The people turned on him, and he only just escaped with his life. It was a satisfying display from Pompey's viewpoint, even if he realised that the mob was fickle enough to change its mind next day. He might have reflected that it was good for one's public persona to have been the target of a projected assassination. Though he had perhaps been as dismayed as Cicero said he was about violent Caesarian politics, in the autumn and winter of 59 Pompey could take stock and probably feel that the struggle was over. He had been thwarted by the die-hards in the Senate ever since his return home, and the fame and high position in society that he thought he deserved had been denied him. His credibility with his veterans had suffered through his inability to put into effect the promised land allotments, and the treaties he had arranged with the client kings and rulers of the east had been left dangling, incomplete. Then in a whirlwind few months all had been effected, at a certain cost to his popularity; but in return he had married a devoted wife who returned his affection, he was wealthy beyond his wildest dreams and he was planning to embellish the city of Rome with its first permanent theatre. It may not have been the pinnacle that he had hoped for, but he was probably content. If Pompey was at all dissatisfied, he may have looked back from a later vantage point, and reflected that in the second half of Caesar's consulship, his life at this time had in truth been as good as it was ever going to be. On the horizon loomed darker moments and grievous associates; one of them was the political delinquent, Publius Clodius Pulcher.[32]

5 The power game

The new tribune Clodius was a member of the Claudian family, but he preferred to use a more quaint form of his name. His political agenda was not partisan or dictated by any powerful magnate, because Clodius was not allied to any party or individual, and worked for no one except himself. Caesar's influence has been detected by some, and just as firmly rejected by others. If Caesar really thought that he could employ Clodius to keep his enemies in check while he was absent, then he had misjudged his man; if there was any hint of an arrangement, as some have supposed, then Clodius did not keep it. Another suggestion is that Caesar merely wanted to intimidate Pompey, a theory formed by extrapolating backwards from a probably intentionally bungled assassination attempt that kept Pompey indoors for the rest of Clodius' tribunate, besieged in his own house by the tribune's mobs. The theory that Caesar was behind it all it is not unanimously considered valid by modern scholars, who point out that Clodius was just as hostile to all factions and all prominent men, who respected the traditional forms only when they worked in his favour.

In order to engender the support of the mob as he embarked on his office Clodius abolished the payments on the corn dole, distributing it free of charge, and thereby attracting many more people to the city who wished to take advantage of the dole. One of his next acts was to legalise clubs and guilds, which had been attacked and supposedly suppressed by previous legislation, but in reality were just waiting underground for someone like Clodius to revive them. The guilds comprised all kinds of men, freeborn, freedmen and slaves, and provided just the sort of intelligence networks at all levels of society that Clodius could use to spread his influence. Cicero accused Clodius of absorbing all the Catilinarians who still lurked in Rome: but perhaps Cicero had a one track mind where these were concerned, and even without the added political agenda of Catilinarians, Clodius could probably have done quite well on his own account.[1]

It was evident before Clodius entered office on 10 December 59 that Cicero was to be his first victim. Clodius had never relinquished the possibility of revenge for Cicero's success in demolishing his alibi at the trial for sacrilege after the Bona Dea scandal; the fact that he had been acquitted made no difference to Clodius' hatred, which he made no effort to conceal. Cicero was fully aware that Clodius intended to arrange an uncomfortable future for him; he wrote to Atticus explaining that Caesar had offered him a post as legate under his command in Gaul, and although he admitted that to accept the post 'would be a more honourable way of getting out of danger', he decided that he preferred to fight. For the same reasons he refused to go on an embassy to Egypt, to assist Ptolemy Auletes. At these refusals both Caesar and Pompey probably washed their hands of him, since there was nothing they could do to remove Cicero from Rome and the fate that Clodius had in store for him, which was to remove him from Rome in a less friendly fashion.[2]

Caesar did not leave Rome until the spring, though he took up his military command and therefore could not enter the city. He lingered near Rome because of the worrying proposal of the praetors Lucius Domitius Ahenobarbus and Gaius Memmius to have his consulship discussed in the Senate with the intention of declaring his acts invalid. The threat to the agrarian bill and all his other legislation was evident. Caesar published speeches against the praetors, but could do very little more himself. Clodius took up the cause. Just before Caesar left for Gaul, he was invited to a meeting of the people in the Circus Flaminius outside the city, specially arranged by Clodius so that Caesar could attend without crossing the city boundaries. The two consuls, Lucius Piso, Caesar's father-in-law, and Gabinius, Pompey's man, spoke about the Catilinarians who had been executed by Cicero, declaring their objections to the procedure. Caesar supported the objections, reminding the people that he had also objected to the death penalty in 63, advocating instead lifelong imprisonment of the so-called conspirators in the houses of prominent men. But he advised against passing any law about the execution of Roman citizens and then applying it retrospectively to past events. Thus Caesar could be seen to have kept his hands clean; he had not gone back on what he had said in 63, and so retained his honour, but he had refused to be actively involved in a witch-hunt that had as its principal objective the consul of 63, Marcus Tullius Cicero.[3]

Clodius had already secured the consuls by passing a law giving them both five year proconsular commands; Piso was to go to Macedonia, and Gabinius, on the first proposal to Cilicia, and then to a more acceptable post as governor of Syria. The fact that Gabinius condoned Clodius' activities in the matter of Cicero, and vociferously blocked anyone who tried to speak out on Cicero's behalf, suggests that his patron Pompey also approved of the policies that Clodius was putting into effect. But Pompey was not responsible for all of Gabinius' actions and did not necessarily strive to control them, allowing Gabinius independence of opinion. However, Pompey did make a point of withdrawing from Cicero, despite his earlier assurances which are recounted in many of Cicero's letters to Atticus that he would protect him; at one point Pompey said that he had effected an agreement with Clodius. It is doubtful if he believed that Clodius had any intention of slackening off in his anti-Cicero campaign. When this campaign was at its height, some of Cicero's friends came to see him at his Alban villa, but Pompey declared that he could do nothing; he was ready to take action only if the Senate should empower him with a specific command. Plutarch relays a story that Cicero himself came to see him, and as he approached, Pompey slipped out at the back door rather than face him. No one else repeats it, and the story has been doubted by modern scholars, but it sums up the position of the two men at the time when Cicero was called upon to pay dearly for his consular zeal in eliminating the dangers to the state that he had detected in 63. Clodius seemed to have no trouble in passing the *lex Clodia de capite civis*, which made it illegal to put Roman citizens to death without trial. At this point Cicero went into voluntary exile, and then Clodius passed another law declaring Cicero an enemy of the state and an outlaw. His property was confiscated and his houses in Rome and the countryside were pulled down. Since Cicero would not accept the safe havens that had been offered to him, and because support for him dwindled as Clodius gained more strength, Pompey perhaps decided to abandon him rather than be dragged down with him. Seager suggests Pompey considered that he could let Cicero go, and then when Clodius was no longer tribune he could use his influence to bring his erstwhile friend back again. Whether or not he thought that by sacrificing Cicero he could save himself from Clodius cannot be known, though it is sometimes suggested that there was a tacit arrangement that if Cicero was sacrificed then Pompey would be left alone.[4]

If Pompey did think that he could avoid attacks from Clodius, then he was soon to be disillusioned. He may have approved of Clodius' neat removal of Cato, but not the task that he was given to get him out of Rome. The kingdom of Cyprus was to be annexed, and its king Ptolemy, Auletes' brother, was to be deposed. When it was thought that Gabinius was to govern Cilicia, the task would have fallen to him; but as governor of Syria it was not within his remit. Someone else would have to go. Clodius proposed that the honour should be given to Marcus Porcius Cato, and when Cato tried to refuse the honour, Clodius berated him for ingratitude in rejecting this favour bestowed on him by the Roman people. No one can imagine that Pompey shed any tears over Cato's removal from Rome, but the annexation of Cyprus could interfere with the eastern settlements so carefully thought out by Pompey, and the relationship of the deposed king of Cyprus with the king of Egypt, also shakily supported on his throne by Caesar and Pompey, could have repercussions on the arrangement.[5]

The primary aim in the Cyprus affair was not necessarily to embarrass Pompey, although this was a possible by-product that Clodius would find acceptable. His other actions concerning the eastern kingdoms definitely were aimed at Pompey. Clodius interfered directly with Pompey's agreement with Deiotarus of Galatia, who had been confirmed as the High Priest of the Magna Mater at Pessinus. This privilege was given to Deiotarus' rival Brogitarus. It is not recorded that Pompey instantly tried to reverse the decision. The next assault on Pompey's arrangements concerned the younger Tigranes. The rebellious prince had been brought as a hostage to Rome, and kept under house arrest by Lucius Flavius, Pompey's man, who had drafted the land bill when he served as tribune, and who was now praetor. Clodius asked to see Tigranes, and promptly kidnapped him. When Pompey and the consul Gabinius went to Clodius to protest they were attacked by Clodius' armed thugs, and Gabinius suffered the indignity of having his lictors beaten up and the fasces they carried smashed. He did not forget the insult, and was uniquely loyal to Pompey when he was harrassed by Clodius from that moment on. There was a serious fight on the Appian Way just outside Rome when Pompey's men met Clodius' gangs who were shepherding Tigranes out of the country; in the skirmish, Marcus Papirius, a personal friend of Pompey's, was killed. Clodius may have received payment from Tigranes and no one really knows what happened in the end, but the irony of the situation probably afforded Clodius a few hilarious moments and made a good after-dinner story, since Caesar and Pompey had tried to remove him from Rome before the tribunician elections to go on a diplomatic embassy to the elder Tigranes.

Pompey did not react with fire and brimstone to the Tigranes kidnapping; it would have gained nothing and made him look petulant. Dio says that he bestirred himself and started to work for the recall of Cicero. On 1 June, the tribune Lucius Ninnius proposed it in the Senate, only to have it vetoed immediately by another tribune. Pompey indicated to Atticus, who relayed it to Cicero in exile, that there should be another attempt after the elections. The consuls who were returned for 57 were Publius Cornelius Lentulus Spinther, who was favourable to Cicero, and Metellus Nepos, who was more inclined to support Clodius. After all, he was Clodius' cousin, and his brother Metellus Celer, who had died in the previous year, had been married to Clodius' sister, the notorious Clodia, who tamed sparrows and drove the poet Catullus and possibly many other men to distraction.[6]

The subject of Cicero's recall had to temporarily dropped, to resurface in the next year when Clodius was out of office. With the aim of ousting Clodius from office before his term expired, a proposal was put forward to allow Caesar to enact all his laws once again but this time through the proper channels, and without the religious disadvantage of his fellow consul watching the heavens for omens and declaring all public business invalid. The one law that would presumably fail was that arranging for the adoption of Clodius into a plebeian family, so that his tribunate could be declared illegal, and all the laws that he had passed could be annulled. Clodius had already threatened to attack Caesar's legislation, and now called the Senate's bluff by declaring that it was not feasible to invalidate one of Caesar's laws without annulling all the others as well; he dared the Senate to do it, and promised that he would carry Cicero home on his shoulders if it happened, translating into modern idiom as a promise to eat his hat. Nothing did happen and Clodius remained tribune.[7]

Pompey could not prevail against him and in fact had withdrawn from public life and shut himself up in his house, when an attempt to assassinate him was foiled. On 11 August one of Clodius' slaves, lingering nearby just as Pompey was about to enter a meeting of the Senate, extracted a knife that he had concealed in his clothing and ostentatiously dropped it. It is more than likely that the assassination attempt was a sham, intended to be foiled, and that there was no real danger of an attack, only a melodramatic demonstration of the potential threat of what might happen if Pompey became too energetic in opposing Clodius. Probably at this point the tribune Quintus Terentius Culleo approached Pompey with the proposal that he should divorce Julia and cut his ties with Caesar, a proposal that Pompey would not entertain, not least because he was happily married, but also because he was not yet ready to renounce his coalition with Caesar. He reinforced this determination to preserve the status quo by sending the tribune Sestius as envoy to Caesar in Gaul, to seek his approval for putting in motion another attempt to recall Cicero. It was not that he was totally under Caesar's thumb, but if Caesar approved he would call off his adherents who could put obstacles in the way of Cicero's return. With the same aims in mind, Pompey and the consul Spinther converted Metellus Nepos to the cause, at least extracting a promise from him not to obstruct the recall of Cicero. Though Pompey did nothing active or visible from August 57 to the beginning of the following year, he presumably made plans for the time when a bill for Cicero's recall was presented as soon as Clodius stepped out of office as tribune.

In January 56 Messius and then Fabricius proposed the measure. Clodius put an end to it in a bloodbath in which Cicero's brother Quintus would have been killed if he had not hidden among a pile of corpses. Clodius had revealed his hand and shown how far he was prepared to go in stopping the bill; so having let all of Rome witness what was at stake, Pompey marshalled his veterans and gave a free hand to the gangs that the tribunes Sestius and Titus Annius Milo had already formed to combat Clodius. It took six months to pass the law recalling Cicero; in June 56 the vote was carried almost unanimously, except for the lone voice of Clodius who voted against the bill. Cicero arrived back in Rome early in September.[8]

There were two problems in which Pompey was involved when Cicero arrived home, both of which had their roots in the previous year. The Egyptian question had arisen once again, since the efforts of Caesar and Pompey to shore up Ptolemy Auletes on his throne had cost a lot of money, which had to be found by the Egyptian tax payers. Resentment had reached such a pitch that Auletes left Egypt in 57 and arrived in Rome, to stay at Pompey's Alban villa, where he embarked on a campaign to secure the support of the Senate to restore him to the throne once again. Pompey arranged for Rabirius Postumus to advance a huge loan to Ptolemy, and later Rabirius went to Egypt to become in effect Ptolemy's finance minister, a post in which he could extract enough from the Egyptian peasants and the Alexandrians to repay his loan several times over. It all ended in tears some time later, when Rabirius was hounded out of Alexandria and then prosecuted at Rome.

In the meantime, while Ptolemy was still in Italy, offending prominent Romans and quietly murdering his opponents who had come to Rome for redress, the tempting possibilities of a lucrative and prestigious command to restore him to his throne were foremost in several people's minds. The consul Spinther was designated as governor of Cilicia once his office expired, so he was eager to take on the task of restoring Auletes; but there were other suggestions. Crassus proposed that a committee of three should be appointed, from among those who had already been invested with *imperium*. Bibulus agreed that there should be a commission of three, but of private citizens and not men with *imperium*. It was also suggested that Pompey should be given powers to restore Auletes. The main debate concerned whether this should be an armed expedition or not. Caius Cato unearthed a prophecy from the Sybilline Books, to which Rome looked when there were bad omens and trouble brewing; the very apposite lines stated that if the Egyptian king should come to Rome to ask for help, he should be treated as a friend, but the Romans must not assist him with a large force, or they would bring onto themselves trouble and peril. As usual, Pompey did not say whether he wanted to be invested with a command or whether he was content to allow someone else to take up the cause of Auletes, but his friends (such as Afranius, Scribonius Libo, Aulus Plautius, and Caninius Gallus) all pressed for his appointment. Caninius wanted to introduce a bill to give Pompey the task, but with no army. In the end opposition in the Senate blocked everything, and the matter lapsed into abeyance. Disappointed and disillusioned, king Ptolemy left Rome to take refuge in Ephesus at the temple of Artemis.[9]

Pompey may have hoped to combine two commands in one with the special task concerning the corn supply. If he was invested with power to organise the food supply, he would have to travel widely over the Roman world, and in the course of his duties he could perhaps go to Egypt. Matters came to a head on the score of the corn supply when Clodius instigated a riot, just after Cicero returned to the city and gave his rapturous speech praising Pompey to the skies. Clodius said that the grain shortages had been caused because Pompey had filled the city with his own supporters when he promulgated the bill for Cicero's recall. The problem had deeper roots than this, and Clodius was no doubt aware of them, but it suited his purpose to blame Cicero. The corn supply was notoriously difficult to regulate at the best of times, dependent as it was on weather, good or bad harvests, shipping, storage and greedy middlemen. The problems of supply and of the distribution of corn dole were to occupy much of Caesar's time and energy, and the same problems kept on surfacing during the long reign of Augustus. Some of their solutions were foreshadowed by those that Pompey instituted when he was given the task of the *cura annonae*. There were two proposals; the consuls Spinther and Metellus Nepos gave him a five year command with proconsular powers and 15 legates, and the tribune Messius suggested a much more wide-ranging command with *maius imperium*, powers greater than the governors of the provinces wherever he needed to operate. This bill was never passed, and Pompey accepted the lesser powers that the consuls proposed for him. It may have been in an exercise to test the water to find out just what the Senate and people would allow, and to be able to include the Egyptian question in the higher command proposed by Messius; or it may have been a demonstration to prove that Pompey did not want or need excessive powers to carry out the task of organising the corn supply. No one was ever very clear as to Pompey's intentions, but no one could doubt his administrative ability. He set about the task with his usual efficiency, choosing Cicero and his brother Quintus as two of his 15 legates; the names of the others, where they operated or what they did are not known.[10]

One of the first problems was to establish who was entitled to the corn dole in Rome, and for this purpose Pompey instituted a census, but it is not clear whether this was a complete count such as Caesar made some time later, or whether Pompey merely counted the new names that would not be included on the full census until the year 55-4. There were many potential new recipients, because people had been freeing their aged slaves in anticipation of the reorganisation of the corn dole. The only source for the numbers of recipients of the corn dole comes from Suetonius' life of Caesar, who is said to have reduced the number from 320,000 to 150,000. These figures do not help in calculating the nature of the problem that faced Pompey. Since he was given control of the whole of the corn supply, from sowing the seeds through harvesting to transport and storage, Pompey had to travel around the Roman provinces and negotiate with landowners, farmers and growers, dealers and merchants, shippers, and harbour masters. He would also have to be present in Rome itself on occasions, so he was allowed to enter the city as and when necessary – not as a blanket ruling, but dispensation was granted whenever he needed to return. The powers and privileges that he was granted in this command were once more anomalous and special, and paved the way to the accumulation of extraordinary powers in the hands of one man that culminated in the principate of Augustus.[11]

Pompey's position while he attended to the corn supply was secure with the people or the mob in Rome, since he was rendering an essential service. His dedication to the task was demonstrated by the anecdote that when he was about to set sail on some mission connected with his duties, he was warned off by the captain of his vessel, who pointed out that the weather was unfavourable. Pompey swept aside all objections with the stern reply that it was necessary to sail; it was not necessary to live. Thus the great man put aside all personal feeling in service to the state and the people; it was not purely altruistic, since the political kudos was priceless. The food supply was a constant concern of the emperors of Rome, whose popularity could be made or broken on the issue. But if Pompey had the temporary support of the people, it was a fickle mob that could change its mind on a whim, and the favour could be easily lost. More important, he was not secure with the opposing factions or with the Senate.[12]

The year 56 was marked by a number of trials of Pompey's and Clodius' associates. Clodius brought Milo to court in February, and when Pompey tried to speak in defence of the erstwhile tribune, Clodius' gangs began to shout him down, hurling insults at him, though he never gave up speaking. Clodius' men were well-primed. He indulged in outrageous pantomime, giving the cues to which the chorus gave their rehearsed replies: 'Who is starving the people to death?' he asked; 'Pompey!' replied the mob. 'Who wants to go to Alexandria?' asked Clodius. The mob shouted 'Pompey!'. 'Who do you want to go?' 'Crassus!'. Then there was a real fight, with Clodius' men spitting at Pompey's crowd, pushing them out of the way, until the tables were turned and Pompey's men, no doubt practised veteran soldiers, cleared the field and threw Clodius off the rostra. A meeting of the Senate was summoned immediately, but Cicero and Pompey went home. The next two days were spent in discussing the riotous proceedings, but only as an excuse for Caius Cato to make a scathing speech about Pompey, whilst praising Cicero, in a thinly disguised attempt to drive a wedge between them. In reporting the incident, Cicero describes how Pompey replied to the tirade with references to the murder of Africanus by Carbo, saying that he would take more care of his life than Africanus had done. He meant that Crassus was plotting against him, and financing Cato and Clodius. The trial of Milo had been adjourned by Clodius until 17 February, and Sestius was also to be tried, and defended by Cicero, who reported that Pompey had summoned his clients from as far away as Picenum and northern Italy, so that he would be much stronger than Clodius.[13]

The acquittals of both Milo and Sestius were achieved at the expense of a loss of popularity for Pompey. His position of pre-eminence was eroded on all fronts, so that he was neither a favourite of the people nor the leader of any strong faction in the

Senate. His relationship with Crassus had deteriorated to the point where only suspicion and distrust remained. Pompey seemed to be fair game for anyone and everyone to criticise. The commission to regulate the corn supply was running out of cash, and failure in this department would be the last straw; so as a means of raising money, among other purposes, Pompey attacked the Campanian land settlements of 59. Most of his veterans were settled by Caesar's first law, so by putting an end to the Campanian settlements Pompey was not seriously damaging his own interests, nor those of his clients. The advantages were that the revenue that was lost to the state by the sale of the lands would be restored if those lands were to be put back into state ownership, thus leaving no excuse for the Senate to refuse Pompey the funds that he needed to continue the administration of the corn supply. Another advantage was that it would demonstrate to Caesar that Pompey still had the upper hand, and at the same time show the Senate that he was not attached to Caesar's apron strings and had a mind of his own. At the end of 57 or early in 56 while Pompey was absent from Rome, the tribune Rutilius Lupus introduced a bill concerning the Campanian lands, as though he had no connection with Pompey at all, explaining that he did not wish the senators to vote immediately because he did not want to act without knowing what Pompey's wishes were. The result was that the senators deferred to Pompey, who did not explain himself fully, and nothing was achieved; but after the Egyptian affair and the trials of Milo and Sestius, Cicero revived the matter in the Senate in April 56. By this time, Pompey had perhaps thought better of the idea, but did nothing to stop Cicero from proceeding.[14]

Within a very short time after Cicero introduced his proposals, Crassus went to visit Caesar who was wintering at Ravenna, presumably to explain what was happening. Then Pompey, who was ostensibly setting off for Sardinia to look into the corn supply, travelled to Lucca to meet Caesar, and possibly Crassus as well, though there is some doubt as to whether Crassus attended the meeting at Lucca. Later sources say that he did, and the little town was filled to overflowing with his and his colleagues' supporters, comprising at least 200 senators and probably an equal number of equites and other hangers on. This is a contradiction in terms, since other sources maintain that the revival of the so-called triumvirate was kept secret for some time, and people were slow to realise that there had been an agreement between the three. If so, then it was a secret known to perhaps one third of the Senate; either it was not kept quiet at all; or the sources about the gathering are false; or the crowds of men who assembled at Lucca were particularly obtuse. The meeting has been labelled the conference at Lucca, and is now indelibly imprinted in the folklore of the late Roman Republic. Some scholars interpret the meeting, so soon after Cicero's proposal concerning the Campanian lands, as a panic attack on the part of Caesar and Crassus at the prospect of an independent role for Pompey, not with them, but operating against them. The story relayed by Suetonius places the emphasis on Caesar, who was supposedly afraid that Domitius Ahenobarbus, who as praetor had tried to wrest the Gallic command from him, would stand for the consulship, and if elected would probably succeed in his quest to remove Caesar from his armies and conquests. There was a proposal to bestow the command of the Gallic provinces upon the retiring consuls of 55, who would be ready to take up their posts in January 54. Caesar had no intention of relinquishing his command by then, or indeed by any other date that might be set by anyone but himself. According to Suetonius' version of the Lucca conference, it was Caesar who arranged it and Caesar who compelled Pompey and Crassus to stand for the consulship of 55.[15]

Whoever it was that brought about the conference, and for whatever reason, it was Pompey who was in the lead for some time, although it is not certain that he had mapped out in advance how to shape Roman political life from that moment onwards. Modern scholars warn that it is unwise to assume that everything that happened after the meeting at Lucca was discussed and prearranged by the three men. At the same time, Pompey had decided upon changing his fortunes, somehow, and ultimately there was no other place for him to turn except to his colleagues. After the meeting at Lucca there was a change for the worse in the flavour of Roman politics. Sulla had shown the way with less subtle methods, but now the three men, whose interests coincided even if their personalities clashed, began to change the world, at first without armies marching on Rome. The only way to entrench their position was to take supreme power and then to attend to the political tangle at Rome; as a by-product, the three of them ensured their future by establishing themselves in long-term provincial commands. Some authors have seen the provincial commands as the driving force behind the conference, and all the other events as subordinate to the purpose of obtaining them. Perhaps the theory of provincial commands, but not the details, were discussed at Lucca.

When the meeting ended, Pompey went to Sardinia as planned, and talked with Cicero's brother Quintus about the situation. The instruction was clear to Cicero: let the matter of the Campanian lands drop. Pompey had decided that this was not the way to reinvent himself, because he knew that even if the bill went through, his popularity with the Senate would be a flash in the pan and over as soon as any other matter arose. He had decided upon more permanent methods, taking no prisoners this time. Writers of novels and film scripts could make much of Pompey's inner convictions at this moment after Lucca; he had reached the nadir of his fortunes more than once since his return from the east, and had lost patience. With his talent for organisation and administration he probably fretted and fumed at the inadequacies of the Roman political system that blocked and harrassed and bled good ideas to death. Before the meeting at Lucca Pompey had arrived at a watershed, and after it he embarked on the path that led ultimately to his doom.

The next most essential task was for Pompey and Crassus to be elected consuls. It is not certain when they decided upon this course. As mentioned above, it is suggested that it was primarily to block Domitius Ahenobarbus, or perhaps to secure the consulship as a preliminary step to obtaining proconsular commands. They achieved their election by subterfuge, intimidation and bribery. They delayed putting their names forward as candidates until it was too late, and the elections were delayed. Somehow they prevented the consuls of 56 from staging the elections until the end of their term of office, and though all the details of how they achieved this have not survived, Pompey and Crassus were both experienced enough to know how to do this with effect. At one point when the consul Marcellinus attempted to hold the elections, C. Cato (who had been bought by the liberal distribution of cash emanating from the coffers of Pompey and Crassus) delivered a message saying that the omens were unfavourable and the proceedings had to be stopped. Marcellinus was foiled for long enough to bring special arrangements into play. If there were no elections within the consular year, an *interrex* had to be appointed to oversee the elections, so it was then necessary to ensure that a pliable appointee was chosen for this task. Another task was to ensure that other candidates for the consulship were removed, and their supporters frightened off, so that when voting took place the only men who did turn up were thoroughly prepared by bribery and all other means of coercion, and the result should be a foregone conclusion. Disuasion of the other candidates was heavy-handed, to say the least. Domitius was wounded in a riot, and one of his supporters was killed. Thus did Pompey and Crassus commence their second joint consulship. Their immediate concern was to hold the elections for the other magistrates and to have as many of their supporters immediately placed in post as praetors, aediles and tribunes, without any time lapse during which prosecutions could be brought against them. A suggestion that there should be a gap of 60 days before the new magistrates entered office was squashed by the new consuls, who thus unequivocally revealed the tenor of their year of office. It was during the violent elections for the aediles that there was a riot, in the course of which Pompey's outer clothing was splashed with blood; he sent his slaves home with the soiled bundle, presumably with instructions to bring him fresh clothes. As a result, his wife Julia, who was pregnant, saw only the bloodstained clothes and assumed that her husband was dead. Before explanations could be given, she collapsed and suffered a miscarriage.[16]

The most important feature of the second joint consulship of Pompey and Crassus was the legislation designed to give them both extensive long-term proconsular commands, and to extend Caesar's command in Gaul. The tribune Caius Trebonius presented the bill to give Crassus the province of Syria (where Gabinius was still governor after a three year term), and Pompey the two Spanish provinces. Each proconsul's command was to run for five years, with the right to levy troops and to make peace or war as they thought fit. This would enable Crassus to start a campaign against the king of Parthia, who was thought to be temporarily compromised by internal dissension among the royal house. Pompey did not envisage such an extensive campaign in his Spanish provinces, and indeed there was no mention of specific campaigns in the bill that Trebonius presented. Naturally there was opposition to the bill, from two tribunes in particular, but with the unspoken agreement of most of the other tribunes. Roman politics were never straightforward and consistency was an unknown concept. Former supporters of Pompey's now turned against him. Extraordinary commands like these would always rouse opposition, but in this case it was not long-lasting or successful. Cato voiced his objections and was imprisoned briefly. The tribunes who had spoken out, Caius Ateius Capito and Publius Aquillius Gallus, were simply forced to desist. Amidst violence and intimidation, the bill became law. The next law perhaps came as no surprise: to extend Caesar's command in Gaul and Illyricum for another five years. The future of the Roman world for the next half decade was divided up between three men, who commanded all the armed forces and most of the political influence at Rome. Some senators probably wondered where it would all end.[17]

The extension of Caesar's proconsulship was most probably one of the topics of discussion at Lucca. Caesar could not come to Rome to seek a further command, but his allies could push through the necessary legislation for him. There might have been a mutual agreement, with benefits promised to Pompey and Crassus, though their five year provincial commands may have come as a surprise to Caesar's adherents. The act to bestow a further five year command upon Caesar may or may not have contained within it a specific terminal date for the command; if it did, no source has preserved it intact, thus causing much anguish to modern scholars who have to discuss the problems that arose in 50 and 49, when the controversy over the recall of Caesar reached critical mass. An unequivocal date would help to establish who was morally right and who was prevaricating and scaremongering, but would not alter the outcome and the decision to go to war.[18]

Apart from the violent legislation to bestow upon themselves and Caesar their five year commands, the consulship of Pompey and Crassus was not noted for sweeping reforms, except for the institution of laws designed to tidy up electoral procedures, which was somewhat ironic considering how they had reached the consulship. Pompey made slight alterations to the composition of the jury courts, leaving untouched the three classes of jurors, but limiting service on the bench to the most wealthy of these groups. He also passed a law designed to curb bribery at elections, and Crassus attempted to bring some order to the elections by passing a law forbidding the use of the *collegia* in drumming up support for the candidates. This may have been aimed at reducing the power of Clodius and his gangs, but during this period of Pompey's ascendancy, Clodius acquiesced in his domination of the political scene – although he then lavished so much praise and attention on his erstwhile enemy that his over-eager attitude descended into mockery. But Pompey probably preferred hypocrisy to open heckling and gangs pounding on his door. He perhaps managed to neutralise Clodius via a marriage arrangement, since his elder son Gnaeus married the daughter of Appius Claudius, Clodius' brother, probably in 55, although the date is disputed and some authors prefer to date this marriage to sometime in 54, during or even after Appius Claudius' consulship.[19]

There were many other enemies to subdue, and the two consuls, aided by Caesar, bought or intimidated as many of them as they could muzzle in one way or another. Their own personal position was almost unassailable, but that of their associates was open to attack. The years after the Lucca conference were marked by trials of the adherents of the three, beginning with Cornelius Balbus in 56, who was accused of unlawfully assuming the Roman citizenship granted to him by Pompey. He was an associate of both Caesar and Pompey, so it was clear to everyone who was the real target behind the prosecution. Both Crassus and Pompey made speeches on behalf of Balbus, and Cicero was persuaded to round off the proceedings with a concluding speech. The jury confirmed Balbus' Roman citizenship. The trials continued in 55.

The accused men were Pompey's associates; Lucius Caninius Gallus was convicted despite being defended by Cicero, on an unknown charge. Titus Ampius Balbus and Lucius Scribonius Libo were also brought to court, both of them men who had assisted Pompey and enjoyed his backing. Libo's accuser was Helvius Mancia from Formiae, who is famous for calling Pompey 'the boy butcher' at this trial. Much of Pompey's time will have been occupied in these trials, in which he appeared in person and made speeches in defence of his adherents.[20]

A more satisfying occurrence was the dedication in August 55 of the great theatre complex that Pompey had begun to build after his return from the east. Besides the theatre itself there were colonnaded walks with works of art on display, and a park that became a famous meeting place and recreational area. Cicero's friend and correspondent Atticus was responsible for the layout of the art works and arrangement of the statues. Within the grounds there was a new Senate House, the *curia Pompeii*, which was close to Pompey's magnificent new house that he built next to the theatre; it would be convenient for him to attend meetings of the Senate almost on his doorstep, especially since the theatre complex was outside the city walls and therefore still open to him as a commander of troops who required concessions to permit travel into the city. There were great celebrations to mark the inauguration of the theatre, including the presentation of plays and dramas, musical performances, and games and gladiatorial shows. Pompey was the most popular man in Rome, until he put on a gladitorial show and brought on a small herd of elephants pitted against the gladiators. The crowd loved the mayhem when one of the animals was wounded and turned on its attackers, hurling their shields across the arena; but gradually the nobility of the animals and their sorrowful plight as they trumpeted and tried to get out of the arena, lifting their trunks as if imploring the crowd for help, penetrated the thick hide of the hardened Romans, and in a rare moment of sympathy the mob turned on Pompey as the author of the terrible suffering. It was said that the people cursed him then, and that this curse sealed his fate, working itself out at Pharsalus. Such fantasies were applied retrospectively to the story. In the scheme of things, as the violence and disorder in Rome increased and finally descended after six years into civil war, the fate of the elephants probably did not occupy more than a few moments of the mob's attention, and did not distract from the enjoyment of the festivities.[21]

The two consuls of 55 did nothing to engineer or block the election of their successors for 54, even though their sworn enemy Domitius Ahenobarbus was a candidate. There was a delay in holding the elections, for reasons unknown, but not because of any violent disturbances such as those of the next two years. Pompey canvassed actively on behalf of Titus Ampius Balbus, but was unsuccessful, and Domitius was duly elected along with Appius Claudius Pulcher. Whether or not the marriage alliance between Pompey's son and Appius' daughter had taken place before the elections or was still to come, Appius pursued an agenda of his own, and was not a mouthpiece for Caesar or Pompey. It promised to be another year of political wrangling.

Pompey was in splendid isolation. Caesar was still in Gaul, earning new laurels for himself by invading the unknown island of Britain, and Crassus left for his province of Syria towards the end of 55. There was violent opposition to his projected attack on Parthia, which was not mentioned in the law assigning him to the province, but was an open secret that everyone knew. The tribune Ateius Capito tried to block Crassus altogether by arresting him, but Pompey showed his hand, accompanying Crassus on the first part of his journey out of Rome to display solidarity. Ateius had to content himself with solemnly cursing the general and the Parthian war; perhaps he was as surprised as anyone else at the effectiveness of his curses when Crassus met with complete disaster in 53.[22]

As the new year opened in 54, Pompey would ordinarily have set off to go to his provinces, having recruited soldiers, like Crassus, within the terms of the laws which bestowed their commands. But Pompey was still in charge of the corn supply, and these duties kept him very busy; instead he sent his loyal adherents Lucius Afranius and Marcus Petreius to the Spanish provinces as his legates, through whom he governed. This was a very important precedent, and underlines his pre-eminent position. It was the basis upon which the emperors, beginning with Augustus, governed the whole Empire. Pompey already had plenty of experience in administering huge areas via legates whom he chose and appointed himself, commanding his troops and carrying out his orders, with a certain amount of flexibility and use of initiative, operating within their own areas and according to a broad remit prescribed by him. Pompey's terms of office in all his extraordinary commands were theoretically finite, and Augustus, whilst recognising the need for continuity if plans were to brought to fruition, was careful to emulate this device, accepting powers from the Senate for blocks of five, then eventually ten years. Domination was less frightening when chopped up into potentially terminable chunks.[23]

The year 54 was marked by squabbles and personal tragedy for Pompey. Trials of his adherents continued unabated, and Domitius Ahenobarbus as consul began to attack Caesar, Crassus, and Gabinius, whose activities in Syria included an unauthorised dash to Egypt to replace Ptolemy Auletes on the throne. In this enterprise he had no orders from the Senate, but had acted on behalf of Pompey, who perhaps hoped to be able to defend Gabinius if he should be prosecuted for leaving his province and entering territory where he had no right to set foot. Pompey had already sorted out a litiginous tangle between Crassus and Gabinius, since the latter had been ousted from his province of Syria by the appointment of Crassus two years before his proconsulship was supposed to end. Further attacks were to be made on Gabinius when he returned home in September 54.

Another Pompeian associate to be prosecuted during the year was Caius Messius, who as tribune in 57 put forward the rejected proposal that Pompey should have command of armed forces to organise the corn supply. Once again Cicero was persuaded to defend the accused, though he perhaps had less repugnance for the task since Messius had tried to have him recalled from exile. He had a much greater moral problem when both Pompey and Caesar dragooned him into defending Vatinius, Caesar's tribune of 59, and praetor in 55. Cicero had virulently attacked Vatinius as a by-product of the trial of Sestius, and now had to take back what he had said. With this in mind, and also the fact that Vatinius had blatantly overstepped the mark and left himself wide open to prosecution, Cicero probably had great trouble in writing his speech on behalf of Vatinius, and more than likely did not deliver anything like the written version.[24]

The consular candidates for 53 were a mixed bunch of mostly anti-Pompeians and anti-Caesarians. Though it cannot be said that political allegiance at Rome was ever consistent or permanent, on their past records none of the candidates promised much for the members of the coalition. The best of a bad lot was Caius Memmius, previously hostile but now reconciled to Caesar and using Pompey's influence in Gaul to gain support. Marcus Aemilius Scaurus ought to have been a safe bet because he had served with Pompey, and being the brother of Pompey's unfortunate second wife Aemilia, he had been Pompey's brother-in-law for a short time. Coincidentally he had also married Pompey's cast-off wife Mucia. Pompey supported him in a lukewarm fashion, not least because Scaurus was undergoing prosecution for extortion in his province of Sardinia. The other candidates were Marcus Messalla and Domitius Calvinus, neither of whom were acceptable to Pompey. The elections were delayed, bribery was so rampant that there were debates about it in the Senate, and then a scandalous scheme hatched by Memmius and Calvinus was brought to light. Pompey forced Memmius to reveal the plan in the Senate; it seemed that the two candidates were in league with the present consuls either to pay them vast sums of money, or to arrange for Appius and Domitius to go to their provinces, by persuading augurs and ex-consuls to swear that laws had been passed on this subject, even though there had been no mention of any such laws and not even a hint of a discussion. This scandal knocked out Memmius from the elections, jeopardised the chances of Calvinus, and threw doubts on the integrity of the consuls Domitius Ahenobarbus and Appius Claudius. This left Scaurus, who was found not guilty of extortion in early September, and Messalla. But the elections were not held until the middle of 53, almost exactly one year later than they should have been, and it was Messalla and Calvinus who were elected.[25]

Meanwhile in September 54 Gabinius returned home, entering the city by night, and when he finally appeared in public he was immediately prosecuted on more than one count. In October he faced a charge of *maiestas* (treason, or specifically crimes against the majesty of the Roman People), but he was acquitted; the jury was proven to be susceptible to bribes, and the prosecution did not press home the charges. Cicero tried to sit on the fence, limiting his part in the trial to a speech as a witness for the prosecution, but without making too much of his case, and not undertaking the prosecution himself because he feared Pompey's reaction. Gabinius also had to face charges of *ambitus* (illegal activities in gaining electoral support) and *repetundae* (extortion). It was this trial for extortion that finished Gabinius' career. His principal enemies were the tax collectors, the *publicani*, a strong element in the trials of more men than Gabinius, who was condemned despite the arrival of a deputation from Alexandria to speak on his behalf, and the activities of Cicero who had been forcibly brought in for the defence by Pompey. Gabinius went into exile, not abandoned by his patron, but defeated all the same because Pompey was not powerful enough to save him without resorting to force.[26]

At about this time, possibly before the trials of Gabinius, or in the course of them, Pompey's wife Julia died in childbirth. This was not just a marriage of convenience for political ends, but a lovematch; Pompey was not just fond of Julia, but genuinely in love with her, as his contemporaries knew. He intended to lay his wife to rest at his Alban Villa, but the people stopped the funeral procession as it was leaving Rome, insisting that Julia should be buried on the Campus Martius – a single honour both to Pompey and to Caesar, who heard of his daughter's death as he returned from his second expedition to Britain. The death of Julia did not cause an immediate rift between Pompey and Caesar, as most authors now point out. There was no political change in either man's attitude to the other, and no personal animosity; as Gruen points out, Caesar did not alter his will, in which he left his estate to his son-in-law, until the outbreak of the civil war.[27]

Since the elections were still delayed, and the candidates had all been prosecuted in the meantime, it was rumoured that Pompey was to be made Dictator. His cousin Lucilius Hirrus loudly announced more than once that he was ready to present a bill to appoint Pompey to the Dictatorship, but Pompey said that he did not want the responsibility. Hardly anyone believed him because that was what he always said when he wanted something. Even Cicero was not sure. In the end nothing happened. Perhaps Pompey was once again testing the water to find out how much support there would have been for the idea, and backing down when he found that it was not popular. In summer 53 in the absence of the consuls who had laid down their office, Pompey presided over the elections for the remaining part of the year. Domitius Calvinus and Messalla took up their office.[28]

Unexpected news arrived that threw Rome into a momentary panic: Crassus' expedition had failed disastrously. Crassus and his son had been killed, and the troops had only just been saved from disaster by Gaius Cassius Longinus, who had been quaestor in 54 and had joined the expedition as one of Crassus' officers. He had rounded up the survivors of the defeat, marched them back to Syria and organised the defence of the province in case the Parthians followed up the attack. Fortunately there was no invasion of the province and for some time Cassius was allowed to remain in command; neither Pompey nor any of his associates rushed out to Syria to take over the army and make war on the Parthians. The death of Crassus was once seen as the last thread that bound Caesar and Pompey together, but scholars deny that there was any discernible change in the political sphere, except that Crassus' clients now needed new patrons, and some of them turned to Caesar to swell the ranks of his followers. But it was not yet a step towards civil war that there were only two men instead of three who wished to control the Roman world.[29]

It may have been now that Caesar made another offer of marriage alliances to secure the bond with Pompey. His suggestion was that Pompey should marry his great-niece Octavia, and he himself should divorce his wife Calpurnia to marry Pompey's daughter Pompeia. These proposals necessitated the break up of three marriages, Caesar's, Octavia's with her husband Marcellus, and Pompeia's with Faustus Sulla; though Pompeia may not yet have married Faustus, she was betrothed to him. Pompey rejected the offer, but no reasons for his refusal survive. He may simply have wished to leave the existing marriages intact, knowing that Caesar did not want to divorce Calpurnia, even though he would make the sacrifice for political ends. Perhaps, too, Pompey respected his own daughter's wishes. There is no firm indication that he intended to turn away from Caesar at this time, though there may have been some of the enemies of Caesar and opponents of the coalition who looked on with interest, trying to discern whether Pompey was at last turning to the camp of the opposition.[30]

The pattern of electoral bribery and violence in the city, which led to delays in holding the elections, continued exponentially in 53 and into 52. The candidates for the consulships of 52 were Plautius Hypsaeus, Metellus Scipio, and Titus Annius Milo. Clodius was standing for the praetorship, so the in-fighting was not limited to words. Since Clodius was more or less reconciled, at least temporarily, Pompey had by now decided that his support for Milo was no longer a good idea, and wanted to block his candidacy. As the elections were continually postponed, rumours that he wanted to be Dictator increased in intensity, but nothing was proposed on this subject. Delays in appointing the consuls could prove useful in removing Milo as a candidate, and Pompey joined forces with the tribune Munatius Plancus in obstructing proposals to appoint an *interrex* to preside over the elections. As events turned out, Milo removed himself from any chance of gaining the consulship. In January, he and his gangs met up with Clodius outside Rome on the Appian Way, and a serious fight ensued, in which Clodius was wounded. He was carried to a nearby tavern, but Milo's men dragged him out and killed him. It was said that Milo decided to finish off Clodius, probably on the grounds that if Clodius survived there would never be an end to the matter, but if he was killed there would be only the charge of murder.[31]

Clodius was given a splendid funeral by the people of Rome, who placed him inside the Senate House and burned him there, along with the building. The mob laid siege to the houses of Milo and the newly appointed *interrex* Marcus Aemilius Lepidus who was lucky to escape with his life, and would probably have been killed when the Clodian gangs broke into his courtyard, had it not been for the arrival of Milo's gangs who threw them out again. Milo found that support for him increased a little after the destruction of the Senate House and the attack on Lepidus, so he returned to the city. The violent incidents polarised the Romans; the enemies of Clodius such as Cicero, Cato and the tribune Caelius supported Milo, while the tribunes Munatius Plancus and Quintus Pompeius Rufus opposed him. The state of affairs demanded extraordinary measures; the Senate passed the last decree, the *senatus consultum ultimum*, empowering the tribunes, the *interrex*, and Pompey to see that the state came to no harm. Pompey already held *imperium* as part of his command to regulate the corn supply and to govern Spain, and he was now authorised to recruit more soldiers in Italy and to conscript all young men of military age. Perhaps as part of a subterfuge designed to discredit Milo, or possibly as a response to information collected by his agents, Pompey let it be known that Milo was planning to assassinate him. The tribunes Plancus and Pompeius Rufus brought the plot to light. Pompey increased his bodyguard, bringing troops to the gardens of his house, where he camped with them as if he were on campaign. Clearly he was taking no chances against Milo, but he also intended to act against him according to the letter of the law.[32]

Despite the seriousness of the disorder and violence, a Dictatorship was still not proposed in the Senate, but a compromise was reached when Bibulus suggested that Pompey should be appointed consul without a colleague. Cato supported the proposal, which was put into effect as soon as possible. There were advantages and disadvantages to being consul rather than Dictator, and it has been suggested that Bibulus and Cato were deliberately trying to limit Pompey's power and authority; but as Seager points out, although as consul Pompey would be accountable when he laid down his office, and would be subject to tribunician veto, he was not limited to the six month period of the Dictatorship. Sulla had been an exception when he was appointed Dictator without a fixed time limit, and in the future Caesar would also be an exception, being eventually and for a very short time appointed *Dictator perpetuo*, Dictator in perpetuity. But there was something distasteful about the Dictatorship, and although a sole consulship was an anomaly and a contradiction in terms, the office held less of a threat.[33]

With characteristic speed and efficiency, Pompey passed laws designed to put an end to the violence, and the bribery and corruption that attended elections, and to bring Milo to trial. He also improved the legal process to streamline the court hearings and make it almost impossible to bribe the juries. First he set a limit on the time scales for court hearings, which were to be completed within four days. Three days were allowed for the examination of witnesses, and on the fourth day the prosecution was allowed two hours for speeches, and the defence three hours. For the juries he selected 120 men of good character from each of the three classes proposed by Aurelius Cotta in 70, making a total of 360 jurors, who were to sit through the first three days of the trials while witnesses were examined; 81 would then be selected for the jury on the final day. The large number of jurors who were present during the beginning of each trial ensured that no one could possibly bribe them all, and the short time scale between the appointment of the final jurors and the last day of the trial gave no one sufficient opportunity to tamper with them. As part of these legal reforms, character witnesses for the accused were forbidden to appear, since more often than not they made irrelevant time-wasting speeches that were nothing to do with the case. According to Appian, Pompey also passed a law enabling anyone to prosecute any office holder, from the date of his first consulship in 70 to the present, in order to cure once and for all the problems of the state. Then he broke his own rules in rescuing Metellus Scipio from prosecution, and making a statement on behalf of Plancus when he was prosecuted for violence in December 53, immediately after his office as tribune expired.[34]

The projected multiple trials of Milo began and ended with his prosecution for using violence. His accusers were Clodius' two nephews, and his defence was conducted by Cicero. There were more accusations lined up (just as Gabinius had been prosecuted under several laws), but it was hoped that the first trial would result in condemnation and exile, so that the other charges against Milo would prove to be simply formalities. Cicero was probably sincere in what he wanted to say on Milo's behalf, but he did not manage to deliver the speech that he intended to deliver, because he was heckled and intimidated by Clodius' supporters and greatly put off by the presence of Pompey's soldiers, who were posted all around the tribunal. The most telling factor would be that even though Cicero may have been sincere in wanting to help Milo, he knew perfectly well that Pompey wanted Milo condemned and removed. It has been argued that the *senatus consultum ultimum* would have authorised Pompey to execute Milo, and the fact that he brought him to trial suggests that he considered him to be innocent. But even if he was not convinced of Milo's guilt, Pompey's attitude seems to have been one of determination to remove him. The result was a foregone conclusion; Milo went into exile, with Marseilles the town he chose as his place of residence. When he received the written version of Cicero's speech, he merely remarked that it was just as well that Cicero had not actually delivered it, otherwise he would never have known the delights of the excellent red mullet of Marseilles.[35]

Looking ahead to the future, Pompey secured his own position by extending his command in the Spanish provinces for a further five years, and was voted money for the upkeep of his troops. It remained uncertain whether he would ever go to Spain. Meanwhile in Rome he rationalised his anomalous position as sole consul. For what remained of the consular year, Pompey chose as his colleague Metellus Scipio. He had married Scipio's daughter Cornelia, who had been widowed when her first husband Publius Crassus was killed on the disastrous Parthian campaign. This alliance has been interpreted as a sign that there was an impending breach between Pompey and Caesar, but this theory is most probably retrospective justification for the outbreak of the civil war. In 52, the civil war was by no means inevitable and Pompey was still co-operating with his colleague, despite the fact that his legislation concerning the government of the provinces and the election of magistrates seemed at first sight to be designed to embarrass Caesar. These laws have been debated by several scholars. Some of them excuse Pompey's actions as those of a blundering incompetent who could not make up his mind whether he opposed Caesar or not, while others have explained that the laws were part of a programme of administrative reform from which Caesar was specifically exempted. The law that concerned Caesar personally is commonly called the law of ten tribunes, which gave him the right to stand for the consulship *in absentia*. The first proposal of the ten tribunes had been to recall Caesar immediately so that he could become consul as Pompey's colleague. This would have solved Caesar's problem of stepping straight from his Gallic command into the consulship, leaving no gaps where he would be a private citizen, vulnerable without either *imperium* or the protection of office. But it was not what Caesar wanted, and probably not what Pompey wanted either. In place of this proposal, Caesar persuaded the tribunes to pass the law allowing him to stand for the elections while still in command in Gaul. Pompey worked hard on Caesar's behalf, determined to push this bill through. His other legislation, however, seemed to contradict this law of ten tribunes, and even to threaten Caesar's command. One of his laws, *lex de iure magistratuum*, stipulated that candidates for election to any of the magistracies must present their names in person. This directly contradicted the law that he had just passed on Caesar's behalf, allowing him to stand *in absentia*; and when this was pointed out by anxious friends of Caesar, Pompey added a codicil to the law, which had already been inscribed, to the effect that Caesar was legally exempted from the provisions of this legislation. Pompey has been accused of several faults, not all of them compatible with each other, including carelessness in drafting the clauses of the law, deceitful subterfuge in the hope that he could quietly annul the law of ten tribunes without alerting anyone, and simple forgetfulness. These explanations are not accepted by all scholars. Pompey was probably highly exasperated by the nitpicking that attended this legislation, and he knew that the codicil had no force in law; but that did not matter because there was an existing law specifically granting exemption to Caesar, and that law had not been repealed. The new law concerning personal attendance at the election of magistrates demonstrated that Caesar was the only candidate, indeed the final candidate, who could stand *in absentia*.[36]

The other law that Pompey promulgated in his sole consulship seemed more directly threatening to Caesar. Its origins lay in the rampant bribery that attended elections, a theme already dealt with in part by Pompey and Crassus when they were consuls together in 55. Candidates for office could afford to borrow and spend money on a lavish scale when they were seeking office, because if they were elected they could each look forward to governing a province after their term came to an end, in which they could reimburse themselves and their creditors at the expense of the provincials. In order to prevent this Pompey's *lex de provinciis* interposed a compulsory gap of five years between a magistracy in Rome and a promagistracy in a province. This was intended to discourage the more ruthless candidates who would require loans and then an immediate method of recouping their cash, but it also had the unfortunate result that a pool of ex-consuls and praetors who had never gone out to govern the provinces could be drawn upon at once, which in turn meant that existing provincial governors could be superceded immediately, because the new governors would not have to wait until their year of office had expired. The system that had been in operation until now was based on a law of Gaius Sempronius Gracchus, by the terms of which the provinces or duties to be assigned to retiring consuls were decided upon before the elections had taken place; on this basis the task of attending to the woods and forest paths had been allocated to the consuls of 59, before Caesar was elected. Pompey's law invalidated this system, and played into the hands of those who agitated for Caesar's recall. Under the Sempronian law, although the enemies of Caesar could still try to arrange for his recall, there would have been a short period of grace while the designated consul took up office and perhaps served the full term in Rome. Now this period of grace was removed entirely, and Caesar's enemies could move in. Pompey's laws had an unwelcome effect on another politician as well as Caesar; Marcus Tullius Cicero had to take his turn as provincial governor. He was sent to Cilicia from the summer of 51 to the summer of 50, and though he did his work well enough he regarded it as almost another period of exile.[37]

The consuls who were returned at the elections of 51 were Marcus Marcellus and Servius Supicius Rufus. Marcellus began to propose anti-Caesarian measures as soon as he took up office. He suggested that since the Gallic wars were over, there was no need for Caesar to remain in Gaul at the head of troops; but according to the law passed by Pompey and Crassus to extend Caesar's command, there should be no question yet of a termination, regardless of the fact that no one knows what the actual final date may have been or even if any such date was fixed at all. This proposal came to nothing, and Pompey weathered the storm of Marcellus' next attack, when the consul claimed that the *lex de iure magistratuum* had annulled the law of ten tribunes and negated the special dispensation granted to Caesar to stand for election without coming to Rome. Pompey made a speech in the Senate opposing Marcellus in March 51. It was proposed that there should be a discussion on Caesar's provincial command, probably in August; whatever the intended date, it was postponed until September, and Metellus Scipio suggested that it should be put off still further, until 1 March 50, when nothing else should be put on the agenda so that full attention could be devoted to the matter. Caesar was not pleased, but at least there was a little breathing space, and he could wait upon events. Marcellus resorted to petty, and ultimately useless, annoying tactics; he flogged a Transpadane Gaul, a citizen of Novum Comum, merely to annoy Caesar who had granted Roman citizenship to that colony; Roman citizens were supposedly protected from this sort of treatment, so Marcellus' action was a direct challenge to Caesar's authority.[38]

Pompey was in an awkward position, harrassed by his own and Caesar's enemies. At one point he said that he would go to Spain, and at another it was rumoured that he would be sent to the east, to settle the worrying Parthian question. Cassius had been left in command and was perfectly competent, but there were threatening signs from the Parthian Royal House, and when Bibulus became governor of Syria he sent messages for help to counter what he thought was to be an invasion. Pompey could have orchestrated a new command for himself had he so desired, but that would merely place him in the same position as he had been in when he returned from the east in 62. In the end he remained in Italy. He did travel to Ariminum, close to Caesar's province of Cisalpine Gaul, and though the two could not have met in person, there may have been some contact and a level of agreement as to what to do in the future. Alternatively, Pompey could have been concerned to find out whether the Gallic war was nearing completion, and whether Caesar really needed more time to organise the provinces. The anti-Caesarian pressures were building up again and promised to continue in 50, since the consuls elect were Gaius Marcellus, a cousin of the consul of 51, and Lucius Aemilius Paullus, who was a declared enemy of Caesar. Perhaps more worrying was the election of Scribonius Curio as tribune. He had been a good friend of the murdered Clodius, and had married Fulvia, Clodius' widow. His political views were staunchly anti-Caesarian, at least right up to November and December before he embarked on his tribunate, so it was assumed that he would continue in this vein and would attack Caesar, whose friends anticipated trouble from Curio and whose enemies welcomed the prospect. Mortal fear of Caesar, and the uncertainty as to whether he intended to march on Rome and take over by force, was being steadily built up by his enemies. This is revealed in the questions that were continually asked of Pompey, whose replies are recorded. He said that he would not agree to Caesar holding the consulship without disbanding his armies; when asked what would happen if Caesar stood for the consulship while still commanding armies, Pompey made the famous reply, with studied calm, 'What would I do if my son were to take a stick to me?', indicating that he thought it highly improbable. The fact that up to this point Caesar had not declared his intention of doing any such thing was irrelevant, but Pompey was manoeuvred into the position of declaring his opposition to such proposals, which were interpreted by a process of wishful thinking on the part of the anti-Caesarians to suggest that Pompey was now in opposition to Caesar.[39]

The beginning of the year 50 was not as tendentious as may have been expected. Curio began his career as tribune with a programme designed to appeal to the people, with proposals to divide the Campanian lands among the poor of the city, to annexe the kingdom of Numidia, to build roads, and to distribute grain to the people. It was the usual paraphernalia of the *popularis* tribunes, but his schemes were perhaps never intended to be fought for seriously. The Senate rejected all the proposals that Curio put forward, including his suggestion that the priests should insert an intercalary month at the end of February. This was necessary from time to time because the Roman calendar was based on a lunar reckoning and had gradually slipped out of synchronisation with the seasons – it was Caesar who eventually rejected the old Roman system and established the solar calendar based on Egyptian calculations. In 50, Curio's suggestion was interpreted as a means of forestalling discussion about Caesar's provinces, which was due to begin on 1 March. So the ploy of inserting an extra month failed, and it was said that at this point Curio went over to Caesar. The ancient authors were convinced that Caesar must have bought him before his tribunate began; but this is open to debate. Gruen suggests that Curio acted independently, not as an agent of Caesar, and that he was determined to split Caesar from Pompey. But the facts are that Curio began to rock the boat in 50, stirred up trouble for Pompey and the Senate, and then finally at the end of the year left to join Caesar in Gaul. He showed his hand when the consul Gaius Marcellus opened a debate, perhaps in February, proposing that since Caesar's command was coming to an end, successors should be chosen to take over his provinces. Curio countered by suggesting that Pompey should also give up his provinces. He explained that he had always been opposed to extraordinary commands, and he would continue to block proposals to send successors to replace Caesar unless Pompey also disarmed. According to Appian, Pompey was in a more precarious position now, having lost popularity because he had succeeded in putting an end to most of the rampant bribery at the elections, which displeased the people because they were far from averse to a little bribery here and there, and had become accustomed to receiving the cash.[40]

Marcellus could make little headway in March, when the matter of Caesar's provinces had been scheduled for debate. His colleague Aemilius Paullus did not support him, and it was widely supposed that his silence had been purchased by Caesar, who was perhaps financing Paullus' building projects. When the discussion about Caesar and his command did begin, Pompey endorsed a proposal that Caesar should be allowed an extension of his command until 13 November. The reason for the choice of this date is not known, but it gave Caesar the opportunity to stand for the consular elections for 49 in the summer of 50, while still in command of his army; he could then arrive outside Rome in the winter with his troops, organise a triumph, hold it, then step straight into office as consul on 1 January 49. Based on all that had gone before this proposal ought to have satisfied all parties and given Caesar everything he asked for. If Pompey thought he had solved the problems, Curio soon disillusioned him by blocking this suggestion. Caesar may have interpreted this move as a trap, since he would be at the mercy of his friend Pompey to keep his options open for him at Rome. What if Pompey decided to postpone the elections? Or perhaps, when the time came to stand for election, Pompey and his friends refused to accept his candidature? Then there was the possibility that Caesar would not be successfully elected, despite the flow of cash that streamed from him to virtually everyone in Rome. No one can be sure of Pompey's intentions when he made the offer of an extension to Caesar. If he was absolutely sincere, hoping to retain his own supremacy side by side with Caesar when he returned from Gaul and became consul, then there is an poignant element of tragedy in the situation. If on the other hand Pompey was anything but sincere, calculating that he could make this eminently reasonable offer to Caesar in the full knowledge that it was not acceptable and would be refused, he could demonstrate his own accommodating attitude and at the same time highlight Caesar's uncompromising obstinacy. It is impossible for modern scholars, knowing with hindsight that the civil war was not averted by any of Pompey's eminently reasonable offers, to discern clearly who intended to wrong-foot whom in the spring of 50. The only certainty is that Caesar did not trust Pompey and did not wish to embark on the next stage of his political career either as his subordinate, or in his debt.[41]

In the summer, Pompey fell ill. He may have already been unwell in April, according to Cicero, and the collapse in the summer while he was at Naples may have been a more serious relapse. The cause is not known, and has been attributed to malaria, and also to stress; but whatever it was, the illness was severe, perhaps life-threatening. Prayers were offered for his recovery, and when he finally emerged, in better health, there was great rejoicing all over the country, a phenomenon that may have convinced Pompey that his popularity was unlimited. While he was ill he wrote to the Senate, recounting his services to the state, praising Caesar's activities, and using his old ploy of suggesting that he was weary of command, since he had accepted his consulship and his provinces only under duress. He offered to lay down his command and affirmed that Caesar would be willing to do the same; and on his return to Rome Pompey repeated these sentiments in the Senate. He may genuinely have intended to renounce his claim on the Spanish provinces, relying upon his pre-eminence to maintain his position. Unfortunately not all of his audience thought him sincere. In a meeting of the Senate, Curio suggested that Pompey was a potential tyrant, and that Caesar's armies were necessary in order to keep him in check; therefore Pompey should be the first to disarm. Pompey did not stay in the Senate House to be further insulted, but swept out, flinging threats at Curio as he went. He was perhaps heartened later on that day by the news that the Senate had thwarted Curio; everything could have gone wrong at this point if the majority of senators had agreed with Curio and voted to divest Pompey of his command, but fear of Caesar prevailed.[42]

By late summer, Pompey's attitude had crystallised. Perhaps he realised that his sincerity would always be doubted, reasonable offers would never be accepted, and since he was continually cast as the villain of the piece by Curio for refusing to disarm, that he had only two choices. Either he could back down, retire into private life and hope to retain some part of his supremacy, or he could resist, in the hope that the worst scenario could be avoided. He had decided that he would not countenance Caesar as consul while still in command of his armies, which was a glaring inconsistency on his part in view of the fact that this was precisely the position in which he stood himself. It was Caesar who now proposed that both should give up their armies, but it was a hollow suggestion that neither contender for power could contemplate, because neither felt safe without an army at his back, to offer protection against enemies and each other.[43]

The Parthian problems surfaced again, sufficiently serious to warrant an assemblage of troops. It was decreed that both Pompey and Caesar should contribute one legion each to the war effort, which in the end never happened. Pompey had lent one of his legions to Caesar, and since his own forces were far away on Spain, and the Gallic war was over, he recalled that legion, and Caesar handed it over without demur, as well as one of his own. This meant that he was now short of two legions, and the news perhaps heartened those in Rome who thought that he was about to march on the city. His friends interpreted this removal of his legions as yet another attack on him, especially as Pompey kept them both in Italy. Talk of civil war began to circulate. Cicero came home from Cilicia to a gloomy situation, and was torn between friendship for Pompey and an ardent wish for peace. In December 50, the consul Marcellus accelerated events; Curio kept on proposing that the two generals should lay down their commands simultaneously, so Marcellus tried to demonstrate how the Senate really felt by proposing two separate motions, firstly that Caesar should give up his provinces and his army, and secondly that Pompey's command should be terminated. The first proposal was passed, the second was emphatically defeated, but Curio upstaged Marcellus by putting forward his usual suggestion that Caesar and Pompey should both lay down their commands, and this motion was passed by 370 votes to 22. Marcellus dismissed the Senate without acting on this overwhelming vote. Rumours began that Caesar was marching on Rome, so without further debate, Marcellus appeared at Pompey's door and placed a sword in his hands, charging him with the defence of the state. He was empowered to take command of the two legions that had been destined for the Parthian war, and of any other troops in Italy. He could also recruit further troops as he wished, a task which Pompey perhaps underestimated as a result of the tremendous enthusiasm that had greeted his recovery from his illness in the summer. He said that he had only to stamp his foot on the ground and troops would rise up; perhaps it was not all hyperbole. He was buoyant because the men of Caesar's legion that had been sent as his

12 *Coin of Caesar, dated to 49, and perhaps struck in Gaul before the crossing of the Rubicon. The obverse shows an elephant trampling a snake, and the priestly implements on the reverse serve as a reminder that Caesar had been Pontifex Maximus since 63*

contribution to the Parthian campaign had been primed to spread the false rumour that the rest of Caesar's army was disaffected, and was on the verge of going over to Pompey. Perhaps on this basis of assured success, Pompey accepted the command, but only on condition that no better solution could be found. At this stage it is possible that negotiation could have settled the immediate difficulties, and it is probable that Pompey imagined that a display of force would be sufficient to persuade Caesar to back down. But by the end of December, in Cicero's opinion, Pompey did not want peace, because he had come to the conclusion that Caesar's intentions were revolutionary, and he would achieve what he wanted by force, even if he gave up his provinces and his armies. Pompey was severely provoked by Caesar's newly elected tribune Mark Antony, who attacked him and his policies in a speech in the Senate on 20 December. But Pompey did not retaliate by resorting to arms; he merely pointed out that if this was how one of Caesar's officers behaved, it would be much worse when Caesar was consul. Despite the contumacious verbal attacks of Antony, the outbreak of the civil war was not inevitable; even now, with Pompey's veterans and soldiers in the city and their general seemingly in a warlike mood, there was still room for negotiation.[44]

In January 49 Caesar wrote to the Senate, via Antony and another tribune Quintus Cassius, proposing that he and Pompey should lay down their commands together, but that he could not lay down his own command while Pompey retained his. Thus he neatly placed all the onus on Pompey for his stubbornness in not backing down. Metellus Scipio then made the proposal that Caesar should give up his armies by a specified date, and it would be deemed a hostile act if he refused. The Senate was willing to adopt this proposal, but Antony and Cassius vetoed it. Pompey summoned the senators to his house after the meeting, and continued the debate. An embassy to Caesar was suggested and volunteers were found who would go and speak with him, but the idea was rejected. In a letter to Atticus written from Formiae in late December, Cicero neatly summed up the alternatives: he acknowledged that one option was to admit Caesar as a candidate for the consulship while he commanded his armies; another would be to persuade him to take up office on condition that he gave up his command. It was a certainty that if his candidacy was refused, Caesar would endure the insult and keep his province, or worse still would invade Italy and obtain what he wanted by force. Then Cicero outlined Caesar's position from the Senate's point of view: he had held a province for ten years, not one that had been allocated by the Senate but one that had been obtained by force. He had arranged the term of office to suit himself, and when it was about to come to an end and the Senate considered appointing a successor, Caesar complained that his candidacy should have been considered. Cicero thought that the time when the coming war should be fought depended on chance, and the plan of campaign on the circumstances; he advocated abandoning the city of Rome if necessary, and stripping it of supplies to deny them to Caesar. He had met Pompey the day before, and talked with him all afternoon; it sounds as though he had listened to a lesson in strategy which he could repeat, but had not seriously taken it in. Perhaps Cicero thought that it would never reach the point where Rome had to be abandoned. He epitomises the anti-Caesarian sentiments that were shared by many; there were now hardliners in the Senate who advocated stronger measures against Caesar. The consuls for 49 were not Caesarians, being yet another Marcellus, brother of the consul of 51, and Lucius Cornelius Lentulus Crus, who was no friend of Caesar. It was Lentulus, together with Cato and Metellus Scipio, who now advocated a policy of resistance to Caesar, refusing to allow any compromise when it was suggested that he should be allowed to keep command of Cisalpine Gaul and Illyricum, or alternatively only one of these two provinces with a single legion. It was said that Pompey was in favour of the proposal to allow Caesar to retain Illyricum with one legion, but Lentulus and his friends would not condone the idea; it is debatable whether this is a retrospective judgement designed to put all the blame for the war on Lentulus, thus absolving Pompey from initial responsibility. In his account of the run up to the civil war, Caesar says more than once that Pompey had been influenced by his friends who were eager to see Caesar defeated. The *senatus consultum ultimum* was passed on 7 January, to authorise the consuls, praetors, tribunes and all the proconsulars near the city to take steps to ensure that the state came to no harm. Significantly the decree did not name Pompey as supreme commander. In their determination to pass the decree, the consuls threatened the tribunes Antony and Cassius with violence if they interposed their vetoes; some sources say that they were ejected from the Senate. Tribunes were supposedly sacrosanct, and to threaten them in this way was tantamount to sacrilege. Caesar was in Cisalpine Gaul, close to the border with Italy, when he heard of the meeting of the Senate and the fact that Antony and Cassius, accompanied by Curio, had fled from Rome and were on their way to his camp. He had one legion with him, the thirteenth; the rest of his army was still in Gaul. Addressing his one legion, Caesar presented the soldiers with a catalogue of all the wrongs that had been done to him in the past. He mentioned that the tribunes' right of veto had been crushed, and that in the past the *senatus consultum ultimum* had been passed only in cases of extreme danger, such as a serious riot of the people, or the seizure of temples and the like. Nothing of this nature had actually occurred in this instance. Whether he actually said this to the troops does not matter; his account of the beginning of the civil war was designed to remind his audience that he had not made the first aggressive move. Whatever he said to the soldiers he whipped them up into a frenzy of righteous indignation on behalf of their wronged commander, and ensured they were ready to follow him wherever he went. Without waiting for the rest of his army to come from Gaul, Caesar began to march to Ariminum (modern Rimini). On the night of 10/11 January he halted for a while at the river Rubicon. This was the boundary between his province of Cisalpine Gaul, and Italy. In the former, he was a legally-appointed governor authorised to command troops; in the latter he would be a rebel if he entered at the head of an army. It was said that he pondered the enormity of what he was about to do. Then he led his troops across the river, on the road to Rome.[45]

6 Civil war

Caesar's invasion of Italy, although it was one of the very events that his enemies feared, seems to have taken them by surprise. Though the calendar was out of synchronisation with the seasons, it was still winter, and Caesar did not have all his forces with him; but even if he had not moved when he did, the politicians who would not compromise with him must surely have foreseen that if peace was not arranged by negotiation, he would march in the spring, which would give them at most two or three months grace. Many people perhaps thought complacently that it would never come to war, and that despite all the spear rattling, ultimately a truce would be arranged, followed by a political deal that would accommodate both parties. Characteristically Caesar did not wait until he had assembled all his forces. If Caesar had waited for a couple of months, Pompey may have benefited from the delay as far as recruitment was concerned, but he could not have expected to train an army in this period. He was too good a general to have forgotten this, so his optimistic and encouraging remarks about his ability to fight the coming war require explanation. Seager maintains that Pompey presumably expected to have much more time to prepare, or that he simply made confident noises in order to boost morale. His claim that troops would spring up in Italy if he simply stamped his foot was challenged by Favonius, who asked him to stamp and see what happened. In truth, recruitment was perhaps not as easy as he had expected, and though he commanded the two trained and experienced legions that had come from Caesar's army in Gaul, he could not trust them, even though one of them was his own. Pompey's caution in this respect directly contradicts the tale that he had been misled by reports that Caesar's army was disaffected and would desert him as soon as the army entered Italy. This is one of the main charges made against Pompey: that he entertained overconfident hopes of weaning Caesar's army away from him, as well as having underestimated the time it would take to raise an army of his own.[1]

There are two schools of thought about Pompey's plans and behaviour at the outset of the civil war. It is possible to interpret his abandonment of Rome and then Italy either as a series of changes of plan as the situation worsened, or as a preconceived idea which was put into operation in stages, but kept more or less secret from the beginning. As to which of these interpretations gains credence, much depends upon opinion of Pompey's ability as a general, and his capacity for forethought and forward planning. The contemporary sources are limited to Caesar's narrative of the civil war with its self-justificatory propaganda, and Cicero's correspondence, which gives much detail but insufficient military insight. Cicero did not at first appreciate Pompey's strategy, influenced as he was by the enormity of the coming war and the abandonment of Rome.[2]

13 *Portrait of Caesar from Turin*

Though Cicero had embraced the principle that if Caesar invaded with hostile intent it might be necessary to withdraw from Rome (to deny him access to money and supplies of food), when it actually happened he could not believe his ears. On 17 January, Pompey left Rome for Capua, his main recruiting ground. He declared that anyone who did not accompany or follow him would be classified as an enemy. The consuls and several senators trailed after him over the next few days; the city was without its chief magistrates for the first time. In haste on 7 January the Senate had appointed provincial governors, breaking all the rules that Pompey had made to insert a five year gap between city magistracies and provincial promagistracies. The provinces of Syria and Transalpine Gaul were designated as consular, and lots were drawn for them; Lucius Domitius Ahenobarbus was appointed to Transalpine Gaul, and Syria was allocated to Pompey's father-in-law Scipio. This appointment provides a hint that Pompey intended to go to the east to fight the war, where he had clients and investments that would pay off; the province of Syria would be a key area and it was necessary to allocate it to someone he could trust. Small wonder that Caesar claimed the allotment was rigged, and not all the names of eligible men were included. As Greenhalgh points out, Scipio's name should never have appeared at all, since he had been consul in 52 and should not have been given a province for three more years. The praetorian provinces included the corn-rich areas of Sicily, Sardinia and Africa, and these went to Cato, Cotta and Tubero. But Cato did not go to Sicily until it was too late, and Caesar was able to win the corn-producing provinces via his own legates.[3]

The appointment of the magistrates and provincial governors theoretically pre-empted anything that Caesar could do on a legal basis when he reached the city – not that the lack of legality was any deterrent to him. To abandon Rome and remove its government was in fact one way of preserving the city, since there was nothing to fight over and nothing to be gained by fighting. Pompey probably realised that when it came to protecting property, many senators would begin to feel nervous about losing their possessions, and might also begin to think in terms of capitulation to Caesar. So he made it clear that they were either for him or against him, and he demanded nothing less than total commitment. This is what Cicero could not quite bring himself to declare. One man who did declare it was Titus Labienus, who for reasons best known to himself, deserted Caesar, with whom he had worked successfully for ten years, and joined Pompey on 22 January. It was said that he was jealous of Mark Antony, whose advancement had been rapid once he came to Caesar in Gaul; or perhaps it was because he was a Picene by birth and in the end preferred to be with Pompey; or he was high-minded enough to refuse to follow Caesar in rebellion against the state. Perhaps there was a little of all these reasons in Labienus' decision. Cicero called him a hero; no one knows what Pompey called him.[4]

While Pompey was still raising troops, it was not known whether he intended to make a stand in Italy, or to leave it altogether. Since the evacuation of his troops demanded the collection of a large number of ships (so many that Caesar could scarcely find one that was seaworthy), either those who, like Cicero, still wondered whether there was to be a final battle in Italy were blind and deaf, or the operation was carried out in complete secrecy until the troops and the ships were suddenly gathered together at Brundisium. Caesar had perhaps got wind of what was happening and was eager to prevent it, because if Pompey escaped intact to another province, the war would be prolonged, and there could be no settlement at Rome while Pompey's troops were present in Spain and wherever else he chose to go. Pompey had sent Lucius Caesar (not a close relation to Caesar, despite the name) as envoy to explain that it was not personal enmity that motivated him, but as always he was thinking of the welfare of the state. Now Caesar returned the messenger to Pompey with suggestions as to how the deadlock might be broken. He may have been sincere, and if he was nothing of the kind then at least he would be able to present himself as the rational, reasonable party who did everything he could to make peace. Caesar proposed that he and Pompey should meet in person to discuss the matters in hand, that both he and Pompey should disband their troops, that elections should be held and the government restored to normal, and that Pompey should go to Spain. Pompey replied that if Caesar returned to his province of Gaul and then disbanded his armies, then he, Pompey, would go to Spain; but if these conditions were not met, then the situation remained the same, and Pompey would continue to recruit and raise armies. There was no positive result from this attempt at negotiation. Pompey and his allies could not seriously expect Caesar to turn back and put himself at a disadvantage, and Caesar would not back down and return to Gaul, presumably because he did not trust Pompey and his allies to leave him unmolested.[5]

The next phase of the war centred on Picenum, where Pompey said he would soon take his army to occupy the territory. If the north could be garrisoned it might be possible to cut Caesar off from Rome, but in the end Caesar occupied it first. At the beginning of February Domitius Ahenobarbus, who was at Corfinium with 26 cohorts and five more under Pompey's cousin Hirrus, was said to be gathering them all together to march to join Pompey at Luceria; then he changed his mind and decided to make a stand against Caesar. Pompey heard of this via other sources, and wrote to Domitius rebuking him for not keeping him informed, and trying very hard to explain that with split forces they could never hope to resist Caesar. He advised Domitius to make a start before it was too late to bring his troops to Luceria, as he had continually asked in earlier letters. This was not the first or the last example of an occasion when Pompey had to deal with colleagues who thought they knew better than he did how to fight the war. On 16 February Pompey wrote again to Domitius, having heard from him that he intended to march to join the main army if Caesar made a move in its direction, but if Caesar remained nearby he would try to resist him. Pompey continued: 'I think you are acting with courage and high-mindedness, but we must be careful to avoid the situation where we are divided and therefore no match for the enemy since he has large forces and will soon have larger'. Domitius presumably knew how many legions Caesar could call up from Gaul, but perhaps thought that he could bring about a swift victory before the whole of the Gallic army had assembled. He may have believed the tales that Caesar had been careful to spread that his troops were weary of war, and would desert him for Pompey. This sort of swift victory, snatched before Caesar's whole army had assembled, called for reliable

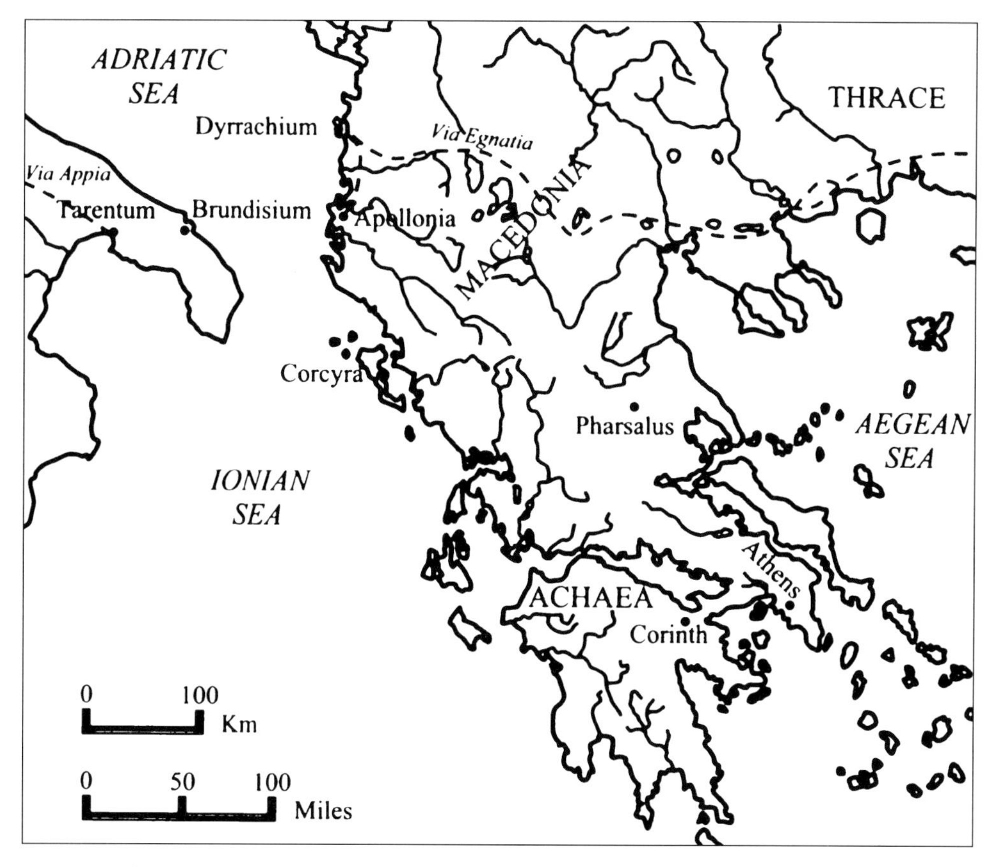

14 *Map of Greece, where Pompey and Caesar fought the battles of the civil war.* Drawn by Jan Shearsmith

intelligence, a good plan with alternatives if it went wrong and, when it was put into action, resolution, activity, and speed. Domitius had none of these attributes, and he was soon writing to Pompey to ask him to come to his rescue, because Caesar was encamped outside Corfinium. Domitius' letter arrived at headquarters just before Pompey's correspondence of 16 February had been despatched, so in haste Pompey replied to Domitius immediately, by adding a short postscript to his first letter. Then he wrote another more detailed reply, dated 17 February. It was no part of Pompey's plan to face Caesar on these terms, and he wrote to tell Domitius that he could not rely on his untrained troops and had no intention of risking the fate of the Republic on one pitched battle in the north. The message to Domitius was plain: you got yourself into this mess, so now get yourself out of it as best you can. It dawned on Cicero with disbelief that Pompey was going to leave Domitius in the lurch, and he now began to worry that he would also evacuate Italy. Two days after receiving the news that Domitius intended to make a stand against Caesar, Pompey started to march his army to Brundisium. Domitius was forced to surrender to Caesar, and was allowed to go free, along with his colleagues Vibullius and Attius Varus. He was even allowed to keep his treasury, worth 6 million sesterces. The troops, however, were absorbed into Caesar's army, and swore the oath of loyalty to him.[6]

Since Pompey did not make a habit of explaining himself to his colleagues, it is impossible to discern whether he had decided to withdraw from Italy from the beginning, and simply kept his plans secret in case anyone panicked, or whether he arrived at this decision by degrees because he had underestimated his own ability to raise and train troops, and had not fully appreciated Caesar's determination and speed of action. Seager makes a case for the evacuation of Italy as a contingency plan, that had been discussed in January; he maintains that Pompey's initial plan was to make a stand somewhere in Italy, but then at the end of January or the beginning of February, he changed his mind, and it may have been the decision to evacuate Italy that provoked Domitius into digging his heels in, hoping to force Pompey into a battle in the north. This theory fits the facts but cannot be proved, because it is not known how much of the overall plan was clear to Domitius. When Pompey gave orders for the march to Brundisium, summoning the consuls to join him, it cannot have been a sudden decision, made without preparation. Though the move began almost immediately after Domitius' attempt to halt Caesar, it was not this event that precipitated the decision to assemble at Brundisium. Given that Pompey's activities in the east during his campaigns and afterwards had brought him clients, wealthy investments, and a knowledge of the terrain and its potential for maintaining an army, it is at least feasible that as war with Caesar became a reality he had decided from the start to fight it in the east. He had troops in Spain under his loyal subordinates, and so if he made his headquarters in Macedonia and Greece he could flank Italy on both sides, and perhaps order a converging march from east and west to regain Rome. Allegedly he said that Sulla had done it, so why should he not do so also – by which he most likely inferred that he could achieve his military objective by removing himself and then returning, not that he intended to follow Sulla's example in the political realm as well.[7]

Speculation as to Pompey's intentions is as frustrating to modern scholars as it was to his contemporaries, and is ultimately unproductive, since history records only what Pompey did, not what he intended at any given point. When Caesar heard that Pompey had started for Brundisium he sent another messenger, a man called Magius chosen from among his Pompeian prisoners, to ask for a meeting with Pompey. It was refused. Caesar then sent Caninius Rebilus to repeat the request for a personal interview. Pompey replied that he could not accede to this request in the absence of the consuls, who had not yet joined him. At this stage it is doubtful that either Caesar or Pompey could have made peace, or even wanted to. The messages were sent as much to delay activity on both sides as to arrange peace talks.

Caesar had by now approached Brundisium and begun his siege works. He had not been able to prevent the departure of most of Pompey's army and the two consuls, who were making for Greece; the transports were to be sent back to pick up Pompey himself and the 20 cohorts that he had held back in Brundisium. Caesar invested the city on the landward side and attempted to block the entrance to and exit from the harbour, by building floating walls from each side. He anchored rafts covered with earth to create a sort of pier, which he protected with screens and towers. Pompey responded by using merchant ships in which he installed towers that were higher than those built by Caesar. There was fighting every day, according to Caesar's narrative, but as Greenhalgh points out, Pompey must have defended the deep water access to the harbour, since his fleet returned to take him and his remaining troops off to Greece. The evacuation is still considered masterly by many authors, and even Caesar admired the measures that Pompey had taken to ensure that he was not pursued too soon. On 17 March Pompey broke out of Brundisium. He had installed light-armed troops on the defences facing Caesar's siege works, and taken off the heavy-armed men with orders to embark in strict silence. At a given signal after the initial embarkation, the defenders left the ramparts and followed their companions onto the ships. Caesar's men were then able to storm the defences, and swarmed over the undefended walls into the town, only to find that the Pompeian delaying tactics inside the defences held them up. Trenches had been dug across the main streets, and pits had been excavated within them, with sharp stakes set inside, and covered with hurdles to disguise them. In addition there were barricades across other streets, and huge palisades guarded the route to the harbour. The inhabitants warned the soldiers of the problems, so they did not fall into the traps, but spent some valuable time circumventing them. By the time Caesar reached the harbour, Pompey had set sail. Two ships were captured by the Caesarians, but that was all. It must have been a tremendous anticlimax for Caesar, and a great relief for Pompey, for he was now committed to his course of action, with no going back.[8]

The campaigns now depended upon sea power. Caesar had several choices, one of which was to try to collect ships and follow Pompey; but he had difficulty in finding vessels and had to organise a shipbuilding programme. He could march overland to try to find and defeat Pompey, but that was an arduous and time-consuming business. He could remain in Italy, but at some point Pompey would have to be faced, and it was necessary to attend to the food supply, by securing the corn-producing provinces, which Pompey had initially tried to take over via legates. Caesar won back control of Sardinia, and despatched Curio to Sicily, and then to Africa, in a curious repetition of Pompey's youthful exploits on behalf of Sulla – except that Curio was not as successful. He won over Sicily without a fight, because Marcus Porcius Cato, the governor whom Pompey had wanted to send out some months before, had refused to go immediately, and then when he did take over, he had to start recruiting and training troops. When he heard that Curio was on his way, he abandoned the island on 23 April. He did however take with him all the soldiers that he had raised, and a number of requisitioned ships, to join Pompey in Greece. In Africa, however, Curio met his match in king Juba. The unofficial governor in Africa was Attius Varus, who had been governor there before, and who had arrived without instruction after Caesar's advance into Picenum had prevented the recruiting drive that Varus had been appointed to carry out. Curio soon bottled up Varus in the city of Utica, but his army was then attacked by Juba and his Numidians and defeated, almost to a man. Curio was killed. After the loss of Sardinia and Sicily, Pompey was perhaps cheered by these events in Africa.[9]

Meanwhile Caesar had turned his attention to Spain. He had briefly gone to Rome to form a government of sorts. He invited Cicero to join him, since the example that would be set by the great orator's presence in Caesar's Senate would encourage others to come over to him. His policy of leniency had already assuaged many a conscience, but there had been a downturn in his popularity since Pompey and the magistrates had left Italy. Cicero had arrived at Brundisium too late to join Pompey, and had then returned to Rome, but he was still attached to Pompey and would not succumb to Caesar's charm. He finally made up his mind to go to Pompey, but by this time Caesar had put a guard on all the ports to prevent anyone from leaving Italy, so Cicero had to ask special permission to leave the country; he finally reached Pompey's camp in June. Eager to attend to the war, and wasting little time in Rome, Caesar attended to the most pressing business. He passed laws to enfranchise the Cisalpine Gauls who had served him so well in his armies, and then appointed Marcus Crassus, the son of his erstwhile colleague, as their governor, in order to secure northern Italy. To take charge of Rome, he appointed Marcus Aemilius Lepidus as prefect of the city. He ordered Mark Antony to assume control of all the troops in Italy, and sent his brother Gaius Antonius to occupy Illyricum; then he departed for Spain. He said that he was going to fight the army without a leader, and then he would return to fight the leader without an army. On his way to Spain he found that the city of Massilia would not open its gates to him and so blocked his route; the citizens said that they owed debts to both Caesar and Pompey, and were friendly to both of them, but would receive neither of them in war. After a failed attempt to take the city by storm, Caesar decided not to waste any more time, and left Trebonius in charge of the siege works, while he himself pressed on to Spain.[10]

Pompey's legates in Spain were Lucius Afranius, Marcus Petreius and Terentius Varro, with a total of seven legions under their command. Caesar brought six legions and a complement of auxiliary troops, 6000 of which were cavalry, most of them highly experienced after ten years of wars in Gaul. Whilst Varro held Further Spain with two legions, Afranius and Petreius joined forces in Nearer Spain. By the time Caesar's first troops arrived under the command of Fabius, they were encamped on a low hill near Ilerda (modern Lerida), on the river Sicoris (modern Serge). At first, Afranius performed well against the measures that Fabius and Caesar employed to dislodge him, beating off an attack by the Fourteenth legion, and attacking one of Caesar's convoys. Eventually he was driven off when Caesar began to create a man-made ford across the river, which would enable him to bring troops across it and prevent the Pompeians from foraging and gathering supplies. Afranius and Petreius moved off towards the river Ebro; Caesar gave chase, managed to overtake and cut them off from their objective, and forced them to turn back. They made for Ilerda, but on the march they were trapped on a hill without access to water, and finally surrendered.[11]

There were profits and losses for Pompey besides this bad news from Spain. The Caesarian Decimus Brutus had defeated a Pompeian fleet, but in turn the Pompeians defeated Caesar's naval commander Dolabella. In Illyricum, Gaius Antonius had fallen foul of the Pompeians and had surrendered. There was further heartening news for the Pompeians when they heard that in the north of Italy Caesar's legions, tired of fighting civil wars with little profit to themselves, had mutinied. But in the end it was not such a serious business, since Caesar had a way with words and knew his men inside out. The most disaffected legion was the Ninth, and Caesar dealt with it roughly, ordering that it should be decimated, that is every tenth man should be killed. When the expected protests were made, he rounded up 120 of the ringleaders and decimated them instead, so for a loss of 12 lives the mutiny was rapidly quelled. The greatest profit for Pompey was the time granted to him to train his army while Caesar was in Spain. He could draw upon his many clients and contacts in the whole of the east for recruits and money. Caesar himself records that Pompey gathered a large fleet by requisitioning ships from Egypt, Phoenicia, Cilicia, Syria, Bithynia, Pontus, Athens, Corcyra, and Asia. These ships presumably came with the crews to man them, drawn from the inhabitants of the areas where he started a program of ship building. He also raised more troops; he had taken five legions with him from Italy, and raised two more from veterans who had settled in Cilicia, Greece and Macedonia. Likewise the consul Lentulus raised two legions from veterans in Asia. In all he had nine legions of Roman citizens, and was expecting two more to come from Spain. Pompey called upon the allied kings whom he had installed after his campaigns, such as Antiochus of Commagene, Ariobarzanes of Cappadocia, and Deiotarus of Galatia, who all contributed troops. He raised auxiliary troops from Thessaly, Boeotia, Achaea and Epirus. Caesar records that he absorbed into these troops the legionaries who had surrendered with Gaius Antonius. Pompey also recruited specialist troops, such as Cretan archers, and two cohorts of slingers. His son Gnaeus brought ships and 500 men from Egypt, from among the men left there by Aulus Gabinius when he mounted his expedition to reinstate Ptolemy Auletes on his throne.[12]

The vast organisation that all this troop raising, fund gathering and ship building required was and still is impressive; it was what Pompey excelled in. Similarly his training programme was energetic and thorough, and he did not shirk the exercises that he put his men through. Plutarch describes how he rode at full gallop in his armour, performed all the sword exercises and hurled a javelin faster and further than many of the young men in the army, even though he was 57 years old (Plutarch says he was 58, but maybe meant that Pompey was in his 58th year). Perhaps because of his display of organisational ability and military skills, he was belatedly made supreme commander by the members of the Senate that had accompanied him. According to Appian, Pompey made a speech comparing himself and his followers with those who had abandoned Athens and then regained it when the city was under threat, and those who abandoned Rome when the Gauls invaded. This may arise from Appian's imagination, but it makes the point that Pompey's strategy was theoretically correct.[13]

The Pompeian government in exile did not elect new magistrates for the new year, but the consuls and praetors that had left Italy in March 49 continued in office as promagistrates instead of magistrates, since by no stretch of the imagination could the claim be made that consuls and praetors had been elected by the people of Rome. Caesar on the other hand had returned to Rome at the end of 49 and set up a rival government there. He was made Dictator, which enabled him to hold the elections; as far as possible he wished to keep within the bounds of legality. The result

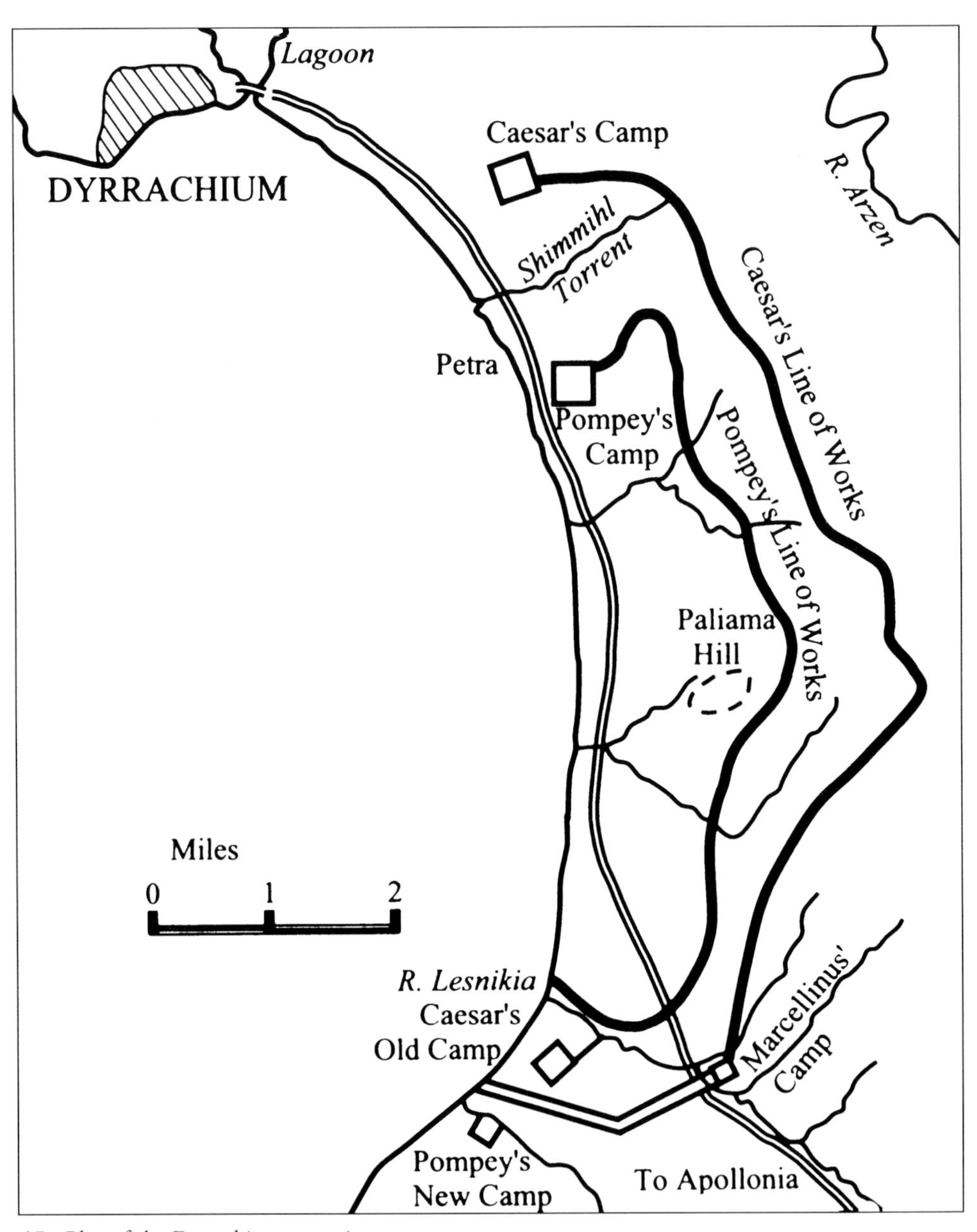

15 *Plan of the Dyrrachium campaign*

of the consular elections was perhaps a foregone conclusion; Caesar himself and Publius Servilius Isauricus were elected. The other magistrates such as praetors and tribunes were appointed, and the vacant priesthoods were filled. He passed some laws in a great hurry, designed to relieve debts and distribute food to the people; both of these problems were potential flashpoints for trouble, and he wished to avoid any possibility of riots while he was absent finding and fighting Pompey. The food supply was the most crucial issue, because Pompey had the upper hand in sea power and could blockade Italy, and he had won back Africa as one of the main corn-producing areas. It would be of no advantage to Caesar to delay in Italy, since the corn supply would only worsen with time.[14]

As soon as he was ready Caesar assembled his troops at Brundisium. They had not all arrived when he got there himself, but that did not matter because he did not have enough ships to transport all of them to Greece. He embarked 15,000 legionaries and 500 cavalry, and leaving Antony in charge of bringing over the rest, he set sail. Pompey had decided to put his forces in winter quarters in Dyrrachium, Apollonia, and in other towns on the coast of the Adriatic. Leaving Scipio in Macedonia with two legions, he marched towards Dyrrachium in January 48, and on the way there he heard that Caesar had crossed the sea, evading the Pompeian fleet under the command of Bibulus, and had landed some 80 miles to the south. Bibulus made up for the fact that Caesar had slipped through the net by capturing about 30 of the transports on their way back to pick up Antony and the rest of Caesar's troops. Where Caesar gave quarter and let his enemies go, Bibulus burnt the ships with the crews still on board. At Pompey's camp, the first news of Caesar's whereabouts and his intentions was discouraging. In need of supplies, Caesar found them where Pompey had stored them at the town of Oricum. The inhabitants decided to open their gates rather than stand a siege and a possible sacking. The next to fall to Caesar was Apollonia, a worse blow because there Pompey thought the citizens loyal to his commander. Having lost control of two cities and the supplies that he had gathered, Pompey made every effort now to reach his objective, because Caesar too was marching to Dyrrachium.[15]

Pompey won the race, and made camp near the city. The advantages that he enjoyed over Caesar included his larger army, his naval supremacy, and the fact that Dyrrachium was already well stocked and could also be supplied by sea. Caesar camped on the south bank of the river Apsus, the boundary between the territory of Dyrrachium and that of Apollonia. Soon Pompey arrived and camped on the northern bank of the river, and there the two armies remained, facing each other but not offering battle. The sources tell of cavalry encounters, and hint that Pompey tried to cross the river, which may have been an attempt to cut Caesar's supply lines. Neither side was in a position to offer battle at this time. Pompey had nine legions, and had summoned Scipio from Macedonia with two more, but none of his men were as experienced as those of his opponent. Although Caesar had this advantage, he was outnumbered and short of supplies. In order to hold off Scipio and the two legions from Macedonia, Caesar detached two legions under Domitius Calvinus to march against him, with the result that Scipio did not join Pompey.[16]

Caesar made the best of a bad situation. He occupied a strip of coastline opposite the Pompeian fleet base on the island of Corcyra, so as to be able to prevent the ships from coming inshore to find fresh water; faced with the blockade of the fleet at Brundisium, Antony did the same, preventing the Pompeian commander Libo from obtaining water. Caesar tried once more to open negotiations with Pompey, sending a message by Vibullius Rufus, who had been captured at Corfinium by Caesar and released, only to be captured again in Spain. Pompey would not listen to Vibullius' message, but turned away, saying that he did not wish to live to a ripe old age courtesy of Caesar. He knew that Caesar was in a precarious position, and would soon be short of supplies; and he also knew that one of Caesar's motives in proposing peace was to cast Pompey and the Senate in the role of intransigent warmongering fanatics.[17]

The Caesarian and Pompeian troops on either side of the river were beginning to mingle on friendly terms; Labienus brutally put an end to this fraternisation, and before it could begin again, Pompey heard that Antony had crossed the Adriatic and landed at the harbour of Nymphaeum, north of Dyrrachium. Caesar would surely join up with him. This must be prevented, so Pompey marched to tackle Antony, planning to trap him on the route southwards at a point where he and his troops would have to march through a narrow pass over the Genusus river. It was a good plan, but fate worked against Pompey. He had failed to win over the Greeks to his cause, and they contacted Antony, so being forewarned he did not walk into the ambush, but camped and waited for Caesar, who marched round to the east and joined up with Antony. Pompey had to withdraw, or be trapped himself. He made for Asparagium, travelling westwards along the Egnatian Way, to protect the route to Dyrrachium. Caesar followed him, made camp opposite him, and the next day drew up his army in battle order; but Pompey did not take the bait. When Caesar moved off the following morning Pompey thought that he was going in search of supplies, but when his scouts returned with the news of where Caesar was heading, it was clear that he would have to follow because there was a danger of being cut off from Dyrrachium. Even so, he allowed his men to rest, and as a result he nearly lost the race. When he reached the area of Dyrrachium he camped on a hill called Petra, and sent out orders for part of his navy to assemble in a safe anchorage in the large bay, and for the supply ships to come to the new base.[18]

Caesar made a camp to the north of Pompey's, and not so close to the sea. He needed to bring about a battle or to wear Pompey down by preventing him from foraging, which would gradually make life very difficult for the cavalry and their mounts. Not having command of the sea, he could scarcely affect the supplies for Pompey's army. He started to occupy the hill tops running in an arc to the east of Pompey's camp, building small forts on them and joining the hills with a series of trenches, intending to enclose Pompey within siege lines. Discerning what Caesar was trying to do, Pompey hastily began to build an inner ring of lines, in order to enclose as much land as possible for foraging; in the end he occupied all the territory from the camp at Petra to the river Lesnikia (modern Gesnike) to the south. Caesar was forced to extend his own lines, stretching his troops to the limit to guard them. At one stage in the proceedings Caesar ordered Antony to occupy and fortify a hill, from where he might have been able to turn his trenches westwards to the coast, thus enclosing Pompey within a much smaller area than he eventually occupied. Fortunately for Pompey, his troops managed to force Antony off the hill, and he carried on extending his lines southward.[19]

In this situation the advantage was with Pompey, whose army could be supplied, while Caesar was in a desperate situation. Pompey knew that inactivity was the best policy while Caesar starved, but had already begun to meet with opposition from the hotheads in his camp. Cicero describes the majority of Pompey's officers, all except Pompey himself and the few genuine leaders, as completely selfish, thinking only of ways in which to get rich quickly from plunder, and so pay off their debts. Plutarch also documents the petty internal squabbles among Pompey's staff. Although Pompey now held supreme command, and could order his subordinates to act rather than recommending a course of action, he still had difficulty in persuading them that his policy of attrition was the correct one. He possessed good cavalry, but was unable to use it effectively, and the animals were suffering badly. In particular, he was losing baggage animals to starvation. Fuller says that he ought to have extracted his cavalry, under a bold commander, and sent it out beyond his lines to harass Caesar's foraging parties and attack his supply convoys. In that way Caesar would have been forced to march off quite soon, and then Pompey could have decided whether to give chase, or to turn his attention to Italy.[20]

Caesar's next ploy was to stop Pompey's water supply. He cut the streams running from the mountains towards the sea, and Pompey's men had to dig wells in the strip of land near the shore. But it was high summer and the wells dried up, so this shortage of water combined with the lack of forage decided Pompey to remove the cavalry to Dyrrachium, where the horses could be properly fed and watered. He now attempted to draw Caesar away from the blockading lines by sending a false message to make him believe that the city of Dyrrachium was ready to open its gates to him. The sources for this story derive from Appian, who says that an inhabitant of Dyrrachium came to Caesar with an offer to betray the town, and from Dio, who writes of Caesar's almost fatal attempt to take Dyrrachium with a small force by night. He was ambushed by troops which had been ferried along the shore in boats, and very nearly killed. While this was going on, Pompey's men attacked Caesar's lines in three separate places, but were repulsed. Caesar insists that he had few casualties in these engagements, and that Pompey sustained at least 2000 dead: but this can probably be put down to hyperbole. The numbers are not as important as the fact that Pompey had not succeeded in driving Caesar off, nor in breaking through his lines. Another disappointment was that Caesar managed to cut off Pompey's cavalry from their foraging grounds, and the horses had to be ferried back by sea to the ground enclosed by Pompey's lines. It was now imperative for Pompey to try to break out. He discovered from two Gauls who had deserted from Caesar's camp that at the southern end of Caesar's lines there was a weak point that could be exploited. There was a double line of trenches, one facing north towards Pompey's camp, and another 200 paces distant, facing south and away from Pompey's lines, in order to protect the Caesarian troops from any attack from that direction. But although

Caesar had placed a camp some distance from the sea, manned by Lentulus Marcellinus in command of the Ninth legion, he had not completed the defence of the area because he had merely dug the two parallel lines to the coast and had not joined them up, so it was possible to get between them. Pompey decided to attack from land and sea. He sent light armed troops by night to sail down the coast and land in two groups, one in the gap between the two lines, and one to the south. The attack went well at first. Pompey's troops rolled back the Caesarians caught in between the two lines, so that in retreat they clashed with the fresh troops that Marcellinus brought up to try to defend the lines. The Pompeians were eventually driven off by the arrival of Mark Antony with 12 cohorts, and then Caesar himself with 13 cohorts. Even though he was forced to abandon the attack, the gains were all Pompey's, since he occupied a camp outside Caesar's lines, to the south near the coast. This meant that he could bring his cavalry to forage in safety, and protect his ships as they approached the coast. He had successfully broken through the blockade. Caesar attempted to take this new camp by storm, before Pompey had moved the whole garrison into it. While it was still defended by only a few men, Caesar attacked, broke through the ramparts and herded the Pompeians together in a corner of the camp; then Pompey arrived with five legions, which panicked the Caesarian soldiers to such an extent that they fled, but found their route blocked by the rampart they had just broken through. Many were trampled to death, and Caesar records that he lost 32 standards, 32 tribunes and centurions, and 960 men. It is recorded that he said Pompey's victory would have been complete if only the troops had been led by a victor, though Caesar himself does not include this turn of phrase in his own account of the battle. Even though Pompey did not follow through and press on to the bitter end after this victory, it nevertheless signalled the end of the blockade, and Caesar decided that the time had come to move off in search of food and forage.[21]

Pompey followed as soon as he knew what was happening, and apart form a skirmish where Pompey's cavalry caught up with Caesar's rearguard at the river Genusus, the two armies peacefully occupied their old camps at Asparagium, facing each other as before. Pompey lost any advantage he may have possessed, since his officers decided to leave the camp to return to their base at Dyrrachium so they could collect their baggage, left behind when the army uprooted itself to chase after Caesar. This gave Caesar a chance to escape while Pompey's camp was in turmoil. Accordingly he moved off and was some few miles away by the time Pompey could gather his troops. There was a pursuit lasting for four days, then Pompey returned to the Egnatian Way, possibly back to camp at Asparagium. There he held a council of war, still advocating his policy of attrition. There were a few alternatives to discuss; Afranius recommended that the Pompeians should prolong the war in the hope of wearing Caesar down; another alternative was to decamp without delay and invade Italy, where it was supposed that Caesar's foothold was tenuous, and in fact just before the final battle Pompey sent part of his fleet to blockade Brundisium and to attack Sicily, moves that could be interpreted as part of his preparation to invade Italy. But if he did so at this juncture, it would mean abandoning Scipio, who would have to face Caesar alone.

According to the ancient sources, Pompey gave way when he was hard-pressed by his supposed advisers and colleagues, and decided on marching to join Scipio, who was now imminently threatened because Caesar was marching to join Domitius in Macedonia, and therefore Scipio would be faced by the combined weight of Caesar's army. There followed a series of marches in Thessaly, in the course of which Caesar approached the city of Gomphi, and found its gates shut against him. Pompey had announced a great victory, and the inhabitants of Gomphi considered that they were dealing with a defeated Caesar, so to open their gates to him might bring Pompey's wrath on their heads. The unfortunate town was soon apprised of Caesar's true status, as he sacked it and made it an example to encourage the others. Thereafter, of all the city-states of Thessaly only Larissa, where Scipio was camped, dared to defy Caesar.[22]

This phase of the war came to an end when Caesar entered the fertile territory near Pharsalus, and made camp. There is some dispute as to whether he camped near Old Pharsalus, or the later settlement, but since the two are only a few miles apart, the argument does not greatly affect the general narrative. It was midsummer according to the seasons, and August by the calendar, and the crops were ripening ready for harvest. Pompey had by now joined up with Scipio, and the two marched to find Caesar. Pompey made camp on a hill, in a defensive position that could be attacked only with great difficulty. Each day, Caesar drew up his troops in battle order, every time a little closer to Pompey's camp; Pompey however would not take the bait, except to parade his men on the hill side, but not in an accessible position that invited Caesar to attack him. The policy of starving Caesar out was working well, since Caesar had just made up his mind to move off to find supplies, then to return and harass Pompey wherever he encamped. Pompey was unaware of this planned move, but he was aware of the fact that as the crops ripened, the policy of trying to wear Caesar down and starve him out would be temporarily redundant, and it would be another long wait before the whole cycle would begin again. On the very day planned for Casesar's departure, Pompey brought his army out and advanced much further than usual down the hill. Many authors since that day have tried to discern what had made Pompey depart from his normal policies, and most have decided that the continual carping of his subordinates and colleagues had worn him down. He was accused of prolonging the war unnecessarily, because he enjoyed giving orders to consulars; he was nicknamed Agamemnon, and king of kings, all of which really only indicates that his supposed subordinates did not like taking orders from him. He may simply have tired of the military deadlock, in the same proportion as he tired of the squabbling. On the eve of the battle, he called a council of war to discuss his plan, and announced that he intended to send the cavalry to attack Caesar's right wing from the flank, and work around to the rear of the enemy, to enclose them in a trap. The plan was sound, since he had an enormous number of horsemen raised from the native contingents of his allies, so the sheer weight of numbers ought to have been overwhelming. In the end the cavalry did not succeed, because Caesar observed its movements on Pompey's left, and guessed what was about to happen. Accordingly he despatched 1000 horsemen to reinforce his right wing, with orders to remain out of sight behind the cavalry and infantry of the right wing. The first clashes of the infantry proved the mettle of Pompey's men, who stood firm and received the attack of the Caesarians without flinching. When Labienus ordered the Pompeian cavalry to attack Caesar's right wing as planned, Caesar brought out his extra cavalry, hurled it against the flank of the attacking Pompeians, and panicked them so badly that some of them turned and fled. The panic spread, and the battle was as good as lost from that point onwards.[23]

In the centre of Pompey's line the men were battling hard and still holding out, and the right wing was also doing well; but on the left the encircling movement that Pompey had proposed was now happening in reverse, and Caesar's men were encircling the Pompeian left. Pompey rode off the field, knowing all was lost. The camp was held by seven cohorts, so the defence of the area and reception of the defeated army must be arranged, but it seems that Pompey did not assert himself energetically to do this, with the result that when Caesar's men broke in, he mounted his horse and rode for Larissa with about 30 attendants. He announced his defeat at the gates but did not enter the city, advising the citizens not to try to resist Caesar. Then he set off for the coast. There is some confusion in the sources as to where he went next. Caesar says that he visited Amphipolis to try to start a recruiting programme, but when he heard that Caesar was following close behind he left after only one night and sailed to Mytilene. This city had sheltered Pompey's wife Cornelia, but after collecting her Pompey continued his voyage, advising the city to surrender to Caesar. He disembarked in one of the coastal towns of Pamphylia, receiving some galleys from Cilicia and reinforcements. He was told that Cato had gathered what troops he could from Dyrrachium and taken them to Africa, where it might be possible to make a stand. He had sent his cousin Hirrus as an envoy to the Parthian court, and it was rumoured that he intended to go to Parthia for aid; but most scholars dismiss this story as a fabrication. Caesar does not mention this tale, and the embassy of Hirrus may have been nothing to do with seeking aid after defeat, but to ensure the neutrality of Parthia in order to protect Syria and the Roman provinces from attack. Pompey's greatest need now was for men and money as well as more ships, even though his command of the sea was not as yet diminished. He could have gone to Africa and made an alliance with Juba, but he did not trust him. Nor did he fully trust the Ptolemies of Egypt, but he had been instrumental in securing the throne for Ptolemy Auletes, and Egypt was a wealthy country where he could perhaps find troops and money, in order to build up another army to continue the war. After a brief dash to Cyprus, where Caesar says he raised 2000 troops, Pompey set sail for Alexandria. One of the major problems that he would encounter there was that the surviving heirs of Ptolemy were engaged in a civil war of their own, with Cleopatra VII driven out of Alexandria, and her younger brother Ptolemy installed there as king, but really as a puppet of his advisers Pothinus, Theodotus and Achillas, who all three decided that it would be better to appease the victorious Caesar than to harbour the defeated Pompey in their midst; 'Dead men don't bite', said Achillas. Thus the greatest Roman of his day met his ignominious end on the Egyptian shore, and his head and signet ring were presented to Caesar when he arrived in Alexandria.[24]

The civil war did not end with Pompey's death; his elder son Gnaeus Pompey fought on and was defeated and killed in Spain, and the younger Sextus took to the seas and made a notorious name for himself, being finally cut down on the orders of Mark Antony in 36. Afranius, Petreius, Labienus, Cato and Scipio continued the Pompeian struggle, to be defeated and eliminated quite soon after Pharsalus. Caesar himself survived only for another four years, but they were crowded and eventful years, as the Republic died and was transformed into the Empire. He bequeathed the Empire to his great-nephew Gaius Octavius, better known as Octavian and then Augustus; but if Augustus owed his career to the fact that he was kinsman of Julius Caesar, he also owed much to the precedents set by Pompey the Great.[25]

16 *Stylised portrait of Caesar's great nephew, Gaius Octavius, better known as Octavian, and eventually as Augustus. Octavian was the political and familial heir of Caesar, but in many ways he was also the heir of Pompey, in that there was a great deal to be learned from studying his career*

7 Legacy

Syme said that if Pompey had won at Pharsalus and returned victorious to Rome he would eventually have been assassinated at the foot of his own statue, by honourable men. Pompey himself was no doubt aware that the majority of the senators would cease to find him useful once the threat of Caesar's domination was averted, and he had probably devoted some thought to what he should do if he won a victory. There were many avenues to explore under the heading of improving and streamlining the functioning of the state; but the difficulty lay in the system itself, which would have to be overthrown before reforms could be instituted – and Pompey did not have the temperament for this. He was a constitutionalist, despite the anomalous position he had occupied all his life; he never aspired to military or political domination, or the kind of prolonged Dictatorship that Sulla had assumed. If he had returned to Rome as victor over the vanquished Caesar, Pompey would very quickly have been faced with two choices, to be relegated to the background while the factional rivalry and violence sprang up again as the scramble for power continued, or to take control much as Sulla did and mould the state according to his own plan. The defeat of Caesar would have left him in virtually the same position as he had been in when he returned from the east, and after the praises had been sung and the honours voted and accepted, he would still have to fight to settle his veterans and retain his position of pre-eminence; the eternal conundrum was that powerful men like himself attracted opposition and consequently had to become even more powerful to rise above it. In a meritocracy without jealousies and rivalries he may have reached the pinnacle and been allowed to remain there, but the reality was that he lived in the Roman world where pre-eminence was achieved at a heavy price and was almost impossible to retain. The modern world knows of Caesar, not Pompey, as the man who shaped the Empire, and of Augustus as the architect who completed the colossal edifice for which Caesar laid the foundations. Yet Pompey had a part to play in the shaping of the Empire, even if his name did not give rise to the hereditary titles of the ruling Emperors. Caesar did not obliterate his memory; his statues were not pulled down and destroyed, his name was not chiselled off the face of inscriptions, and his adherents were studiously accepted into the fold. Augustus actively promoted the memory of Pompey, in direct proportion to his need to divorce himself from the memory of Caesar the Dictator. It has been pointed out that when Livy praised the achievements of Pompey it did not take great courage to do so because it was not an act of defiance. Even as late as Augustus' death, long after the civil war, Pompey was still remembered, and his image was carried in Augustus' funeral procession.[1]

17 *Pompey's sons survived him, and issued coins depicting him. Gnaeus Pompeius took his troops to Spain, where he held out until Caesar arrived. He was killed at the battle of Munda in 45, and may have issued this coin at Corduba in the same year.* Drawn by Jacqui Taylor

As a youth Pompey liked to be compared to Alexander the Great, adopting the name Magnus in emulation of his hero. His friend Theophanes commemorated him as the Roman Alexander in his contemporary writings, and Sallust and Plutarch drew on the comparison in their works. Few historians would deny Pompey his military reputation; his military skills were what brought him to prominence and kept him at the forefront as the first man in Rome. The world that nurtured Pompey was shaped by war; it was the whole focus of his youth and early manhood, and he excelled in it. He had the qualities of leadership that made men believe in him and his cause, and obey him. He made mistakes but rectified them without extravagant cost, and his men knew that he would take the best care of them that he could. Though rightly called the boy butcher for his zeal in eliminating enemies when he fought for Sulla, he did not waste lives unnecessarily, and did not instigate proscriptions to rid himself of opponents once he rose to power.[2]

In the military sphere he was an anomaly, holding extraordinary commands while under age and without the senatorial experience that was normally a pre-requisite of such commands – but he operated in extraordinary times and circumstances. He was the first and last equestrian to celebrate two triumphs, but he had worked hard for them, and he was a hero, such a youthful one at that, so these anomalies could be forgiven. Once he entered the political scene, the anomalies were more glaring. He entered the Senate as consul, without having held any of the magistracies that ought to have preceded such high office. His sudden rise marked him out as an outsider, ambitious, possibly dangerous, a man to be watched. And a man to be used in times of crisis, which he knew perfectly well. His motives were never clear and he never intended that they should be. Pompey may at first have been an innocent in a corrupt world, but later he utilised that image of simple honesty and innocence as the front that he presented to the world. He had a talent for self-advertisement but it was brash, redolent of pride and vanity. He reminded people of his achievements whenever there was need, and indulged in spectacular display at his triumphs and in his public entertainments and games. Compared to Augustus he was too heavy-handed, and in this way he served as a negative example, for though Augustus was much more thorough about selling himself, he was also much more subtle.[3]

His dearest wish was to be of service to the state, Pompey protested, but he ensured as far as possible that when he did serve the interests of that state it was on his own terms. He has been accused of provoking crises when he was at a loose end and could discern a niche for himself, but this is not to suggest that he created them from nothing. The problems were already there, so he embellished them and ensured that the idea was implanted that he would be the best man to solve them. Inactive while his friends put pressure on the Senate to call upon him and grant him the necessary powers, he burst into purposeful activity once he was appointed, whether it was a war against the pirates or to put an end to electioneering and rampant bribery. There were no half measures with Pompey, but always the grand plan, presumably thought out some time before he gained the appointment and then meticulously applied with energy and determination. Perhaps the only difference between Pompey and Caesar as curators of the state was that Caesar did not wait to be asked. In this respect Augustus was as much the heir of Pompey as of Caesar. Despite the violent opposition to the bills that gave Pompey his special commands, the Senate had tolerated him in various roles with unprecedented powers, provided that the need and the purpose were clearly demonstrated and the depressing concept of permanence could be avoided. When there was talk of making him Dictator to attend to the corn supply, Pompey avoided the appointment and the title, and in 52 when the elections had been postponed he preferred to accept a sole consulship, even though it was once again an anomaly, whereas the Dictatorship was a properly constituted office – but one which terminated after six months. It was perhaps less of an aberration to become sole consul than to agitate for an extension of the Dictatorship. While holding office as sole consul, Pompey also controlled his Spanish provinces via legates whom he selected

18 *Gold aureus issued by Pompey's younger son Sextus, in 40. The obverse shows the head of Sextus with the name Magnus adopted from his father, and Pius, by which he demonstrated his loyalty. IMP ITER refers to the fact that his troops hailed him as Imperator. After Pharsalus, Sextus took over the Pompeian fleet, and his command of the seas was indisputable. His maritime activities caused problems for the Triumvirs, Antony, Octavian, and Lepidus, the successors of Caesar. For a brief period, the Triumvirs came to an agreement with Sextus, recognising his command, as shown on reverse of this coin showing the heads of Pompey and his elder son Gnaeus, with the legend PRAEF. CLAS. ET ORAE MARIT. EX S.C., indicating that Sextus was now officially commander of the sea and shore of the Mediterranean. It was not an enduring situation. In 36 Octavian and his admiral Agrippa defeated Sextus at the naval battle of Naulochus*

and appointed himself, and many scholars have declared this the key to Empire. When Augustus had established himself at the head of the state he required some means of controlling the armies without too blatantly overt a command or the implication of aggression. He renounced his office as triumvir, because a terminal date had been set for it, and he could not hope to retain it forever without causing protest. He needed some means of adopting the power of the office without actually holding the office; and Pompey had shown the way to do that, when he chose legates to govern Spain while he was in office as consul. This is to oversimplify matters, but the point at issue is not the legal niceties of the commands but the precedents set by Pompey that could be turned to good account later on by Augustus.[4]

As a politician, Pompey has been on the one hand derided as an ineffectual ignoramus, and on the other praised as a shrewd and astute manipulator. It is true that he proved ineffective against the opposition when he returned from the east, but he began at a disadvantage, having been absent for so long, and having made enemies of Lucullus and Metellus. He could have obtained what he needed by calling on his veterans and forcing the issues, but then he would have had to hang on to power by force for the rest of his life. He did not want to dominate, he wanted to be accepted, and he had tried to gain acceptance into the ranks of the ruling classes by the usual means of marriage alliances, but in the end found himself adrift. Cato refused his offer, and the opposition would not relent, so he was thrown into the arms of Caesar, and there made the marriage alliance which proved to be a happy and contented relationship, but did nothing to gain the acceptance that he desired. Once again he did not fit the pattern, and remained an anomaly.

As an individual Pompey inspired respect, loyalty and love in his friends and family. His marriages to Julia and Cornelia were said to have been happy, and he did not seem to be the sort of husband who suppresses his wives or tries to mould them in an image that he desired. As a father all that is really known is that his two sons who fought on after his death honoured him in their coinage, and were not prepared to renounce their ancestry. The following that Pompey built up was a large one, drawn from all strata of society, and from several provinces. He invested widely in clients and in financial deals, and having accumulated wealth he distributed it to gain clients; he was probably more wealthy than Crassus, since he owned vast estates in Picenum, and elsewhere in Italy, and after the wars in Spain and the east his list of clients included chiefs and kings. He liked to be seen in public in Rome surrounded by crowds of his followers, not just to keep his enemies at a distance but to advertise his importance. Anderson distinguishes between two types of friends that Pompey gathered around him, firstly the necessary nobles as far as he could affiliate himself to them, and secondly an inner circle of close friends and advisers mostly drawn from the equestrian classes, almost foreshadowing the *amici* of the Emperors. All prominent men had their circles of intimates, but perhaps Pompey developed and regularised the system. He bestowed patronage on a variety of people all over the Roman world, without seeming to demand pay back. It has been said for instance that he did not cultivate the right friends to help him to achieve his ends, and in particular he did not establish a powerful faction in Rome while he was absent in the east. His candidates were either defeated at the elections, or if successful at that stage they were crushed later when they tried to introduce legislation on his behalf, perhaps because they refused to resort wholeheartedly to strong-arm tactics. When Pompey made use of the one man who did not flinch from such tactics, Titus Annius Milo, everything ultimately went wrong and backfired. It was not the means by which he wished to rise or to retain power, but he finished what he had started and brought soldiers into Rome to make certain of a conviction. If his followers overstepped the mark Pompey abandoned them; Gabinius too was convicted, despite the initial efforts on Pompey's part to save him. Perhaps it was callousness that made him turn away when the law had been flagrantly broken, so that he emerged upright and above suspicion; perhaps he briefed his assistants first and made it clear that he wanted to obtain results but within firmly drawn parameters, and beyond these boundaries they were alone.[6]

The crucial point as the ancient authors saw it was that Pompey would not tolerate an equal, and he had risen as high as any man could in the Roman Republic without becoming a monarch, which was the final step that he would never take. The problem was that he was enigmatic, not given to saying directly what he wanted, so even if he claimed that he did not want to become king, people would not believe him, uncertain whether or not he was sincere. Later historians thought of him in a more derogatory light than perhaps his contemporaries did. Tacitus called him the maker and breaker of his own laws, and classified him in the same category as Marius or Sulla – but more devious than either. Dio's opinion was that both Pompey and Caesar aimed at monarchy. Appian admitted that what the Roman state required was the guiding hand of one man with authority, provided that the right candidate could be found, a man with a loyal and sufficient army, and a friend of both the people and the Senate. Appian enjoyed the benefit of hindsight and knew how the Empire developed, and in this passage he describes what Pompey could have been, and what Augustus became.[7]

Notes and references

1 Son of Strabo

1. For a succinct precis of Marius' career see Greenhalgh (1980, 108, 1-2), and Shotter (1994, 29-34, esp. 33-4) for Marius as a new man dependant upon the army for influence because he had no ready made place among the oligarchy and no following. Brunt (1971, 96-100) summarises the main points about the political impact of Marius, and claims that he wanted dignity and influence, and never craved to be sole master of the state: that was a phenomenon that began with Sulla. For an account of the wars of Marius see *CAH* (IX 1932, 135ff).
2. The Pompeii acquired their estates in Picenum at some time before the Social War, possibly before Strabo's birth. Syme (1939, 28) says that they hailed from Picenum where they held their lands, but Seager (1979, 1) points out that Picenum was not their original homeland, because the tribe that they belonged to, the Clustumina (see *ILS* 8888), did not belong to that region. See Velleius Paterculus (2.21.4; 2.53) on the family in general, and on Pompey's birth. Strabo's father was Sextus Pompeius, and he had a brother, probably his senior in years, also called Sextus; see *ILS* 8888, where Strabo is named *Gn. Pompeius Sexti filius*, and his brother is listed as a member of his consilium; see Mattingly (1975). Pompey's mother Lucilia was related to the satirist Lucilius, and her nephew was C. Lucilius Hirrus, tribune in 53 (Velleius Paterculus 2.29.2; Anderson 1963, 12). It is possible that Pompey himself arranged his sister's marriage with C. Memmius after the death of Strabo (Anderson 1963, 10). Memmius was killed in 75 (Greenhalgh 1980, 234; Plutarch *Pompey* 11; *Sertorius* 21); his nephew, also called C. Memmius, was tribune in 66 with C. Manilius, and though his political stance is unknown it is likely that he supported the Manilian law to appoint Pompey to the command against the pirates.
3. With regard to Roman citizenship, the aims of the Italians differed; some wanted independence within an alliance with Rome, some wanted to found a separate Italian state, and others were content with the protection and privileges that citizenship afforded (Shotter 1994, 36). Beard and Crawford (1985, 80-1) point out that when Rome ceased to found colonies, Roman citizenship became more remote for the Italians, who were debarred from any participation in decision making in Rome.
4. Livius Drusus is chiefly remembered for his attempt to enfranchise the Italian allies, but in fact he did not introduce this aspect of his legislation until late in the day. See *CAH* (IX 1932, 178) for a résumé of the accounts of the ancient authors: Cicero portrayed Drusus as the champion of the Senate; Velleius Paterculus says that the franchise bill was not introduced until later in his programme, while Appian implies that the franchise bill was of paramount importance. The Social War was not a spontaneous uprising, but was premeditated and planned, and Roman politicians could probably foresee it. A law was passed in 95 to allow for the prosecution of those Italians who had usurped the citizenship, and it is possible that the consul responsible for promulgating the law, Lucius Licinius Crassus, together with Livius Drusus, saw the grant of citizenship as a timely means of avoiding war

(Brunt 1971, 100). Otherwise Drusus acted primarily in the interests of the nobility, and his programme included increasing the numbers of senators from 300 to 600, admitting equites to the Senate – but membership was denied to the *publicani*. He also wished to reform the law courts. None of his legislation survived him, and it is possible that the franchise bill was never discussed.

5. See Seager (1979, 1-2) on the early stages of Strabo's career. The Spanish cavalrymen of the *turma Salvitana* who were rewarded by Strabo are listed on an inscription (*ILS* 8888), which also names the men of Strabo's *consilium*. As Seager (1979, 2 n.11) points out there is a preponderance of men from Picenum.
6. The *lex Plautia Papiria* granted Roman citizenship to all Italians south of the river Po. As consul in 89 Strabo passed the *lex Pompeia* which granted Latin rights to the Transpadane tribes, or the Gauls north of the Po. Latins could achieve Roman citizenship by serving on their town councils. Pompey derived great benefits from this connection with the Transpadane Gauls, not least for recruiting (Seager 1979, 2 n.16). See Cicero *Ad Quintum Fratrem* 2.3.4; Asconius 3; Pliny *Naturalis Historia* 3.138.
7. On the early contacts between Cicero and Pompey see Ward (1970a). For the leader of the Marsi see Cicero *Philippics* 12.27; Seager (1979, 2).
8. The Marsi claimed that there had never been a Roman triumph without them (Greenhalgh 1980, 4). Strabo's break out from the blockade at Firmum gave rise to rejoicing at Rome (Seager 1979, 1 n.5; Appian *BC* 1.47).
9. See Seager (1979, 2-3) on Strabo's activities as consul.
10. Strabo's colleague L. Porcius Cato was killed in the war (Appian *BC* 1.52.227). The siege of Asculum is reported by Appian (*BC* 1.48.207ff) and Velleius Paterculus (2.21.1).
11. Beard and Crawford (1985, 7-8) outline the increasing mutual dependence of soldiers and commanders; the soldiers had no lands or wealth when they returned home, so their generals were forced to enter the political arena in order to obtain land settlements, a process which could become violent, as evidenced by the efforts of Saturninus, the tribune acting for Marius. See Brunt (1962). Pliny (*Naturalis Historia* 33.47.134) reports the opinion of Marcus Licinius Crassus that no one could think himself wealthy unless he could equip and pay an army.
12. The source for Strabo's triumph is Asconius 17; see Seager (1979, 13 n.17).
13. On Mithridates see Appian *Mithridatica* 1-63; Plutarch *Sulla* 11-26. For the expansion of the Mithridatic kingdom and the rebuff by the Romans see *CAH* (IX 1932, 211-238, esp. 237 on the intervention of Sulla in 92).
14. Beard and Crawford (1985, 80-1) point out that outside Rome itself Italians and Romans were perceived as one and the same, because both were the beneficiaries of Roman rule and exploitation.
15. According to the ancient sources Sulla tried to stop all public business (Appian *BC* 1.55.244; Plutarch *Sulla* 8.3). See also Greenhalgh (1980, 6-7) and Seager (1979, 3).
16. Sulla's infamous march on Rome is reported by Appian, who says (*BC* 1.57) that the soldiers followed their general because they were promised rewards once they arrived in Greece to fight against Mithridates. Sulla's officers would not accompany him; see *CAH* (IX 1932, 205-6). Gruen (1974, 383-4) points out that Sulla did not march as a rebel, but as the legally-appointed consul, to fight against a group of men who had usurped his authority.
17. Leach (1978, 19) thinks that Sulla regarded Strabo and his army as a potent rival. Seager (1979, 3 n.26) says that the Senate appointed Pompeius Rufus to the command of Strabo's army; see also Greenhalgh (1980, 7-8). Appian (*BC* 1.63.283) says that a law was passed to transfer Strabo's troops to Pompeius Rufus, but he does not specifically state that it was Strabo who murdered him.

Greenhalgh (1980, 234) and Seager (1979, 4 n.27) refer to other sources that do blame Strabo, such as Valerius Maximus (9.7 ext. 2).

18. Velleius Paterculus (2.21.1) accuses Strabo of negotiating with both sides; see Seager (1979, 4).
19. Plutarch (*Pompey* 3) elaborates upon the plot to kill Strabo and his son. Seager (1979, 4 n.32) suggests that the story is false or garbled because the soldiers had just killed Pompeius Rufus on behalf of Strabo, and would not so soon declare for Cinna by deserting in droves. This implies a complete uniformity and constancy of opinion among Strabo's soldiers, which would be rare; and it does not allow for the work of Cinna's agents inside Strabo's camp, converting a number of men, but not all of them, perhaps in a short time.
20. For Strabo's defence of Rome see Appian (*BC* 1.66-8); Seager (1979, 4); Greenhalgh (1980, 8-9).
21. Appian (*BC* 1.66-8) describes how Strabo still persisted in trying to negotiate with both sides; Dio (52.13.2) says that Strabo was intent on reaching a second consulship.
22. Appian (*BC* 1.68.312; 80.366), Velleius Paterculus (2.21.3) and Orosius (5.19.18) all say that Strabo was struck by lightning; see *CAH* (IX 1932, 264). But Velleius also says in the same passage that Strabo died of disease. Plutarch (*Pompey* 1) describes how Strabo was hated by the mob because of his avarice and cruelty; see also Syme (1939, 28 n.4) quoting Asconius 70.
23. For Strabo's funeral and the behaviour of the mob see Seager (1979, 3 n.40); Licinius 22-3; Velleius Paterculus 2.21.3; Plutarch (*Pompey* 1). Leach (1978, 17; 237 n.12) thinks that Strabo's evil reputation derives from later adverse propaganda.
24. See note 21 (above) on Strabo's ambition to attain a second consulship.
25. Cinna's men trashed Pompey's house (Greenhalgh 1980, 10). On the prosecution of Pompey see Seager (1979, 7) quoting Schatzman (*Historia* 21 1972, 195) and Gruen (1968, 244) who thinks there was a financial motivation behind the court case. Philippus and Hortensius spoke for Pompey (Cicero *Brutus* 230). For Antistius see Cicero (*Brutus* 224) and Seager (1979, 7 n.2) for the view that Plutarch (*Pompey* 4) is mistaken when he says that Antistius was praetor, since according to Velleius Paterculus (2.26.2) he was only an aedile when he was killed.
26. On the death of Cinna see Plutarch (*Pompey* 5) and Seager (1979, 8).
27. Marcus Licinius Crassus raised a private army for Sulla (Plutarch *Crassus* 4-6), as did Metellus Pius (Appian *BC* 1.80). According to Plutarch (*Pompey* 6.4) Pompey raised three legions all at once, but Appian (*BC* 1.80) says that he raised only one originally. Gelzer (1949, 37) says that he raised one initially and then he was free to raise two more in the respite afforded after his first victories. Gelzer (1949, 36) also points out the difference between Pompey, who was an under-age private citizen, and Metellus, who ranked as proconsul, legally entitled to command troops. See also Seager (1979, 9) and Greenhalgh (1980, 14; 234).
28. Anderson (1963, 13) suggests that Lucius Afranius may have joined Pompey now when he was recruiting his first troops; Afranius was a legate in Spain by 75, and so may already have been associated with and well known to Pompey by then. For Afranius' later career in the service of Pompey in the wars against Sertorius and Mithridates see Plutarch (*Sertorius* 19; *Pompey* 34). See also *ILS* 878. Aulus Gabinius may also have been an early associate (Anderson 1963, 14); see also Sanford (1939). Titus Labienus was probably another of this group (Anderson 1963, 14), and though he served with Caesar for many years, he returned to Pompey from personal loyalty and because he was discontented with Caesar (Dio 41.4.4). Marcus Petreius was older than these men and could have served with Pompeius Strabo; he was already a serving soldier in 92 (Anderson 1963, 14; Sallust *Catilina* 59.6). Syme (1939, 31) discusses Pompey's adherents from Picenum, and adds Marcus Lollius Palicanus,

attested by Sallust (*Historiae* 4.43), who may be a relative of Lucius Lollius, one of Pompey's officers in the east (Appian *Mithridatica*, 95). Aulus Gabinius was married to Lollia, (Suetonius *Divine Julius* 50.1), who may be a relative of Palicanus.

29. Three senatorial armies converged on Pompey, but they did not join up, so Pompey attacked the nearest one first (Gelzer 1949, 37; Greenhalgh 1980, 15; Appian *BC* 1.79-80).
30. For Sulla's battles see Plutarch (*Sulla* 22-33).
31. Sulla hailed Pompey as Imperator, which implied that he equalled Metellus in rank and endorsed his position as an independent commander (Gelzer 1949, 38; Seager 1979, 8; Appian *BC* 1.80.367; Plutarch *Pompey* 8; Valerius Maximus 5.2.9).
32. For the campaigns against Carbo and Marius see *CAH* (IX 1932, 227ff).
33. Carbo withdrew to Ariminum (modern Rimini), while Pompey won a battle at Sena Gallica (Greenhalgh 1980, 17; Appian *BC* 1.88).
34. See Greenhalgh (1980, 19; 40-2) on Sertorius going to Spain and gaining a foothold there. For sources on Sertorius see *CAH* (IX 1932, 318 n.2).
35. Sulla chased the Samnites to Rome and entered into battle as he arrived (Greenhalgh 1980, 20; Plutarch *Sulla* 33).
36. Plutarch (*Crassus* 6.3-4) says that the rivalry between Pompey and Crassus stemmed from the fact that Crassus was not sufficiently rewarded for his part in saving Rome at the battle of the Colline Gate, while Pompey was brilliantly rewarded all through his early career.
37. For Sulla's comment on the young Marius see Greenhalgh (1980, 20).

2 *Adulescentulus carnifex*

1. The term *adulescentulus carnifex* derives from a speech by Helvius of Formiae, reported by Valerius Maximus (6.2.8); see Syme (1939, 27) and Leach (1978, 225-6). On the marriage to Aemilia see Plutarch *(Sulla* 33.3; *Pompey* 9). The alliance with the Metelli is discussed by Seager (1979, 9) and Anderson (1963, 5). See also Twyman (1972) on Pompey and the Metelli.
2. Julius Caesar could not be persuaded to divorce his wife Cornelia; his defiance of Sulla is related by Velleius Paterculus (2.41.2); Suetonius (*DJ* 1.1); Plutarch (*Caesar* 1.1-3).
3. The annual turnover of magistrates prevented the institution of continuous and consistent policies, for which permanent power was necessary. The acquisition and retention of such power always implied tyranny, and the way in which Sulla went about it earned him the opprobrium of contemporaries and modern scholars. Taylor (1949, 19) says that Sulla reorganised the Roman government not as a tyranny, but as an aristocracy. For a sympathetic view of Sulla see Keaveney (1982), and for collected sources see Broughton (1986, 73ff). The problem of lack of continuity to put through far-reaching reforms was not solved until Augustus took power and patiently introduced reforms during his long reign.
4. On the original Dictatorship which had disappeared by 202, see Robinson (1997, 8), who describes the Dictatorships of Sulla and Julius Caesar as merely cloaks for arbitrary power based on military force. Appian's statement (*BC* 1.99.462) that Sulla was given powers to make laws (*legibus scribundis*) is doubtful, but it is clear that Sulla did have legislative power (Brunt 1971, 107). Plutarch (*Sulla* 33.1) says that the *lex Valeria* by which Sulla was made Dictator gave him the power to put his opponents to death, but it is certain that there was a law concerning the proscriptions (Cicero *In Verrem* 1.47.123).

5. Gruen (1974, 411-12)outlines the havoc wrought by the proscriptions because of Sulla's determination to extirpate whole families and connections of the proscribed men, disenfranchising their heirs, and ignoring the murders that took place under cover of the official proscriptions. See Broughton (1952, 69).
6. On the main points of Sulla's government see Gruen (1974, 8-10); Brunt (1971, 107ff); *CAH* IX (1932, 282-308). The attack on the tribunate is a persistent theme in modern works (Beard and Crawford 1985, 9), perhaps given more prominence than it deserves (Gruen 1974, 23-4); but Greenhalgh (1980, 236) thinks that although it may not have been important historically, Gruen does not make sufficient allowance that the curtailment of tribunician power was very important for Sulla. Legislative powers may have been removed from the tribunes; Taylor (1941, 121; 1949, 19) says that their rights of initiating legislation were abolished; Gruen (1974, 23) writes that these rights were curtailed, possibly abolished; Brunt (1971, 107) suggests that tribunes could not initiate legislation without the approval of the Senate.
7. Authors are divided on the issues of the tribunician veto and whether it was abolished. Brunt (1971, 108) says that he limited it but it is not known precisely how it was done, and Gruen (1974, 23) also opts for restrictions on the veto. According to Caesar (*BC* 1.5; 1.7) the right was retained, but Cicero (*In Verrem* 2.1.155) says that the tribune Opimius in 75 issued his veto 'against the Cornelian law' (*contra legem Corneliam*).
8. Gruen (1974, 29) describes the issue of the jury courts as a political football, and analyses retrospectively from the point of view of the reform of the courts under the law passed by Lucius Aurelius Cotta (Gruen 1974, 28-32). In part, Sulla was perhaps trying to provide more personnel for the courts, since the duties had become too frequent and onerous (Gruen 1974, 30). Brunt (1971, 108) says that Sulla's design was to entrench the authority of the Senate against both plebs and equites; others would not see the overall plan as quite so divisive.
9. Sulla's motives in elevating equites to the Senate was possibly an insurance policy for their good behaviour; Gruen (1974, 8-9) points out that the equites who were promoted would perhaps be less likely to turn against the system. See Robinson (1997, 6-10) for a brief synopsis of the Senate and magistrates of Rome, with reference to the changes that Sulla made. See also Gruen (1974, 162ff) on the quaestorship and praetorship before and after Sulla.
10. Beard and Crawford (1985, 42-3) describe the censorship and the duties of censors. On Ofella see Appian (*BC* 1.101); Greenhalgh (1980, 235). Seager (1979, 9 n.14) prefers Afella, following Badian (1967).
11. Appian (*BC* 1.92-96) and Orosius (5.20-21) give accounts of the Marians in Sicily and Africa. Pompey was granted propraetorian rank according to Plutarch (*Pompey* 10) and Cicero (*de Imperio Cn. Pompei* 61).
12. Appian (*BC* 1.96.449), Plutarch (*Pompey* 10), and Valerius Maximus (9.13.2) tell the story of Carbo's execution.
13. Seager (1979, 9-10) discusses whether Carbo was one of the proscribed, and whether his consulship had been revoked before his death; see also Valerius Maximus (6.2.8) and Orosius (5.21.3).
14. On the 6000 Samnites see Greenhalgh (1980, 21).
15. Plutarch (*Pompey* 10) and Cicero (*In Verrem* 2.2.83) describe Pompey's friendship with Sthenius of Himera.
16. For the African campaign see Greenhalgh (1980, 23-7) and Seager (1979, 10).
17. For the gold-digging episode see Greenhalgh (1980, 25).
18. Plutarch (*Pompey* 11-12), Appian (*BC* 1.80) and Sallust (*Historiae* 1.53) describe the war with Domitius.

19. Domitius was probably already proscribed (Seager 1979, 10); on his execution see also Plutarch (*Pompey* 10; 12) and Orosius (5.24.16). Seager (1979, 10 n.28) points out that there is an alternative tradition that Domitius died fighting (Orosius 5.21.13).
20. On Hiarbas and Hiempsal see Greenhalgh (1980, 235); Orosius (5.21.11-14).
21. The comparison of Pompey with Alexander is recounted by Sallust (*Historiae* 3.88) and Plutarch (*Pompey* 2). The soldiers hailed Pompey as Imperator and then as Magnus (Plutarch *Pompey* 12; 13).
22. After the lightning campaign of 40 days Pompey was asked to send his legions back to Italy, and to wait for the appointment of a successor (Plutarch *Pompey* 13). Seager (1979, 11) thinks that the rioting of the soldiers was encouraged by Pompey, as a result of one of the lessons that he had learned from Strabo, but he discounts the idea (1979, 11 n.30) that Pompey was ready for rebellion, and was a serious threat to Sulla, as postulated by Badian (1958, 274).
23. Greenhalgh (1980, 27) recounts the emotional scenes between Pompey and his men, but it is unlikely that Pompey ever lost control of his troops; Seager (1979, 10) points out that in Sicily after the fighting was over his discipline was extreme. With regard to the interaction between the civilians and the soldiers he even went as far as to seal up the men's swords in their scabbards (Plutarch *Pompey* 10). Hillman (1997, 106) re-examines Plutarch's account of the recall of Pompey, and concludes that the young general was not responsible for masterminding the near mutiny of his troops in Africa, and had no intention of military blackmail when he returned to Rome.
24. Plutarch (*Pompey* 13) says that Sulla greeted Pompey as Magnus when he arrived home, and instructed everyone else to do the same. The demand for a triumph and the famous quote that more people worship the rising sun is recounted by Plutarch (*Pompey* 14); see also Appian (*BC* 1.80.368). As Seager points out (1979, 11 n.35) the African war against Hiarbas and the installation of Hiempsal sufficed to describe the war as an external one, a necessary qualification because a triumph over Roman citizens was to be avoided. Caesar held four triumphs in succession after the civil wars were over, but there was no reference to anything other than foreign enemies. Greenhalgh (1980, 236) refutes the suggestion that the Metelli were involved in persuading Sulla to allow the triumph to go ahead.
25. Frontinus (*Stratagems* 4.5.1) describes how Pompey foiled the mutinous soldiers who threatened to ruin his triumph. See Deutsch (1924) on Pompey's triumphs in general, and Seager (1979, 12 n.44) for references and discussion of the first triumph and its date. Badian (1955) refutes the theory that it was held as late as 79; Leach (1978, 237-8 n.20) follows his argument and opts for the earliest possible date for the triumph; see also Twyman (1979).
26. See Greenhalgh (1980, 235-6) for a discussion of the marriage with Mucia and the date; it is likely that Pompey married in 80 when he returned home from Africa and not immediately after the death of Aemilia (Ward 1970). Plutarch (*Pompey* 9) deals with the marriages to Antistia and Aemilia, but makes no mention of Mucia until he discusses the divorce in 62 (*Pompey* 42-3).
27. The Lepidus episode and Pompey's part in it are described by Plutarch (*Pompey* 15-17; *Sulla* 34), Appian (*BC* 1.107) and Sallust (*Historiae* 1.55.18; 1.77.4). Seager (1979, 14) thinks that Pompey supported Lepidus because he could foresee that there would be disturbances that he would then be called upon to quell. See Gruen (1974, 13-16) for an assessment of the impact of the Lepidus revolt. *CAH* (IX 1932, 316) considers that Lepidus was puny compared to other troublemakers, which with hindsight is true, but at the time no one could be sure how serious the potential civil war would be.
28. Greenhalgh (1980, 236) points out that Lepidus was allowed to stand for the elections because he had done nothing illegal and fulfilled all the criteria, not because Sulla had lost the capacity for eliminating him. Greenhalgh (1980, 33) says that Sulla made the two consuls swear an oath that they

would not use force against each other; Seager (1979, 15) suggests that the Senate pressurised them when Lepidus had already started to take up the cause of the disaffected rebels in Etruria; see Appian (*BC* 1.107.502); Sallust *Historiae* (1.77.1).

29. The exact date when Sulla retired is disputed; see Gruen (1974, 12 n.7). Appian (*BC* 1.97.103-6) describes the death and funeral of Sulla; see also Valerius Maximus (9.3.8). See Carney (1961) for the theory that syphilis may have been the cause.
30. For Pompey's arrangements for the funeral of Sulla see Plutarch (*Pompey* 15; *Sulla* 38). See also Appian (*BC* 1.105); Sallust (*Historiae* 1.54).
31. See note 27 above.
32. See Appian (*BC* 1.107) and Sallust (*Historiae* 1.65-6) for the revolt in Etruria. Seager (1979, n.15) points out that Lepidus had inherited clients in the Cisalpine region; see Badian (1958, 276). Gruen (1974, 15-16) says that Lepidus did not join the insurgents until the last moment, and that he had no definite policy, but was just an agitator who saw an opportunity.
33. On Philippus and the *senatus consultum ultimum* see Sallust (*Historiae* 1.77.22). Seager (1979, 15-6 n.19) discusses whether Pompey was to be subordinate to Catulus or whether he had an independent command.
34. For the death of Brutus see Plutarch (*Pompey* 16; *Brutus* 4). Gelzer (1959, 44-5) suggests that Brutus may have been proscribed in 82, and endorses Pompey's actions, but Seager (1979, 16 n.27) disagrees, pointing out that it is unlikely that Brutus would have been appointed as legate to Lepidus if he had been condemned in 82.
35. Lepidus was not declared *hostis* until he began to march on Rome (Seager 1979, 16).
36. Pompey refused to disband his troops after the suppression of the revolt (Plutarch *Pompey* 17). He probably did not have designs on taking over the state at this point any more than he had thought of it in Africa; see Hillman (1992, 106). It is not known at what point Pompey began to think of taking on the Spanish command; Seager (1979, 16) calls him 'an implausible dictator', and adds that it is possible that Metellus had already asked for help (1979, 17 nn.32 and 34).
37. Greenhalgh (1980, 236) points out that Philippus was the senior consul and would have the right to recommend that Pompey should be sent to Spain. Seager (1979, 17 n.34) adds that even if Pompey was granted proconsular power, it would not injure Metellus too much if the younger man were sent out, rather than another consular. In any case no one wanted to go. Cicero (*de Imperio Gn. Pompei* 62) reports Philippus' phrase *non proconsule sed pro consulibus*, and says that Catulus also endorsed the appointment of Pompeius, which Seager (1979, 17 n.36) thinks not unlikely even though Catulus and Pompey previously had a contretemps over Pompey's unwillingness to resign his command. See also Cicero (*Philippics* 11.18); Valerius Maximus (8.15.8); Appian (*BC* 1.108.508).
38. The campaign in the Alps and in Gaul is attested in the letter that Pompey wrote to the Senate during the war with Sertorius; Sallust (*Historiae* 2.98). In the text of the letter Pompey says that he has opened a new route across the Alps, an alternative to the one that Hannibal took; but as Greenhalgh (1980, 236-7) points out, there is no possibility of identifying this route.
39. Plutarch (*Sertorius*) gives most detail about the war in Spain; see also Appian (*BC* 1.108-15). On Sertorius generally and on the war in Spain see Spann (1987). Greenhalgh (1980, 40-57) gives an account of the campaigns, and in the footnotes (1980, 237-8) outlines the problems of determining an exact chronology from the ancient sources, which contradict each other. On Sertorius and Pompey see Wylie (1992a).
40. Plutarch (*Pompey* 19.6; *Sertorius* 21.5) describes how Pompey could be supplied by sea and Sertorius, reliant upon supplies from the interior, was in difficulties until the Mediterranean pirates in alliance with Sertorius closed the ports, enabling him to reverse the situation.

41. On the siege of Lauron, and on the difficulties of giving an account of the Spanish campaign, see Greenhalgh (1980, 46-8; 237); Spann (1987, 92-3). No ancient source gives great detail; the relevant books of Livy's history exist only in epitome (Livy *Epitome* 91-7), and book 91 breaks off after an account of the campaigns in 76, and does not resume until Pompey and Sertorius met at Lauron.
42. Appian (*BC* 1.110) puts Metellus and Pompey together at the battle of the Sucro, but all other sources say that Pompey did not wait for him to come up; see Greenhalgh (1980, 237). Plutarch (*Pompey* 18)gives an account of the battle, and in *Sertorius* (19) he mentions the success of Afranius in capturing and then being driven out of Sertorius' camp.
43. Livy (*Epitome* 92) is the only source to mention Clunia by name, whereas Plutarch (*Sertorius* 21) merely says that Sertorius retreated after the battle of the Turia into a strong city in the mountains.
44. For the text of Pompey's letter to the Senate see Greenhalgh (1980, 51-2). Spann (1987, 120-1) comments on the rhetoric in the letter, adding that a young proconsul with Alexandrian pretensions might well talk of a 40 day conquest of Gaul, and would pass off the battle of the Sucro as a victory, while not actually mentioning Lauron or Segontium. In saying that the war could be brought to Italy, it has been suggested that Pompey meant that he would throw in his lot with Sertorius, but Seager (1979, 19) discounts this implication; it is also doubtful if Sertorius would in fact have followed him to Italy, but perhaps contemporaries were not so certain of this. Spann points out (1987, 122) that the threat of carrying the war into Italy was partly exaggeration and partly fear on Pompey's part, but at Rome it was viewed differently. There was genuine panic in Rome because it was thought that if Pompey fell back on Italy, Sertorius might overtake him, arriving before the senatorial army.
45. Badian (1958, 279) and Ward (1970b, 64) think that the Senate deliberately obstructed Pompey and denied him supplies and money; Seager (1979, 19 n.54) and Gruen (1971, 8) disagree. Ward (1977, 37) accuses the Senate of dilatoriness rather than obstruction. Lucullus was one of the prime forces behind the schemes to help Pompey, but as Seager (1979, 19-20) points out Sallust (*Historiae* 2.98.10) mentions both consuls, not just Lucullus. Mithridates offered Sertorius an alliance, reported by Sallust (*Historiae* 2.71; 2.78) and Orosius (5.23.1-15; 6.2.12); see also Spann (1987, 99-104). Greenhalgh (1980, 53) and Seager (1979, 20) make the point that Mithridates would prefer to see Pompey tied up in the west so that some of Rome's resources were not available for the war in the east. The date of the proposed alliance is not clear; Greenhalgh (1980, 237-8) discusses the evidence, and opts for 74, after the death of Nicomedes of Bithynia and its annexation by Rome. See also Broughton (1952, 99).
46. For the course of the war in 74 and 73 see Greenhalgh (1980, 53-4); Spann (1987, 123-39). Frontinus (*Stratagems* 2.11.2) reports on Pompey's capture of Cauca.
47. Greenhalgh (1980, 55-6) documents the split in Sertorius' forces.
48. On Perperna see Plutarch (*Sertorius* 27).
49. On Pompey's recruitment of clients see Seager (1979, 21). The grants of citizenship were ratified by law; see Cicero (*Pro Balbo* 19; 32; 38). Leach (1978, 53) suggests that the law was passed at Pompey's request. The consuls of 72 were appointed censors in 70 during the consulship of Pompey and Crassus, when the censorship was revived, so it is reasonable to suppose that there was friendly contact between them and Pompey, and that they supported him
50. Pliny (*Naturalis Historia* 3.18) and Sallust (*Historiae* 3.89) record the building of Pompey's monument in the Pyrenees, at Col de la Perche. See Spann (1987, 138-9) on the absence of the name of Sertorius on the monument, and the desire of both Pompey and Metellus to portray their campaigns as part of a foreign war in order to earn a triumph.

3 Consul and Imperator

1. On the episode of Spartacus see Seager *(CAH* 9 2nd ed. 1994, 221-3). Crassus raised his own army to fight Spartacus (Plutarch *Crassus* 8-11); for this purpose he was able to recruit many Sullan veterans (Appian *BC* 1.104). See Brisson (1959) on Spartacus, and Marshall (1973) on Crassus' command.
2. There is debate as to whether Pompey was officially recalled from Spain, or whether he returned to Italy simply because he had completed his campaigns. Appian (*BC* 1.119-20) says that he was recalled, but it is not clear if this was by senatorial decree; Cicero (*de Imperio Gn. Pompeii* 30) also indicates that Pompey was asked to return, since aid was sought from Pompey though he was far away. See Greenhalgh (1980, 238), who points out that these two sources are probably more reliable, but less credence can be bestowed on Plutarch because he contradicts himself; in his life of Crassus he says that before the gladiators escaped from the siege lines in Bruttium, Crassus wrote to the Senate recommending the recall of Lucullus and Pompey, but later regretted it (Plutarch *Crassus* 11.2). The account in the life of Pompey makes no mention of any recall; Plutarch says that Pompey returned to Italy and by chance met up with the fleeing slaves while the servile war was at its height (Plutarch *Pompey* 21.1).
3. On the escape of Spartacus, the final battle, and Pompey's part in rounding up the fugitives see Leach (1978, 57-8); Greenhalgh (1980, 62-4).
4. The number of people turning out to meet and greet the returning generals on their homecoming was not just a matter of spontaneous enthusiasm, but conveyed great importance in measuring the general's popularity; see Lacey (1996, 17-56).
5. Syme (1939, 29) infers from the fact that Pompey kept his army together after his homecoming that he intended to extract the consulship from the Senate by the threat of force; see *CAH* (IX 1932, 332-4) for a similar harsh view. Seager (1979, 22-3) accepts Pompey's word that he was waiting for the arrival of Metellus and his army so that they could hold a joint triumph. Seager points out that though the troops were at the gates of Rome while Pompey canvassed for the consulship, it does not mean that he wished to use them to force the issue; he maintains that Pompey had no designs on taking over the state. Greenhalgh (1980, 239) concurs that Pompey had no need to demand the consulship under the threat of force. Plutarch (*Pompey* 21) says that Pompey promised to disband his troops once he had held his triumph. The Senate waived the legal requirements on behalf of Pompey, who was still under age and had not held any of the requisite magistracies (Livy *Ep.* 97; Plutarch *Pompey* 21; *Crassus* 12).
6. It is not known if there were any other candidates for the consulship of 70; as Leach (1978, 59) suggests, perhaps no one would have been foolhardy enough to try to stand against Pompey and Crassus. Plutarch (*Crassus* 11-12) reports on Crassus' progress from the end of the servile war to the consulship; he says that Crassus approached Pompey for his support for his candidacy. Greenhalgh (1980, 239) says that Pompey and Crassus recognised the need for cooperation, which need not imply that they had no personal quarrel with each other. Rivalry between Pompey and Crassus had probably begun when they first fought for Sulla. According to Plutarch (*Crassus* 11) the fact that Pompey held a triumph while Crassus was allowed only the lesser *ovatio* was the root of the animosity between the two men, but it perhaps merely increased feelings that were already established. Since Crassus had fought a slave army in Italy, his war could not be regarded as an external one, fought against an honourable enemy for the glorification and expansion of Rome. Seager (1979, 23 n.82) says that Pompey and Metellus were anxious to have their war against Sertorius classified as an external war so that they could justifiably hold their triumphs. Crassus could have held no such hope that he could hold a triumph. For Pompey's consulship in general, see Stockton (1973).

7. On Pompey's triumph see Velleius Paterculus (2.30. 1-2); Dio (36.25.3); Valerius Maximus (8.15.8). See also Deutsch (1924), who examines all Pompey's triumphs. Pompey's friend Terentius Varro wrote a handbook on senatorial procedure for Pompey, who had never attended a meeting of the Senate; see Aulus Gellius (*Noctes Atticae* 14.7.2); Seager (1979, 27 n.111); Leach (1978, 60). On Varro see Astbury (1967).
8. Pompey made a speech to the people outside Rome, while consul designate. He was waiting to celebrate his triumph, still in command of his troops, and so could not enter the city. See Sallust (*Historiae* 4.45); Plutarch (*Pompey* 22); Appian (*BC* 1.121) for the speech. Since the demise of Sulla several attempts to restore tribunician power had been made. See Gruen (1974, 23-8) on the struggle for the tribunate; he says that the 'smokescreen of propaganda' about the achievements of the consuls of 70 in restoring the power of the tribunes obscures the earlier work that had gone on for a decade before. See also Broughton (1952, 126). C. Aurelius Cotta succeeded in removing the ban on holding further offices so that the post of tribune no longer stultified careers; see Greenhalgh (1980, 65); Seager (1979, 18); Asconius (67). One of the men who agitated for reform was Lucius Quinctius in 74; he was defeated by the efforts of Lucullus, and though he backed down, Quinctius took his revenge when he had the opportunity at a later date to intrigue against him, discrediting Lucullus during his eastern command; Seager (1979, 20; 31-2); see also Cicero (*Pro Cluentio* 110). In the following year C. Licinius Macer linked Pompey's name to the campaign, even though the latter was still in Spain. Macer implied that the *optimates* in the Senate were delaying action because they were unsure of Pompey's opinion; Seager (1979, 21) dismisses this as ludicrous. Macer went on to say that Pompey would be sure to use his influence to restore legislative power to the tribunes; for his speech see Sallust (*Historiae* 3.48.21-23). It is not possible to ascertain whether Macer was just name dropping or whether he had sounded out Pompey's intentions. Seager (1979, 24 and n.91) points out that Pompey and Crassus co-operated only once, in passing the act to restore full legislative powers to the tribunes; he dismisses claims that the law was passed by Pompey alone, since both consuls would desire the fame and kudos resulting from their act, and both would hope to utilise the tribunes in the future. Marcus Lollius Palicanus, of Picentine origin, contributed much to the law, but it is not certain that he acted in concert with Pompey; see Badian (1958, 283) and McDermott (1977).
9. On the jury courts see Gruen (1974, 28-30) who points out that the business of the courts had increased so much that complaints were recorded about the excessive burden, so that broadening the base of jury members released the pressure. Gruen also highlights the fact that the reform of the courts was not a victory of the equites over the Senate, and that the author of the act, Lucius Aurelius Cotta, was not a demagogue but a member of the nobility. Pompey was not as actively interested in the reform of the courts, and though he supported Cotta, he simply allowed him to get on with it and did not hinder him (Seager 1979, 25-6; Gruen 1974, 29-30). Greenhalgh (1980, 238) suggests that the date of Cicero's first speech in the trial of Verres, given on 5 August, 'is a *terminus post quem* for the recomposition of the courts'. Pompey's interest in the trial of Verres was limited to helping Sthenius of Himera, in whose interests Palicanus was also active; the suggestion that Pompey and the Metelli were at loggerheads over the trial is unfounded, see Seager (1979, 25-6 esp. n.102).
10. The games that Pompey arranged, fulfilling his vow that he made in Spain, are reported by Cicero (*In Verrem* 1.31). The *transvectio* of the equites was arranged by the censors; see Plutarch (*Pompey* 22).

11. Plutarch (*Crassus* 6.4; 7.1; 11; *Pompey* 21.2) and Appian (*BC* 1.120-1) describe the rivalry between Pompey and Crassus. For their reconciliation at the end of their consulship see Plutarch (*Crassus* 12; *Pompey* 23). See also Seager (1979, 27), quoting from Ward (1977, 109), in pointing out that Crassus' speech in praise of Pompey was 'two edged'.
12. After his consulship, Pompey was conspicuous by his absence, and when he did appear in public, he was always surrounded by large crowds of clients and supporters (Plutarch *Pompey* 23.3). Leach (1978, 64-5) assumes that he concentrated on the formation of a Pompeian party in Rome and that he devoted some time to thinking about the Mediterranean and the eastern campaign while he was in semi retirement.
13. On Mucia see Seager (1979, 12; 73; 77); Ward (1970, 126 n.37), who dates the marriage to 80. See also Bauman (1992, 78-9). Gnaeus Pompey has attracted less attention than Sextus, who survived his father's death by several years; see Hadas (1930). Pompeia was married to Faustus Sulla (Suetonius *Divine Julius* 27.1).
14. According to Cicero (*Ad Att.* 6.1.3). in 64 Pompey was able to make a loan of 40 million sesterces to Ariobarzanes of Cappadocia, impoverished because his kingdom had suffered in the Mithridatic wars. This means that he had already built up his personal fortune before this date. As Leach points out (1978, 90) there were probably more recipients of Pompey's loans while he was in the east, and after his campaigns he monitored his investments closely. Leach concludes that Pompey was one of the wealthiest men in the Roman world.
15. Gaius Lucilius, a relative of Pompey's mother, died in 102, and Pompey inherited his estates near Tarentum (Leach 1978, 15; 237 n.5).
16. The consul Piso would not allow Palicanus to stand for the consulship (Valerius Maximus 3.8.3). Seager (1979, 30 n.18) concludes that the *optimates* in the Senate resorted to bribery to keep Pompey's candidates out of the running and to put their own men in influential posts.
17. The land settlements for the veterans of Metellus Pius and Pompey were authorised by the *lex Plotia*, but the law was never put into effect. Leach (1978, 63; 240 n.11) says that the commission to settle the veterans probably ran into financial difficulties. On the *lex Plotia* see Smith (1957); see also Seager (1979, 31).
18. On the pirates see Greenhalgh (1980, 77-80); Seager (1979, 32-3). Rickman (1980, 50-2) describes the effects of the pirate raids on the corn supply of Rome and documents the various campaigns that the Romans mounted to eradicate the nuisance. The capture of Caesar and his subsequent revenge are described by Suetonius (*Divine Julius* 4.1-2).
19. On the *lex de piratis* and the command of Antonius in 102 see Rickman (1980, 50); Broughton (1951, 568). P. Servilius Vatia confiscated the pirates' lands (Cicero *In Verrem* 2.1.56; Orosius 5.23).
20. Mithridates encouraged the activities of the pirates to harass Roman shipping and commerce (Rickman 1980, 50; Appian *Mithridatica* 63). Sertorius was helped by the pirates who blocked the ports, preventing supplies from reaching Pompey and Metellus (Greenhalgh 1980, 50; 78; Plutarch *Pompey* 19.6; *Crassus* 10).
21. For a brief account of the Roman offensives against the pirates up to the time of Pompey see Rickman (1980, 50-1), and for a fuller survey see de Souza (1999, 97-148). In 67 the pirates attacked Ostia and killed the consular commander (Greenhalgh 1980, 79; Cicero *de Imperio Gn. Pompeii*. 33; Dio 36.22)
22. On Gabinius in general see Sanford (1939); Badian (1959). For the *lex Gabinia* see Plutarch (*Pompey* 25) and Dio (36.37.1); see also Loader (1940); Jameson (1970a). On Cicero and the bill see Davison

(1930); Ward (1969). Seager (1979, 33 n.44) says that there is no doubt that Gabinius and Pompey collaborated on this bill, and Rickman (1980, 51) says that Pompey saw the matter of the pirates as a Mediterranean-wide problem requiring large-scale operations to eradicate it. For an examination of Pompey's motives in accepting the command, and his methods of operation, see de Souza (1999, 161-78). Dio (36.25) records Pompey's apparent reluctance to take on the command, and the objections of the Senate to the unprecedentedly great powers bestowed on him.

23. The debate about *imperium aequum* or *imperium maius* is not helped by the contradictory sources. Velleius Paterculus (2.31.1) compares Pompey's powers to those of Antonius in 74, declaring that he held *imperium aequum*, whereas Tacitus, writing about Corbulo in the reign of Nero, says that he held *imperium maius*, like Pompey during his Mediterranean command. Seager (1979, 36) opts for *imperium aequum*, concluding that Velleius is correct. See also Ehrenberg (1953) on *imperium maius*. More recently Ameling (1994, 17-8; 22) examined *imperium aequum/maius* in the context of the commands of Augustus and Agrippa, comparing their powers with Republican precedents, when tasks were allotted for specific purposes and limited duration. Pompey's command was to last for three years; for the terms of the original bill see Dio (36.23.4; 34.3; 37.1) and Appian (*Mithridatica* 94).
24. Opposition to the Gabinian bill was violent, and according to Plutarch (*Pompey* 25) the consul Piso warned Pompey that if he intended to act like Romulus then he would end like Romulus. Caesar supported the bill; for the controversy over whether this was the Gabinian bill or the Manilian bill, or both, see Seager (1979, 33 n.49). Hortensius said that no one should be granted the huge powers that Gabinius proposed, but if they were to be given to someone, Pompey was the most deserving (Cicero *de Imperio Gn. Pompeii* 52). On Cicero and the Gabinian bill see Davison (1930) and Ward (1969).
25. See Plutarch (*Pompey* 25) and Dio (36.24.1) on the tribunes Trebellius and Roscius. The speech of Catulus is reported by Sallust (*Historiae* 5.24); Velleius Paterculus (2.32.1); Valerius Maximus (8.15.9). Seager (1979, 35 n.61) says that there is no need to interpret the reply of the mob as ironic, when Catulus asked who could replace Pompey.
26. When Gabinius' bill was made law, the number of ships, legates, and troops voted to Pompey were increased (Plutarch *Pompey* 26; Livy *Ep.* 99; Appian *Mithridatica* 94). According to Plutarch there were 24 legates in total, while Appian says there were 25. An additional law was passed to appoint Pompey to the command (Seager 1979, 35), and as soon as he was appointed, the price of bread, which had been forced up because of shortages caused by pirate activity, fell dramatically (Plutarch *Pompey* 25; Velleius Paterculus 2.31; Appian *Mithridatica* 94); see also Rickman (1980, 51).
27. Although Cicero (*de Imperio Gn. Pompeii* 68) was arguing in favour of the Manilian law the points raised in his speech about the extraordinary commands granted to Scipio Aemilianus and Marius are applicable in general to the command proposed by Gabinius. Seager (1979, 41 n.128) adds the comment that neither Scipio nor Marius was a private citizen at the time when their commands were granted, whereas Pompey held no office when he was appointed, which is what made the command against the pirates doubly unprecedented.
28. Plutarch (*Pompey* 26.3) says that the Mediterranean was divided into 13 regions, but does not name the commanders. Appian (*Mithridatica* 95) names 13 legates, as does Florus (3.6.7-14 = 1.41, translated in Leach 1978, 231-2) but only 9 names are common to both lists. Leach (1978, 71) says that it is a tribute to Pompey's standing and the respect that was held for him that two of the legates commanding the coastal areas on either side of Italy were the consuls of 72, who were the two censors appointed during the consulship of Pompey and Crassus. If such high-powered men were willing to subordinate themselves to one supreme commander they presumably had faith in his ability to achieve

his aims. The point about the command of Marcellinus, responsible to Pompey and not to the Senate is raised by Leach (1978, 73-4) quoting Reynolds (1962). According to Plutarch (*Pompey* 26) there were 24 legates in total, while Appian (*Mithridatica* 94) says there were 25, but no source states where the remaining 11 or 12 legates operated after the maritime ones had been allocated to their stations. Some probably commanded land forces (Greenhalgh 1980, 240), which perhaps consisted of a large number of local levies who knew the terrain and coastal hiding places (Leach 1978, 74).

29. Pompey cleared the western half of the Mediterranean first in order to enable the corn ships from Sardinia, Sicily and north Africa to resume operations (Rickman 1980, 51-2). Rome did not yet command the resources of Egypt, which became the major source of cereals only after the fall of Alexandria to Octavian in 30 BC. The whole operation to clear the western seas took only 40 days, according to Plutarch (*Pompey* 26.3-29.6) and Appian (*Mithridatica* 94-6). As Greenhalgh notes (1980, 93) the figure of 40 days is very commonly cited for all sorts of events. For the Piso episode see Plutarch (*Pompey* 27); see also Greenhalgh (1980, 94) and Leach (1978, 79-81).
30. Cicero (*de Imperio Gn. Pompeii* 12.34) gives 49 days for the clearance of the eastern Mediterranean and the final battle against the pirates. See Leach (1978, 72) on the siege of Coracaesium, and Greenhalgh (1980, 95).
31. Plutarch (*Pompey* 28) recounts that Pompey made the pirates live in cities and farm the land, while Appian (*Mithridatica* 96) names the cities of Soli, Mallus, Epiphaneia, Adana and Dyme as the cities where pirates were settled. Strabo (8.7.5) names Dyme and Soli. Lucan (*Pharsalia* 2.579) waxes lyrical about the pirate settlements, saying that they humbly begged some land on which to make their homes.
32. On the incident with Metellus, Leach (1978, 74) says that the episode highlights the difficulties of trying to organise Roman foreign policy through proud and independent commanders who would not necessarily cooperate with each other. Pompey does not emerge unscathed from the affair; Plutarch (*Pompey* 29) thinks that he acted badly, but Dio (36.17a-19) also puts the onus on Metellus for his stubborn behaviour.
33. Manilius was prosecuted in 65, and Pompey sacrificed him probably because he was 'a dubious asset' (Seager 1979, 57-8). According to Plutarch (*Pompey* 30), when he heard of the passage of the Manilian law giving him the eastern command, Pompey protested about his endless tasks which made him the object of envy and kept him from settling peacefully in the country with his wife and family. Leach (1978, 75) says that Pompey was touring the Cilician cites overseeing the settlements of the pirates when he heard the news; Seager (1979, 42) points out that the news distracted Pompey from waging war on Metellus.
34. Seager (1979, 31-2) is not in doubt about Pompey's involvement in the agitation to discredit Lucullus. See Plutarch (*Lucullus* 33) on the efforts made in Rome to bring Lucullus down. Dio (36.4-11) records Lucullus' loss of territory in the north and the failure to conquer Armenia.
35. See Dio (36.2.2) for the appointment of Marcius Rex to Cilicia. Cicero (*de Imperio Gn. Pompeii* 26) and Sallust (*Historiae* 5.13) record Gabinius' law giving the command of Pontus and Bithynia to Acilius Glabrio.
36. Manilius proposed that the command of Cilicia, Bithynia and Pontus, together with the Mithridatic war should be given to Pompey (Plutarch *Pompey* 30; *Lucullus* 35). See also Velleius Paterculus (2.33.1). On the consulars who voted in favour of the bill see Seager (1979, 40) and Cicero (*de Imperio Gn. Pompeii* 68).
37. On Manilius' bill see Plutarch (*Pompey* 30; *Lucullus* 35); Velleius Paterculus (2.33.1); Livy (*Ep.* 100). The content of Cicero's speech in favour of the proposals is reported in Seager (1979, 40-2) and

Greenhalgh (1980, 102-5). Greenhalgh (1980, 104) does not believe that Pompey masterminded the whole project put forward by Manilius.

38. Sherwin-White (1984, 189) points out that Cicero's speech on the Manilian law does not reveal much of its terms and how it affected Pompey's resources, but it is to be presumed that Pompey retained all the materials and manpower allocated to him by the Gabinian law. Most of the legates that Pompey had appointed for the campaign against the pirates probably retained their posts; the new legates that he chose for the Mithridatic war included Gabinius and Lucius Afranius; see Leach (1978, 75-6) and Seager (1979, 43). Seager points out that Gabinius and Afranius owed nearly everything to Pompey, while Metellus Celer and Metellus Nepos associated with him only as long as it suited their purpose.
39. Greenhalgh (1980, 106) accepts the embassy of Metrophanes to Phraates, but Seager (1979, 45) rejects it as fiction. See Sherwin-White (1984, 190-1).
40. The main sources for the Mithridatic war are Plutarch (*Pompey* 30-42); Appian (*Mithridatica* 97-119); Dio (36.45-54; 47.1-23). As Leach points out (1978, 79), these sources are contradictory and not always reliable.
41. On the diplomatic mission to Phraates see Dio (36.45.3); Leach (1978, 79); Seager (1979, 44-5); Greenhalgh (1980, 106).
42. Mithridates asked for a truce (Dio 36.45.3-4; Appian *Mithridatica* 98). Leach (1978, 79) says that this would simply grant more time to Mithridates to recoup his losses and build up his strength, while Seager's opinion (1979, 45) is that Pompey could not afford to end the war so quickly, so in order to ensure that Mithridates had no choice but to fight he offered very harsh (if not impossible) terms.
43. Pompey's meeting with Lucullus at Danala is described by Plutarch (*Pompey* 31; *Lucullus* 36) and Dio (36.46.1-2).
44. For brief accounts of Pompey's pursuit of Mithridates see Leach (1978, 79-80) Seager (1979, 46); Sherwin-White (1984, 192-3). Greenhalgh (1980, 109-155) describes the events at greater length. Tigranes would not receive Mithridates and put a price on his head (Plutarch *Pompey* 32; Dio 36.48.2).
45. Tigranes suspected that Mithridates had encouraged the younger Tigranes to turn against him (Seager 1979, 46 n.19; Dio 36.50.1). The submission of Tigranes to Pompey is described by Plutarch (*Pompey* 33); Dio (36.52.2); Valerius Maximus (5.1.9). According to Velleius Paterculus (2.37.3) Tigranes said that he would surrender to no one but Pompey, and would be willing to bear any condition that was imposed on him by Pompey. Plutarch adds that Tigranes was allowed to keep his kingdom, minus Syria, Phoenice, Cilicia, Galatia and Sophene, and he had to pay an indemnity of 6000 talents. Seager (1979, 50) points out that Syria was counted as a Roman possession from the moment that Tigranes gave it up.
46. The younger Tigranes was given Sophene, according to Plutarch (*Pompey* 33) and Dio (36.54.2). Appian (*Mithridatica* 105) says that Tigranes received Gordyene as well, but Seager (1979, 47 n.30) disagrees, since this is refuted by Frankfort (1969, 270). Seager (1979, 47-8) suggests that Pompey thought of the grant of Sophene to Tigranes purely as a temporary measure. For the arrest and imprisonment of Tigranes see Plutarch (*Pompey* 33). The arrest disturbed Phraates, whose understanding with Pompey was now on shaky ground; Phraates sent an embassy at a later date to Pompey to ask if the frontier would be the Euphrates (Plutarch *Pompey* 34; Velleius Paterculus 2.40.1; Strabo 11.11.6; 11.3.5; 11.4.5). The date when Afranius was sent to take over Gordyene is not certain, but it was most probably after the battles with the Albanians and the Iberians; see Plutarch (*Pompey* 36); Seager (1979, 49, quoting Dio 37.5.4); Greenhalgh (1980, 130-1).
47. Oroeses attacked Pompey because he thought that he would be next on the list to be targeted; see Leach (1978, 83-4); Greenhalgh (1980, 120-1); Dio (36.54.1). Seager (1979, 49) says that the con-

quest of Albania was forced on Pompey, and should not be dismissed as mere ostentation, as Magie (1950, 359) suggests that it was.

48. On Artoces and the conquest of the Iberians see Plutarch (*Pompey* 34) and Strabo (11.3); see also Leach (1978, 84-5); Greenhalgh (1980, 122-4). Oroeses put up a further resistance and was defeated at the river Abas (Strabo 11.4.5).
49. See Leach (1978, 86-7) for the work of Pompey's legates, and for the scientific aspect of the expedition to the Caspian. Greenhalgh (1980, 129-30) gives a more detailed account of the Caspian adventure. Sherwin-White (1984, 210) describes the independent operations of Pompey's legates, who were enabled to undertake tasks far removed from the direct control of Pompey himself, as a result of the flexible approach instituted by the Gabinian and Manilian laws.
50. Metellus Celer and Valerius Flaccus had commanded two of Pompey's three divisions when they were all attacked by the Albanians in winter camp. These two officers returned to Rome and were elected praetors for 63. Similarly Ampius Balbus and Labienus returned home and were elected tribunes for 64/3. Their activities were thwarted by Cicero; see Leach (1978, 106); Seager (1979, 64-5). Pompey never considered any other solution except annexation for Syria (Seager 1979, 50); for discussion of the reasons why he did not restore kingship, see Sherwin-White (1984, 209-10). On Antiochus XIII and the annexation see Dio (37.7a); Appian (*Syriaca* 49.349); see also Leach (1978, 90). Plutarch (*Pompey* 38) describes the march south from the headquarters at Damascus.
51. Ptolemy Auletes sent gifts to Pompey when he arrived in Syria (Appian *Mithridatica* 114; Leach 1978, 100). For Crassus' proposal for the annexation of Egypt see Seager (1979, 60, esp. n.32 where he discusses and rejects the theories advanced by some authors that all this was done for the benefit of Pompey). Phraates invaded Gordyene again (Plutarch *Pompey* 38; Dio 37.6.2). Dio (37.7.2) suggests that Pompey had not sufficient confidence to wage war on Parthia, but Greenhalgh (1980, 140) thinks that he did not wish to jeopardise the organisation of Asia Minor. Instead of invading Pompey sent three officers to negotiate a peace between Tigranes and Phraates (Dio 37.7.3; Appian *Mithridatica* 106); see also Greenhalgh (1980, 139-40). Envoys from Mithridates may have arrived at the same time as the embassy from Phraates; see Leach (1978, 92) and Seager (1979, 50 n.48) who admits that it could have been as late as the Syrian campaign in 64, since the main source (Appian *Mithridatica* 107) is not clear as to the chronology.
52. Aristobulus won support from Aemilius Scaurus when he was sent to Judaea, possibly in 66, though the date is not certain; see Josephus (*BJ* 1.127; *AJ* 14.29). When Pompey met Aristobulus and Hyrcanus at Damascus, as he had promised, he still made no pronouncement in favour of either of the brothers (Josephus *BJ* 1.131; *AJ* 14.40; Dio 37.15.3). Sherwin-White (1984, 216-7) says that it is not clear why Pompey should have involved himself in the affairs of Judaea and Nabataea, since they were independent states and had not allied with any of Rome's enemies; the real focus of the campaign was Damascus. Bellemore (1999, 118) concludes that the Roman intervention in Judaea was neither necessary nor inevitable. On the news of the death of Mithridates see Josephus (*BJ* 1.139; *AJ* 14.53) and Dio (37.11).
53. Aristobulus at first resisted and then tried to negotiate, but was arrested (Josephus *BJ* 1.139; *AJ* 14.55; Dio 37.15.3). Hyrcanus was installed as High Priest, not king of Judaea, and his territory was much reduced; some of it was placed in the hands of the governor of Syria, and Judaea became a client state of Rome; see Greenhalgh (1980, 142-3) and Leach (1978, 93-4). See also Grant (1973, 53-8) for the whole episode from the point of view of the Jews, and Bellemore (1999) for the view that Josephus' account in the *Antiquitates Judaicae* is pro-Roman and derived from pro-Roman sources, whereas that of the *Bellum Judaicum* is derived from Jewish sources.

54. On Pharnaces see Plutarch (*Pompey* 42). See also Leach (1978, 96); Seager (1979, 52).
55. For Pompey's eastern arrangements in general see Leach (1978, 96-101), who comments that he took into consideration the local customs in drawing up his administrative arrangements; see also Seager (1979, 52-5); Greenhalgh (1980, 147-67); Sherwin-White (1984, 226-34); Freeman (1994). Dio (37.20.2) comments that Pompey's administrative settlements were still in operation in his own day. On the organisation of Bithynia-Pontus see Marshall (1968). Seager (1979, 52) says that Pompey's organisation of Pontus was his finest work. He also points out (1979, 55) that Pompey was not granted lasting power such as Augustus procured for himself, which was what was required to oversee the long term development of the eastern provinces.
56. Strabo (12.3.1) describes the 11 districts that Pompey created in Bithynia, with an urban centre in each one. Leach (1978, 98-9) points out that the frontiers of Bithynia are not fully known, despite descriptions in literary sources. The urban centres that Pompey set up were probably only administrative, rather than true cities with flourishing trade and large populations. Deiotarus received Lesser Armenia as part of his extended kingdom, but there is dispute over whether he received it from Pompey or the Senate. Seager (1979, 53 n.94) suggests that Pompey granted it to him and the Senate confirmed it. On the territorial adjustments between various client kings see Appian (*Mithridatica* 114-5).
57. Rewards to Pompey's troops totalled 384 million sesterces (Leach 1979, 101); see also Appian (*Mithridatica* 116); Strabo (11.14.10).
58. Mucia tried to curb the excesses of Nepos (Leach 1978, 112-3). Pompey commissioned drawings of the theatre at Mytilene, generally considered to be the basis on which he designed his theatre in Rome (Greenhalgh 1980, 166-7).

4 Tarnished triumph

1. The disbandment of the soldiers at Brundisium dispelled alarm at Rome that Pompey intended to follow the example of Sulla; see Leech (1978, 113); Seager (1979, 72); Greenhalgh (1980, 166-7). The towns through which Pompey and his retinue passed treated him as a hero and a great crowd welcomed him outside Rome (Plutarch *Pompey* 43; Appian *Mithridatica* 116).
2. As Leech (1978, 102) points out there was no strong Pompeian party in Rome during the wars in the east from 66-62, though Cicero wrote of the Pompeian officers (*manus Pompei*) who returned to Rome, whose help he sought in standing for the consulship (*Ad Att.* 1.1).
3. On Pompey's offer of a marriage alliance with Cato see Plutarch (*Pompey* 44; *Cato* 30). Cicero said that the divorce of Mucia was approved in Rome (*Ad Att.* 1.12.3). See also Seager (1979, 73) who adds that Metellus Celer and Metellus Nepos were offended by the divorce, but given that Nepos' track record was hardly successful as far as Pompey's interests were served, Pompey perhaps considered that he would be better off without him.
4. The conspiracy of Catiline in 65 was probably fabricated, by Cicero and anti-Caesarians after the events of 63, which were also very largely a product of Cicero's imagination and thirst for glory; see Seager (1964; 1979, 56-60) and Leach (1978, 105); see also the views of Frisch (1948) and Lacey (1978).
5. Cicero was piqued because Pompey had not given him enough praise for the heroics of his consulship (Leach 1978, 110-11; Greenhalgh 1980, 192).

6. Cicero in his speech on the agrarian bill presented the terms of Rullus' land bill as injurious to Pompey; on Cicero and Rullus see Sumner (1966). Gruen (1974, 389) describes the points that Cicero raised as 'studiously nebulous' and that the assertion that the bill was harmful to Pompey is not credible. Seager (1979, 62-3) thinks it much more likely that Rullus was operating on Pompey's behalf than against him; see also Sumner (1966). On Rullus and the Sullan veterans who were already settled see Drummond (2000), and on Pompey's possible involvement in the bill see Leach (1978, 107-8). Greenhalgh (1980, 180) calls the land bill a 'superficially healthy agrarian reform' and has more sympathy for Cicero's doubts about it, hinting at the machinations of Crassus.
7. For a discussion of the terms of Rullus' bill and Cicero's main arguments against it see Gruen (1974, 398-96); Seager (1979, 62-4).
8. Crassus and Caesar were suspected of scheming together in various projects; see Leach (1978, 105; 111); Seager (1979, 60; 67). Drummond (2000, 153) concludes that the Rullan bill was closer to that of the tribune Flavius in 60 and to Caesar's land bill in 59 than has previously been assumed.
9. Nepos prevented Cicero from making his speech at the end of his consulship (Plutarch *Cicero* 23.26), and Caesar co-operated with him in wresting the contract for rebuilding the temple of Jupiter from Catulus; see Seager (1979, 69); Syme (1939, 35) and Gruen (1974, 393) comment on the efforts that Caesar made in working with Pompey's adherents, devising honours for him, and trying to curry favour with him.
10. Plutarch (*Cato* 26.26) and Dio (37.43.1) mention only the proposal to recall Pompey, and do not say anything about the possibility of election as consul *in absentia*. Syme (1939, 32 n.6) treats the two ideas as though they were alternatives; either Pompey should be recalled to establish order, or he should be elected consul. Leach (1978, 109) and Seager (1979, 68-9) both think it impossible that Pompey could have been involved in the proposals, since communication between him and Nepos would not have been rapid enough. Seager suggests that Pompey gave Nepos a free hand to exploit any opportunity that came his way.
11. See Seager (1979, 70-1 and n.93) on the postponement of the elections to allow Piso to reach Rome in time (Dio 37.44.3); there may have been two requests for postponement of which only one was granted, or one request covering both Piso and Pompey himself, but only Piso returned to Rome. Syme (1939, 32) suggests that the Senate acquiesced because of fear of civil war.
12. Cicero reported to Atticus (*Ad Att.* 1.12) that a great scandal had been caused because 'P. Clodius, son of Appius, was discovered in woman's clothes in C. Caesar's house'. In another letter (*Ad Att.* 1.14) Cicero described how Pompey had been questioned at a public meeting, and again in the Senate, about various aspects of the trial. His answers were studiously neutral. See Seager (1979, 74-5).
13. For a full description of the triumph see Greenhalgh (1980, 168-77); Plutarch (*Pompey* 45-6); Appian (*Mithridatica* 115-17); Velleius Paterculus (2.40.3-4). Plutarch (*Pompey* 46.1) comments that it would have been better if Pompey had died at this point in his life, then his reputation would have remained high.
14. For the Alban villa and the projected theatre see Leach (1978, 117-8); Greenhalgh (166-7). For the temple above the theatre see Hill (1944).
15. Cato tried to stop the election of Afranius, whose consulship was ineffective, indeed some said disgraceful, but without giving details; see Cicero (*Ad Att.* 1.16; 1.18.5; 1.19.4; 1.20.5), who labelled Afranius 'the son of Aulus', and indicated that his candidacy was unpopular, and that he was worse than useless as consul. Broughton (1952, 130 n.5) says that Afranius was praetor in 71, but as Seager points out (1979, 77 n.22) Afranius had no experience and no other support save

Pompey's, so although he had hoped to stand for the consulship of 61, he waited instead for Pompey's return. Pompey canvassed on behalf of Metellus Celer (Dio 37.49.1), and according to Syme (1939, 33) Celer swallowed the insult of the divorce from Mucia in order to benefit from the support of Pompey. Cicero (*Ad Att.* 1.18; 1.19) sings the praises of Celer, noting that 'he is an admirer of mine'. On Afranius and Celer see Leach (1978, 116); Seager (1979, 76-7). Flavius' land bill was opposed by Cicero, who still thought that by doing so he was rendering good service to Pompey (Syme 1939, 34). In a letter to Atticus (*Ad Att.* 1.19.4), Cicero said that the only claim to popularity for Flavius' bill was its supporter, Pompey. Cicero outlined the modifications to the bill that he had suggested, including the removal of clauses that impinged on private rights of ownership. When Celer was imprisoned over the bill, Pompey backed down (Cicero *Ad Att.* 2.1.8; Dio 37.50.1).

16. Caesar's proposals to hold the triumph that had been voted to him, and to stand for the consulship *in absentia* were blocked by Cato (Plutarch *Caesar* 13; *Cato* 31; Appian *BC* 2.8.30; Suetonius *DJ* 18.2). See also Seager (1979, 81-2) and Greenhalgh (1980, 201) who says that if Caesar gave up the triumph so readily it meant that he was sure of the election, and Greenhalgh extrapolates from this surmise that Caesar must have enjoyed Pompey's support. He also suggests that Pompey must have devised a land bill that would satisfy all the opponents and quell all the contentious issues that had prevented the passage of the earlier bills.
17. Syme (1939, 34) says of Cato's bribery: 'Cato gathered a great fund to carry by bribery the election of Bibulus, his daughter's husband. He should have made certain of both consuls'.
18. Florus (2.13.11) mentions all three members of the so-called first triumvirate together, listing what each of them got out of the agreement. See also Sanders (1932); Mitchell (1973) for Cicero's viewpoint; Leach (1978, 121); Greenhalgh (1980, 201). On Pompey's need to maintain his position see Knight (1968). Suetonius (*DJ* 19.2) says that Caesar reconciled (*reconciliavit*) Crassus and Pompey, and made a compact with them both, that no step should be made in public affairs which did not suit any one of the three; see also Plutarch (*Crassus* 14). For Crassus as financier see Plutarch (*Crassus* 3.1), who says that no interest was charged on any of the loans that Crassus made because his motive was not economic, but political; see also Plutarch (*Crassus* 7.2) on how Crassus expanded his client base. Gruen (1974, 68-9) points out that 'the extraordinary power wielded by Crassus is confirmed again and again by contemporary evidence'. After the marriage of Pompey and Julia, Caesar began to ask Pompey to speak first in the Senate, whereas previously he had always asked Crassus (Suetonius *DJ* 21); see Seager (1979, 86) and Gelzer (1968, 80).
19. On Lucceius see Suetonius (*DJ* 19.1); Syme (1939, 35). Greenhalgh (1980, 201-2) says that Caesar duped Lucceius into thinking that he stood a chance of election as his colleague, but the partnership was perhaps not forged in such a callous way; defeat of Bibulus and his backer Cato may just have come about if Caesar and Lucceius allied. In the opinion of Seager (1979, 82) 'it was Cato who threw Pompey and Crassus together'.
20. On Caesar's agrarian bill see Gelzer (1968, 72), who points out that no one in Rome could deny that there were lots of idle poor and landless men in Rome, while uncultivated lands abounded in Italy. In connection with the previous land bill put forward by Flavius, Cicero (*Ad Att.* 1.19) supported the suggestion that land should be purchased, 'thinking that the city might be emptied of the dregs of the populace, and the deserted parts of Italy peopled'. See also Dio (38.1.3). On Vatinius see Seager (1979, 85). Plutarch (*Cato* 31) and Dio (38.1) both knew that the land bill that Caesar put forward was so careful that no one could find anything to object to.

21. For the provisions of the land bill see Seager (1979, 86), especially on the commission of 20 men, which is unusually large, and the executive group of five men within the 20. Seager points out that both of the two groups of commissioners belong to the first law to settle Pompey's veterans, so it is not the case that there were 20 men on the first commission and five on Caesar's second agrarian law concerning the Campanian lands. Cicero (*Ad Att.* 2.6.2 and 2.7.3) writes of commissions of 20 and five. See *ILS* (XLVI) for the five; Marcus Valerius Messalla was one of the group, as was Marcus Atius Balbus, the grandfather of Octavian-Augustus. Gelzer (1968, 74) speculates that Terentius Varro was another of the five; with Pompey himself and Crassus, this may be the full membership. On the stormy scenes in the Senate, the imprisonment of Cato and the actions of Marcus Petreius see Dio (38.2-3).
22. Dio (38.4.1-3) reports on Bibulus telling the crowd that they would not get the bill this year, and in another passage (38.5.1-2) he relays Pompey's speech reminding the people that the agrarian bill of 70 had never been put into effect because of lack of money, but now that he had conquered the east and brought wealth to Rome, there was no excuse this time for not passing and effecting the land bill. Pompey said that if anyone raise his sword in defiance of the bill then he would raise his shield (Plutarch *Caesar* 14.2-6; *Pompey* 47.5-8). The riots as the bill was passed are described by Suetonius (*DJ* 20.1); Plutarch (*Pompey* 48.2-3); Appian (*BC* 2.38-41); Dio (38.6.1-3). See also Greenhalgh (1980, 207). Cato, Metellus Celer and Favonius refused to swear the oath to protect the agrarian law, but eventually gave in (Dio 38.7.1-2; Plutarch *Cato* 32; Cicero *Ad Att.* 2.5.1).
23. The eastern settlement was ratified without opposition (Dio 18.7.5; Plutarch *Pompey* 48.4; Appian *BC* 2.46; Velleius Paterculus 2.44.2). Plutarch (*Lucullus* 4.2.6) says that Lucullus fell on his knees begging for Caesar's mercy in connection with the agrarian law, but Suetonius (*DJ* 20.4) places the incident with the eastern settlement, in which Lucullus would have greater interest (Gelzer 1968, 75). Leach (1978, 124) suggests that the hard-working Vatinius did most of the work in making all the necessary arrangements, including confirmation of treaties. Leach says that the eastern settlements were made law in February; Seager (1979, 87) opts for March.
24. Dio (39.12.1) describes the work by Pompey and Caesar to have Ptolemy Auletes recognised as king of Egypt, and the payments made to them in return for this service; according to Suetonius (*DJ* 54.3) the full amounts were never paid. See also Caesar (*BC* 3.107.2) and Gelzer (1968, 76). Seager (1979, 87) suggests that the Egyptian affair was arranged at the same time as the eastern settlements, and possibly the eastern tax contracts (see note 25 below) that Crassus had tried to sort out were also dealt with in the same period. It would make sense to attend to all eastern matters, which in any case overlapped, in one connected series of legislation.
25. On the tax contracts and Caesar's advice to the *publicani* not to bid too high next time, see Cicero (*Ad Att.* 1.17.9; 1.18.7; 2.1.8; 2.16.2).
26. On the adoption of Clodius into a plebeian family see Suetonius (*DJ* 20.4), who attributes the reason for Caesar's action in arranging the adoption to the speech of Cicero deploring the state of the times. See also Dio (38.11-12). Seager (1979, 92-3) thinks that Pompey and Caesar had not thought through their actions properly. It may have been Pompey's idea to send Clodius on an embassy to Tigranes, perhaps with the purpose of delaying his return until after the tribunician elections, but Clodius would not go; he threatened to stand for the tribunate and pass laws to rescind all Caesar's legislation, which had been carried out without regard to Bibulus and his withdrawal from public life to watch the heavens (Seager 1979, 93-4). On Clodius' career see Lintott (1967) and Gruen (1966).
27. Caesar's second agrarian law features in several of Cicero's letters to Atticus; he is puzzled as to how Caesar will ever find a solution to the land bill that will not meet with opposition, then wonders

what 'our friend Gnaeus' is doing to let himself be carried so far (*Ad Att.* 2.15-18). See also Velleius Paterculus (2.44.2); Suetonius (*DJ* 20.3).

28. Pompey's marriage to Julia is reported by most sources (Plutarch *Caesar* 14.7; *Pompey* 47.10; Suetonius *DJ* 21; Appian *BC* 2.50; Dio 38.9.1; Velleius Paterculus 2.44.3). Cicero heard of the betrothal in May and said that Pompey was running amok, calling him by the nickname Sampsiceramus, after one of the eastern potentates (*Ad Att.* 2.17.1). Gelzer (1968, 80) and Seager (1979, 94-5) interpret the betrothal as an attempt on the part of Caesar to bind Pompey more closely to him because he thought that their current unpopularity might turn Pompey against him. There is some confusion as to the identity of the Quintus Caepio to whom Julia was betrothed; see Syme (1939, 34) who says it is Marcus Brutus; Seager (1979, 96 n.68) says that it is not certain whether Marcus Brutus or his adoptive father is meant. See also Leach (1978, 126). Cicero (*Ad Att.* 2.24) reports retrospectively to Atticus that Bibulus had warned Pompey to be on his guard against plots on 13 May; see also Leach (1978, 127-8); Greenhalgh (1980, 219).
29. The tribune Vatinius presented a bill to give Caesar Cisalpine Gaul and Illyricum with three legions for five years (Dio 38.8.5; Plutarch *Pompey* 48; Appian *BC* 2.13.49; Velleius Paterculus 2.44.5). Pompey moved that Caesar should be given Transalpine Gaul with one legion; Suetonius (*DJ* 22.1) says that Caesar was granted Gallia Comata, where he did eventually operate, but it was not the original province of Pompey's proposal. Plutarch (*Caesar* 14) mentions that Caesar was given four legions by the first bill, which is true only after Pompey had recommended that he should govern Transalpine Gaul. Gelzer (1968, 67-8; 84-5) accepts that the mundane tasks that had been assigned to the retiring consuls of 59 were designed to curb Caesar's ambition, but Seager (1979, 83) disagrees on the basis that the troubles in Gaul required that the Senate should keep the consuls in reserve in case of a war. Cicero mentioned that the Aedui had fought a great battle, that the Helvetii were armed and dangerous in 60, and that the consuls of that year had been assigned to the two Gallic provinces (*Ad Att.* 1.19).
30. Cicero (*Ad Att.* 2.19) reports that at the games of Apollo the actor Diphilus made an attack on Pompey with the line that 'by our misfortunes you are great', which was encored several times. In the same letter Cicero relates how Caesar was greeted with silence when he entered the throng, but the young Curio was treated to a rapturous standing ovation. Cicero said that Caesar immediately wrote about the incident to Pompey, who was at Capua.
31. The Vettius affair has been variously interpreted and not even contemporaries were certain of who was behind it all. Cicero reported the whole affair to Atticus (*Ad Att.* 2.24); he thought that Caesar was the culprit, and went on to say that 'as far as we can see' (*ut perspicimus*), Vettius promised Caesar that he would lead Curio into trouble. Leach (1978, 127-8) suggests that there may well have been a plot, and having heard of an attempt to be made on his life from Bibulus in May, Pompey and perhaps Caesar may have deployed Vettius to find out more as an undercover agent. Greenhalgh (1980, 225) prefers to see Vettius as slightly unhinged and acting on his own initiative. Seager (1979, 100-01) detects the hand of Clodius, as part of his ongoing programme directed against Caesar and Pompey; by making Pompey nervous and distrustful, he could be weaned from Cicero's side, and leave the latter unprotected.
32. Bibulus issued a decree, probably in July 59, just before the consular elections would have been held, postponing them until 18 October (Cicero *Ad Att.* 2.20; see also 2.21). If the elections had been held at the normal time, it is possible that Pompey's candidate Gabinius would not have succeeded in being elected; but by October, after the news of the plot on Pompey's life had been made public, there was more sympathy for Pompey, and when Caius Cato tried to prosecute Gabinius, and denounced Pompey as a *privatus dictator*, he was almost lynched (Cicero *QF* 1.2; Seager 1979, 100-01; Greenhalgh 1980, 225).

5 The power game

1. On Clodius generally, and whether he was acting on behalf of Caesar or anyone else, see Gruen (1966) and Lintott (1967). Velleius Paterculus (2.44-5) had only disgust for Clodius, labelling him reckless, with no limits to his speech or actions except those he imposed for his own good. On Clodius' gangs see Dio (38.12-14) . Cicero (*Ad QF* 13) said that Clodius had gathered the remnants of Catiline's followers. On the corn doles and the legalising of clubs and guilds see Greenhalgh (1981, 3) and Seager (1979, 103).
2. Caesar offered Cicero a post as legate in Gaul, and it was suggested that he should go to Egypt to remove him from Clodius, but he would not accept any postings; see Cicero (*Ad Att.* 2.19) where he says that he can see that it would be an honourable way out, but he preferred to stay and fight. See also Plutarch (*Cicero* 39.3-5) and Dio (38.17.1-2).
3. Domitius and Memmius attacked Caesar's consulship (Suetonius *DJ* 23), and all that Caesar could do was respond verbally; see Greenhalgh (1981, 2); for the meeting in the Circus Flaminius see Seager (1979, 105) and Gelzer (1968, 97-8).
4. On the five year proconsulships for Piso and Gabinius see Seager (1979, 103) and Greenhalgh (1981, 5). On Clodius' law forbidding the execution of Roman citizens without trial (*lex de capite civis*) see Velleius Paterculus (2.45.1); Plutarch (*Cicero* 30.4); Appian (*BC* 2.15); see also Gruen (1974, 244). According to Plutarch (*Cicero* 31.3) when Cicero went to see Pompey as Clodius' campaign was at its height, Pompey slipped out from his villa unseen as Cicero approached from the front; Seager (1979, 103) does not believe the story, whereas Leach (1978, 131) accepts it. See also Dio (38.17.3). Seager (1979, 104) suggests that Pompey broke with Cicero, allowing him to go into exile, knowing that he could recall him later when Clodius was out of office.
5. The removal of Cato is described by Plutarch (*Cato* 34; *Pompey* 48; *Caesar* 21); Velleius Paterculus (2.45); Dio (38.30.5). According to Cicero (*Dom.* 22) Caesar congratulated Clodius on his successful appointment of Cato to the Cyprus command. Seager (1979, 105) points out how neatly Cato was trapped; he had always argued against extraordinary commands, but having been forced into accepting one, he would have to have his acts ratified when he returned, as Pompey had done, which meant that Cato could not attack Clodius' legislation without jeopardising his own command and the arrangements he made in Cyprus.
6. On Deiotarus see Cicero (*Dom.* 129); Seager (1979, 105-6), and on Brogitarus see Magie (1950, 1235-6). Rawson (1973) says that Clodius was interested in expanding his client base. For the Tigranes episode, the attack on Gabinius and the skirmish on the Appian Way see Seager (1979, 106-7); Greenhalgh (1981, 11-12); Plutarch (*Pompey* 48); Dio (38.30.1-2); Cicero (*Ad Att.* 3.8). Dio (38.30.3) says that the kidnapping of Tigranes spurred Pompey on to recall Cicero.
7. Greenhalgh (1981, 16-7) says that there was no danger in the threatened attack on Caesar's legislation, because Clodius' intention was to attack it unsuccessfully, which would only demonstrate its strength, thereby protecting his adoption and therefore his tribunate. Seager (1978, 107) suggests that the proposal to re-enact all Caesar's laws had one purpose only, to omit the adoption of Clodius and render his tribunate invalid. Clodius said that if the Senate would annul Caesar's legislation, he would bring Cicero home on his shoulders (Cicero *Dom.* 40).
8. Cicero (*Pro Sestio* 69) gives the date of 11 August for the discovery of the so-called plot against Pompey, whereupon the great man went home and did not re-emerge until the end of the year; see also Seager (1979, 109) and Greenhalgh (1981, 276) on the sources. Plutarch (*Pompey* 49) reports

that the tribune Quintus Terentius Culleo tried to persuade Pompey to divorce Julia and cut his ties with Caesar, but Pompey refused and instead started to call in his clients from the north of Italy, and condoned the assembly of gangs organised by the tribunes Milo and Sestius, to rival those of Clodius. He sent Sestius to Caesar to secure his agreement to the recall of Cicero (Cicero *Pro Sestio* 71); see Seager (1979, 109), who says that Caesar's consent was grudgingly given.

9. Cicero wrote to Atticus as soon as he arrived in Rome, explaining his circumstances (*Ad Att.* 4.1); politically he was restored to his former position, but financially he was in dire straits. He went on to describe his journey home, the crowds who came to meet him, and the speech he gave in the Senate on 5 September, the day after he arrived. The Egyptian affair was debated in the Senate while Ptolemy Auletes stayed as Pompey's guest at his Alban villa; for the various solutions proposed see Greenhalgh (1981, 24-5; 31-2); Leach (1978, 137-8); see also Siani-Davies (1997).
10. Cicero described to Atticus how Pompey was given control of the corn supply (*Ad Att.* 4.1); on the day of the proposal there were only two men of consular rank in the Senate, but on the next day there was a full house, willing to grant Pompey anything. He asked for 15 legates and chose Cicero as the first of them; see also Cicero (*Dom.* 8); Plutarch (*Pompey* 45). Pompey's ambivalence is neatly conveyed by Cicero (*Ad Att.* 4.1) when he describes Messius' proposals for much greater powers for Pompey, contrasted with the more seemly proposal of the consuls: 'the law that the consuls propose is now considered quite moderate; that of Messius perfectly intolerable. Pompey says he prefers the former; his friends that he prefers the latter'. See also Seager (1979, 112); Leach (1978, 135-6).
11. Statistics on the consumption of corn in the city, the cost, and the numbers of recipients at any one time, are difficult to establish. Suetonius (*DJ* 41) gives the only reliable figures when he says that Caesar reduced the number claiming the dole from 320,000 to 150,000. Rickman (1980, 169-71) documents the history of the corn doles, and suggests that Cato may have doubled the number of recipients when the pirates, the disruption caused by Catiline, and general food shortages all threatened the state at the same time, and some cosmetic action was required to calm the people. When Clodius abolished the charges for the dole, crowds of people came into Rome, and many slaves were freed in anticipation of the free food (Rickman 1980, 174). Pompey organised a census of the recipients, but it is not certain whether he counted all of them, or only the new ones who had arrived in the city or had just been freed (Rickman 1980, 175). Cicero (*Pro Sestio* 55) says that when Clodius abolished the charge for the corn dole, the cost to the state of providing the corn amounted to one fifth of the annual revenue. Without a balance sheet, the value of this fraction is impossible to calculate. See Greenhalgh (1981, 276) on the increase in revenue brought in by Pompey's eastern conquests, and the vagaries of the information derived from the ancient sources. Rickman (1980, 170) points out that the figures used to calculate the cost to the state are not connected to each other.
12. On Pompey's administration of the corn supply, and the quote 'It is necessary to sail, it is not necessary to live' see Plutarch (*Pompey* 50-1). Dio (39.9; 39.24.1-2) comments on the need for Pompey's appointment and the high market prices of corn, from various causes. Seager (1979, 110-11) suggests that Messius' proposal was to test senatorial reaction. See Cicero (*Ad Att.* 4.1) for an account of the proceedings in the Senate. Clodius objected to the appointment of Pompey because it was unwise to entrust so much power to one man (Plutarch *Pompey* 49). Leach (1978, 136) describes how the administration may have been carried out, from planting, to harvest, to distribution of the corn. Pompey obtained special dispensation on an *ad hoc* basis to enter the city even though he held a command.

13. On the trial of Milo and Clodius' heckling of Pompey see Cicero (*Ad QF* 2.3); on the background to the trial see Cicero (*Ad Att.* 4.3). Pompey made a speech in his defence against the attack of C. Cato, comparing himself to Africanus, hinting that Crassus was plotting against him (Cicero *Ad Att.* 1.14). See also Leach (1979, 139-40); Seager (1978, 119-20); Greenhalgh (1981, 33-5).
14. Pompey was in an invidious position in the 50s with no allies; see Gruen (1974, 100-01; 106-9) for an analysis of his followers, and the lack of men of consular rank or political influence among his friends. Seager (1979, 114) says that to offer the Campanian lands back to the Treasury would be 'a potent demonstration' of Pompey's goodwill towards the Senate. On Lupus see Cicero (*Ad QF* 2.1); see also Stockton (1971, 207). Cicero revived the question of the Campanian lands (*Ad QF* 2.4), probably thinking he was doing Pompey a favour, in which case he was correct but not in the way that he hoped, since he wanted to detach Pompey from Caesar, not force them back together. Gruen (1974, 311) says that Pompey was able to put pressure on Caesar with the unwitting assistance of Cicero; Seager (1979, 121) endorses the opinion.
15. On the conference at Lucca see Lazenby (1969); Gruen (1969); Luibheid (1970). Crassus reported to Caesar at Ravenna as soon as Cicero brought up the Campanian settlements; Seager (1979, 122 n.48) does not agree with the suppositions of Marshall (1976, 124) or Ward (1977, 262) that Crassus had worked in the background to bring about the situation. Gruen (1974, 72; 101) thinks that the numbers of senators and others who gathered at Lucca were mostly Crassus' clients and followers; Seager (1979, 122-3) doubts that Crassus was even at Lucca and suggests that the meeting was held between Pompey and Caesar alone. He points out that here is no contemporary account of the meeting, and the nearest source is dated two years later; this is Cicero's letter to Spinther in 54 (*Ad Fam.* 1.9), which Seager interprets to mean that Crassus met Caesar at Ravenna and then went away without meeting Pompey at Lucca, not least because their relations were already strained. See also Plutarch (*Pompey* 51.3; *Caesar* 21.2); Appian (*BC* 2.17), who says that there was a meeting somewhere in the Po valley, and does not name Lucca. Dio (39.27.1) does not describe a meeting, but says that the three men came to an agreement. Suetonius (*DJ* 24) says that it was the ardent attempts of Domitius Ahenobarbus to remove Caesar from his command that forced Caesar to call the conference and ask Pompey and Crassus to block Domitius' candidacy for the consulship.
16. All the ancient authors who describe the meeting or the agreement made at Lucca (see above note 15) assume that the consulship of 55 for Pompey and Crassus was discussed and arranged on the spot. This may not have been the case. Leach (1978, 143-4) discusses the possible occasions when Pompey and Crassus decided to stand for the consulship; he says that it is important not to assume that the political developments that occurred after Lucca were in fact on an agenda for discussion by the three in 56. See also Greenhalgh (1981, 51-2) who assumes that Pompey did not want to be consul, but had to stand for election because there was no one else who could oppose Domitius and secure the appointment of friendly magistrates. Plutarch (*Pompey* 51; *Crassus* 15) and Dio (39.27-30) describe how Pompey and Crassus evaded questions and managed to delay the elections by putting their names forward at the last moment; Seager (1979, 128) and Greenhalgh (1981, 44) explain how they bought and utilised the disruptive talents of their erstwhile enemy C. Cato. On the violence at the elections see Plutarch (*Pompey* 52; *Crassus* 15); Dio (39.31-2). For the disturbances at the aedilician elections, and the story of Julia's subsequent miscarriage see Plutarch (*Pompey* 53.3-4); Dio (39.32.2).
17. Seager (1979, 129) says it is unlikely that the provincial commands for Pompey and Crassus were worked out in detail at Lucca. Cicero visited Pompey at Naples in April (*Ad Att.* 4.9.1; 4.10.2) and nothing had been arranged then, though Pompey was never as forthcoming about his plans as

Cicero would have liked. On the provincial commands see also Velleius Paterculus (2.46.2; 2.48.1); Plutarch (*Pompey* 53; *Crassus* 15; *Caesar* 28); Dio (38.33.2). Pompey chose Spain because it afforded him a chance to control what happened in the west (Seager 1979, 130), but there was justification for the five year command since the tribes of those areas untouched by Pompey's campaigns against Sertorius had risen in revolt and defeated the governor Metellus Nepos (Leach 1978, 145). As Greenhalgh (1981, 49) points out the Roman world was divided up between the three men for the next five years. Pompey sent his legates to Spain immediately after the passage of the bill into law, according to Dio (39.39), and Crassus also sent legates to Syria, where Gabinius was still technically in command (Dio 39.60).

18. Leach (1978, 146; 244 n.43) thinks that the extension of Caesar's command was one of the main items discussed at the conference at Lucca. Caesar was confirmed in command of both Gallic provinces and also Illyricum for the next five years; see Cicero (*Ad Att.* 8.3.3); Velleius Paterculus (2.46.2). Seager (1979, 131 n.27) points out that the law to extend Caesar's command could have been promulgated by Trebonius, just as he put forward the laws granting five year commands to Pompey and Crassus; the usual name for the law granting Caesar another five years is *lex Pompeia Licinia*. Unfortunately there is no clarity as to the terminal date of Caesar's command; see Greenhalgh (1981, Appendix I, 292-5) and Seager (1979, Appendix 2, 193-5) for discussion and references; Seager concludes that neither law concerned with Caesar's command would contain a precise terminal date. See also some of the literature of the past 70 years on this subject: Adcock (1932); Stevens (1938); Elton (1946); Cuff (1958); Stocker (1961); Jameson (1970b). Dio (39.33.3; 44.43.2) says that Caesar's command was for three years.
19. The second consulship of Pompey and Crassus was not noted for reforms, which lends support to the theory that all they wanted was the provincial commands (Leach 1978, 145). Pompey and Crassus seemed to be principally concerned with preventing others from reaching the consulship as they had done, via bribery and intimidation. Pompey reformed the composition of the jury courts and Crassus prevented the use of the *collegia* in canvassing for the elections (Seager 1979, 129); Dio (39.37.1). See also Gruen (1974, 230-3) for more detailed discussion of the laws and how they were applied. The muzzling of the enemies of Pompey, Crassus and Caesar was achieved by purchase, or perhaps by negotiation and fear. See Seager (1979, 128 n.1) for the date when Clodius was temporarily tamed, probably after Lucca, and for his outrageous flattery, which could not have been sincere (Dio 39.29.1); see also Leach (1978, 145). Greenhalgh (1981, 62-3) attributes the taming of Clodius to the marriage between Pompey's son Gnaeus with the daughter of Appius Claudius Pulcher, Clodius' brother. Gruen (1974, 148; 454) suggests that this marriage took place after the elections for the consulship of 54; Syme (1939, 38; 45 n.3) portrays Appius Claudius angling for an alliance with Pompey while he was consul, and places the marriage of Gnaeus at the same time as that of Brutus with another daughter of Appius Claudius, which according to Cicero (*Ad Fam.* 3.4.2) took place in 54.
20. On the trial of Balbus see Gruen (1974, 312-3), who adds that Balbus was adopted by Pompey's friend Theophanes at the same time that Pompey married Julia; see also Seager (1979, 131-2). Greenhalgh (1981, 42-3) says that the failure of the opposition either to convict Balbus, or previously to remove Caesar from his command, is an indication of Pompey's restored power. The fate of Caninius Gallus is not known; Gruen (1974, 313) and Seager (1979, 131 n.32) think that he may have been condemned. On the trials of Ampius Balbus and Scribonius Libo see Gruen (1974, 314); Seager (1979, 131-2). The date is not known, but Gruen (1974, 314 n.17) opts for 55; see Valerius Maximus (6.2.8).

21. Pompey's theatre was famous long after his day; see Plutarch (*Pompey* 52); Pliny (*NH* 7.34-6); Tacitus (*Ann.* 14.20); Dio (39.38.2). For architectural studies of the theatre see Platner and Ashby (1929, 146; 428; 515) and Nash (1968, vol.2 plates 1216-23). Seager (1979, 131) presents the building of the theatre as an attempt by Pompey to restore his lost popularity, but the building must have occupied several years before Pompey found himself in his current position. The episode of the elephants is recounted by Pliny (*NH* 8.20); Dio (39.38.2).
22. Leach (1978, 148) says that Pompey and Crassus were not like Sulla and made no attempt to control the elections for 54, which perhaps means that Pompey was prepared to allow the normal government machinery to run. See also Seager (1979, 132-3); Gruen (1974, 141-50) on the general lack of control of the elections by the coalition; see especially Gruen (1974, 148-51; 451) where he says that conventional politics were allowed to return by the coalition, and that none of the three could manipulate the elections to their taste in the 50s, unless they all acted in concert.
23. On Pompey governing the Spanish provinces while still in Rome, see Seager (1979, 132 n.42) who says that this system when regularised formed the basis of Augustus' governmental scheme, and that the ancient authors understood the position perfectly, explaining that Crassus held Syria, Caesar held Gaul and Pompey the city of Rome. See also Leach (1978, 146); Greenhalgh (1981, 62). Dio (39.39.4) says that Pompey used the excuse that the control of the corn supply kept him near Rome. Syme (1939, 32) points out that three men held the most important provinces and most of the armed forces, amounting to about 20 legions between them.
24. Domitius attacked Caesar, Crassus and Gabinius as soon as he was in office (Seager 1979, 133). See Cicero (*Ad Fam.* 5.8.1); Dio (39.60.3). Gruen (1974, 148 n.115) says that Appius Claudius had an agenda of his own, and was not acting on behalf of the coalition, but according to Syme (1939, 38) neither Domitius not Appius was strong enough to do any harm to Pompey. Domitius also attacked Gabinius, who had restored Ptolemy Auletes to the throne of Egypt on the orders of Pompey, whereas foreign policy ought to have been the prerogative of the Senate (Leach 1978, 148); see also Dio (39.55.3). As Siani-Davies (1997, 337) points out the attack on Gabinius was really aimed at Pompey, who had perhaps underestimated the strength of the opposition to his preponderant influence in Egyptian affairs. Gruen (1974, 330) describes how 13 adherents of the members of the coalition were prosecuted in the two years following the trial of Balbus; most were acquitted. On Messius see Gruen (1974, 109; 316); Cicero (*Ad Att.* 4.15.9), and on Vatinius see Gruen (1974, 317); Cicero (*QF* 2.15.3; 3.9.5; *Ad Att.* 11.5.4; 11.9.2; *Ad Fam.* 5.9); Plutarch (*Cicero* 26).
25. The delay in holding the elections for the consulship of 53 was caused by the scandalous bribery that attended canvassing, but it has been interpreted as deliberate obstructionism on the part of Pompey in order to create a situation in which he could be called upon to save the state; Gruen (1974, 149 n.20) disagrees with this theory. The situation has also been thought to indicate the beginning of a split between Caesar and Pompey, but Seager (1979, 134-6) refutes the idea. Cicero (*Ad Att.* 4.18; 4.19) mentions that rumours of a Dictatorship were circulating in 54. See also Greenhalgh (1981, 64-5).
26. Cicero did not prosecute Gabinius because he felt that this would incur the wrath of Pompey and perhaps precipitate an alliance with Clodius (Seager 1974, 138 n.87; Greenhalgh 1981, 67-8). He spoke as witness for the prosecution, but not very forcefully. In letters to Atticus (*Ad Att.* 4.18; 4.19) he says that Gabinius was helped in the first trials because there was talk of a Dictatorship for Pompey, so the jurors were frightened to do anything other than acquit. When the trial for *repetundae* came up, Pompey forced him to defend Gabinius. On the various trials see Fantham (1975); Gruen (1974, 322-

8); Seager (1979, 136-8). Syme (1939, 66-7) and Gruen (1974, 143) point out that Gabinius' character was blackened by Cicero, but in reality Gabinius had been responsible for salutary legislation for the defence of provincials, and had demonstrated genuine interest in administrative and constitutional reform. Syme (1939, 67 n.2) says that Gabinius was sacrificed to the *publicani*, and that Pompey was not sincere about having Cicero defend Gabinius,; he could have saved him if he had so wished, but preferred to conciliate the financial lobbies at Rome. See also Dio (39.55.6; 39.62-63) who suggests that the condemnation of Gabinius was a surprise to Pompey.

27. For the death of Julia see Plutarch (*Pompey* 53; *Caesar* 23); Suetonius (*DJ* 26.1); Velleius Paterculus (2.47.2). Cicero (*QF* 3.1.17) places the death in September, and Dio (39.64.1) dates it to the same time as the trials of Gabinius; see Seager (1979, 138-9). Julia had formed a strong bond between Caesar and Pompey (Dio 41.6; Valerius Maximus 4.6.4); Syme (1939, 38) says that the potential split between Caesar and Pompey because of the deaths of Julia and then Crassus was not realised; Gruen (1974, 450-1) who points out that the two men continued to co-operate politically until well into the year 50.
28. Rumours of a Dictatorship had been circulating since the delayed elections of 54, and Pompey's cousin Lucilius Hirrus proclaimed that he was ready to introduce a bill; see Cicero (*QF* 3.8); Seager (1979, 139). Greenhalgh (1981, 72; 279) dates the episode of Hirrus well into the year 53, envisaging that Pompey was absent from Rome while dealing with the administration of the corn supply, and Hirrus, helped by the tribune Vinicianus, devised the bill to make Pompey Dictator. His friends denied that he wanted to be made Dictator, but when he returned to Rome he presided over the elections, presumably with authorisation from the Senate.
29. On the expedition and the death of Crassus see Plutarch (*Crassus* 17-33); see also Plutarch (*Pompey* 53; *Caesar* 28); Appian (*BC* 2.28.66); Dio (40.27); Velleius Paterculus (2.46.4). Gruen (1974, 453-4) detects no evidence of the slightest rift between Caesar and Pompey after the death of Crassus, even though some of the clients of Crassus went over to Caesar; Pompey was preoccupied with the next elections, and especially the need to block the candidacy of Milo. Seager (1979, 140-1) says that the danger of a split between the remaining members of the coalition was increased by the death of Crassus, even though it was not an immediate cause of the civil war.
30. The only source for the marriage offer that Caesar made to bind Pompey more closely to him is Suetonius (*DJ* 27). The date when the offer may have been made is not known, and Suetonius does not provide a chronological context. Gruen (1974, 453) places it in 53 perhaps just after the death of Crassus, but others argue that it was in 52. Gruen also points out (1974, 453 n.18) that the refusal of the offer did not offend Caesar, and that having made his son-in-law Pompey the chief beneficiary of his will, he did not alter the will until just before the outbreak of the civil war; see Suetonius (*DJ* 83.1) who says that from his first consulship until the outbreak of the civil war, it was Caesar's custom to name Pompey as his heir and to have this read out to the soldiers, but in his last will he named Octavian, Lucius Pinarius and Quintus Pedius. Seager (1979, 141) suggests that when Pompey refused Caesar's marriage alliance he may have considered that it would have been a waste of their dynastic resources, and that it would have been better to ally themselves with other families to spread their influence; but the opposition would have viewed Pompey's refusal as a step in their direction.
31. Dio (40.46.3) and Asconius (48) attest to the violence in 53 connected with the candidates for the magistracies of 52. Pompey joined forces with Munatius Plancus to block the appointment of an *interrex*: see Seager (1979, 142). Greenhalgh (1982, 74-5) places the marriage offer made by Caesar in this context, because in addition to his struggles to conquer Gaul at this point Caesar had many enemies in Rome as well, and Pompey was becoming stronger by the minute.

32. For the whole episode of Clodius' death and his impromptu funeral see Dio (40.48-9); Appian (*BC* 2.21.75-7); Asconius (31-2). Cicero (*pro Milone* 91) argued that Clodius set an ambush for Milo, so he fought in self-defence. See Seager (1979, 142-3) and Greenhalgh (1981, 75-7) on Milo's popularity after the Senate House was burned, and the rescue of Lepidus by his gangs. Cicero, Cato, and the tribune Caelius supported Milo, against the opposition represented by the tribunes Plancus and Pompeius Rufus (Seager 1979, 145; Greenhalgh 1981, 78). The *senatus consultum ultimum* is attested by Cicero (*pro Milone* 13; 61; 67; 70); Asconius (34) and Dio (40.49). The split between Milo and Pompey was complete; according to Cicero (*pro Milone* 65f) the tribunes Plancus and Pompeius Rufus asked Pompey if he had heard rumours that Milo was plotting against him, and he affirmed that he had. He refused to see Milo when he asked for an interview (Asconius 35). Caesar (*BG* 7.1.1) heard of the Senate's decree when he returned to Italy from his campaign in Gaul in 52, and immediately took advantage of the authorisation to recruit soldiers in Cisalpine Gaul. Pompey increased his bodyguard and lived in the gardens of his house, encamped with his soldiers whom he had summoned to Rome (Syme 1939, 39). Seager (1979, 145) says that Pompey acted as if Milo was about to assassinate him; whether it was a real danger or feigned to cast suspicion on Milo is not clear, but as Greenhalgh points out (1981, 79) Pompey did not need Milo now that Clodius had been eliminated.
33. For the clamouring of the people to make Pompey Dictator, and the suggestion of Bibulus that he should be consul without a colleague see Plutarch (*Pompey* 54; *Caesar* 28; *Cato* 47); Dio (40.50.3-4); Appian (*BC* 2.23.84); Velleius Paterculus (2.47.3); Suetonius (*DJ* 26.1). Plutarch and Appian both hint that Pompey prolonged the disorder in order to be made Dictator (Greenhalgh 1981, 79). Cato said in the Senate that no one except Pompey could govern the state (Greenhalgh 1981, 80); Seager (1979, 144) comments that it must have been gratifying to Pompey to see Bibulus and Cato humble themselves. When he was made sole consul, Pompey broke the regulation that there should be a 10 year gap between consulships (Greenhalgh 1981, 279). Seager (1979, 144 n.22) discusses the theory of Appian (*BC* 2.23.84) that Bibulus proposed the consulate rather than a Dictatorship because Pompey would be subject to tribunician veto and called to account at the end of his term of office, and points out that in 52 Pompey's power should not be underestimated.
34. See Gruen (1974, 150-5) for Pompey's sole consulship in general. Greenhalgh (1981, 81-2; 279) outlines the legislation that Pompey immediately pushed through, designed to streamline procedure and make it clear that justice must be seen to be done; see Plutarch (*Pompey* 55); Appian (*BC* 2.23.87); Dio (40.52.1; 40.55.2). Syme (1939, 39) says that it was not to be expected that Pompey would adhere to the letter or the spirit of his own legislation; Tacitus (*Annals* 3.28) is more laconic, describing Pompey as the maker and breaker of his own laws.
35. On the trial of Milo and Cicero's role see Plutarch (*Pompey* 55); Appian (*BC* 2.24.90-3); Dio (40.51.3; 40.53.1). Greenhalgh (1981, 86) points out that Cicero was nervous not only because of Clodius' gangs shouting abuse, and the presence of Pompey's soldiers, but also because he realised that Pompey did not really want to see Milo acquitted. On the other hand Berry (1993, 503) suggests that since Pompey could have executed Milo after the *senatus consultum ultimum* was passed, he presumably thought that he was innocent. In order to protect Cicero, Pompey gave him a bodyguard (Cicero *Ad Fam*.3.10).Seager (1979, 146-7) points out that in further trials Milo's associates were acquitted, while Clodius' friends were condemned, and when Metellus Scipio and Hypsaeus were accused, Pompey somehow arranged for their acquittal. Greenhalgh (1981, 88) recounts how Pompey invited all the jurors to dinner and made it clear that he supported Metellus, and no charges were actually made against him.

36. The ancient sources differ on the extension of Pompey's Spanish command. Plutarch (*Pompey* 55) says that Pompey was voted 1000 talents for the maintenance of his army, and that Spanish command was extended for a further four years, which Greenhalgh (1981, 280) says is unlikely, since other sources give the more normal five years; see Dio (40.44.2; 40.56.2). Appian (*BC* 2.24.92) says that Pompey was voted two more legions, and Plutarch (*Caesar* 28.8) erroneously adds Africa to Pompey's command. On Pompey's marriage to the daughter of Metellus Scipio see Plutarch (*Pompey* 55) who places the event after Pompey's entry to the city as consul, but the date is not certain; see also Greenhalgh (1981, 74; 88); Seager (1979, 146-7). On the law exempting Caesar from personal attendance at the elections see Dio (40.51) who says that Pompey arranged this law through the tribunes; he also implies that Pompey did not want Caesar as a consular colleague. Suetonius (*DJ* 26.1) explains that Caesar wanted to stand for the consulship *in absentia* so as to avoid having to leave the province prematurely and without finishing the war. See also Appian (*BC* 2.25.96). Seager (1979, 147-8) points out that Caesar planned well ahead for special dispensation that would allow him to remain in Gaul while also standing for election, and Gruen (1974, 455) champions Pompey who worked strenuously to pass the law granting Caesar special dispensation. Cicero met Caesar at Ravenna in the winter of 53-2 and promised to use his influence on Caelius, tribune elect for 52; but although he endorsed the bill at the time, he later said that he did not support it (Gruen 1974, 455 n.25; Cicero *Ad Att.* 7.1;.7.3; 7.6; 8.3). The *lex Pompeia de iure magistratuum* is described by Dio (40.56); Suetonius (*DJ* 28); Cicero (*Ad Att.* 8.3), who says that Pompey confirmed the law of 10 tribunes in his statute. Seager (1979, 148-9) says that the codicil that Pompey added would have no validity in law. Gruen (1974, 456-7) dismisses those historians who suggest that Pompey was forgetful or did not draft the bill carefully enough, since he was hardly likely to forget that he had fought very hard for Caesar's dispensation, and the drafting of the bill would be a joint effort and subject to close scrutiny, although even then loopholes could appear. There was no intention to harm Caesar in this law.
37. The *lex de provinciis* stipulating that there should be a five year gap between magistracy and provincial command was proposed in 53 (Dio 40.46) but not drafted until 52 (Dio 40.56). Caesar (*BC* 1.85) interpreted the law as hostile in intent, but as Greenhalgh (1981, 280) points out this is retrospective justification for his actions in the civil war, and does not count as evidence for Caesar's opinion in 52. Seager (1979, 148) says that the law was in line with the attempts to reduce bribery at elections, since candidates could not then recoup losses so quickly or easily, but the unfortunate result of the application of the law was that it reduced the one year's grace that would have attended normal procedure. Stockton (1975) says that Caesar must have known that whoever was appointed to succeed him in Gaul was bound to be an enemy, and that it is unlikely that Pompey was scheming so pettily to remove him by means of the law on the provinces.
38. Pompey held the elections just after he took Metellus Scipio as his colleague, and Marcus Marcellus and Sulpicius Rufus were elected consuls. On taking up office Marcellus attacked Caesar, saying that the war in Gaul was over, so there was no further need for Caesar to remain in office, though as Seager (1979, 150) points out the *lex Pompeia Licinia* granting Caesar's extended command could not yet have expired; see Caesar (*BG* 8.53.1). (Greenhalgh 1981, 94-5) says that the terminal date was almost certainly 1 March 50. Marcellus claimed that the law on magistracies had annulled the law of the 10 tribunes, and Pompey replied to this charge in the Senate (Dio 40.59; Suetonius *DJ* 28). Marcellus then proposed that the colonists of Novum Comum should have their citizenship retracted, and to prove the point he flogged one of the men from the colony (Dio 40.59; Suetonius *DJ* 28.3; Plutarch *Caesar* 29; Appian *BC* 2.26.98; Cicero *Ad Att.* 5.2.3; 5.11.2). Caelius reported to Cicero (*Ad Fam.* 8.4) that

Curio had been elected as tribune, and that a debate on Caesar's provinces was due to come up in the Senate in August. In another letter (*Ad Fam.* 8.9) Caelius reported that the debate was postponed, and that Metellus Scipio proposed there should be no discussion until 1 March 50, when there should be nothing else on the agenda. Seager (1979, 152) suggests that Pompey was being fair and reasonable since the extension of Caesar's command would have run out by then.

39. Gruen (1974, 464-5) says that Pompey was playing a difficult game in 51, not wanting to break with Caesar but still hoping for pre-eminence. The Parthian problem was raised from time to time, and some suggested that Pompey should be given the command, while others proposed that Caesar should be sent (Caelius *Ad Fam.* 8.10.2). In September 51 Cicero wrote to Atticus from his province, explaining that the Parthians had crossed the Euphrates, and expressing the opinion that Pompey could not possibly be sent because of the situation in Rome (*Ad Att.* 5.18); early in 50 Cicero thought that Pompey would take the command (*Ad Att.* 6.1).When Pompey went to Ariminum he could have had some contact with Caesar (Gruen 1974, 467), possibly to find out for himself if the Gallic campaign was concluded and how much time Caesar would need to finalise the administrative details. Caelius (*Ad Fam.* 8.9.5) illustrated the sort of questions that were being asked when he reports that Pompey said that he would not agree to Caesar continuing to hold his provincial command and his armies while consul. According to Caelius when Pompey gave the answer 'What if my son should beat me with a stick?' he said it with the utmost gentleness; see Seager (1979, 153) and Greenhalgh (1981, 106-7). Gruen (1974, 469-70) suggests that Caesar was prepared to wait and see what happened on 1 March 50, and if the verdict was unfavourable he would then find some means of prolonging his command.
40. For Curio's first proposals in the Senate see Caelius (*Ad Fam.* 8.6; 8.10); Dio (40.61-2); Appian (*BC* 2.27). Gruen (1974, 473) points out that the programmes for road building and the division of the Campanian lands were all stock tools for demagogues. The proposed intercalary month was seen as a device to help Caesar to remain in his province for longer, but on the other hand some thought that it was because this idea was refused that Curio changed sides and went over to Caesar; see Caelius (*Ad Fam.* 8.11); Dio (40.62.1); Greenhalgh (1981, 283); Seager (1979, 155). For Curio's earlier hostility to Caesar see Cicero (*Ad Att.* 2.18; 2.19); Suetonius (*DJ* 50). The ancient authors thought that Curio had been bribed by Caesar; see Dio (40.40.2); Plutarch (*Pompey* 58.1; *Caesar* 29.2-3); Appian (*BC* 2.26). Gruen (1974, 473) disagrees that Caesar had bought Curio, arguing that Curio acted independently, determined to drive a wedge between Pompey and Caesar. Pompey had lost some of his popularity because he had curbed the bribery that attended elections (Appian *BC* 2.27). Marcellus proposed that Caesar should be replaced as governor, and Curio responded with the proposal that both Pompey and Caesar should give up their commands simultaneously; Cicero (*Ad Att.* 5.20.7); Appian (*BC* 2.27); Suetonius (*DJ* 29); Plutarch (*Pompey* 58; *Caesar* 30); Dio (40.62.3); Velleius Paterculus (2.48.2).
41. On Paullus see Caelius (*Ad Fam.* 8.4); Cicero (*Ad Att.* 6.3); Appian (*BC* 2.26); Plutarch (*Pompey* 58.1; *Caesar* 29.2-3); Suetonius (*DJ* 29.1). Caelius (*Ad Fam.* 8.11.3) reports the proposal made by Pompey to extend Caesar's command until 13 November; Seager (1979, 155-6) says that it is impossible to decide upon the chronology of Curio's proposals and this move by Pompey, and that although the suggestion would give Caesar the opportunity to retain his command and also stand for the consulship, he would be dependent upon Pompey's goodwill and would owe everything to him. The fact that Curio blocked the proposal suggests to Seager that Caesar had already decide that he would not be placed in that position. Seager (1979, 156) and Greenhalgh (1981, 112) consider that Pompey was more than fair to Caesar. On the other hand Gelzer (1968, 181) says that the

offer was made by Pompey in the knowledge that it would be no help to Caesar, since it would leave him disarmed all through 49.

42. On Pompey's illness, the prayers for his recovery and the ecstatic demonstrations when he did recover, see Cicero (*Ad Att.* 6.3); at a later date Cicero (*Ad Att.* 8.16) retrospectively judged the ardent prayers a sham. See also Dio (41.6.3); Appian (*BC* 2.28); Velleius Paterculus (2.48.2). Plutarch (*Pompey* 57) reports that the effect on Pompey after the rejoicing at his recovery was to make him think that the population was solidly behind him, and because of this he boasted that he had only to stamp his foot and troops would rise up in Italy; as Seager expresses it (1979, 157) Pompey thought that all those who had turned out to meet him on the way back to Rome would also turn out to fight for him. Appian (*BC* 2.28) describes the letter that Pompey wrote to the Senate offering to give up his command, which Greenhalgh (1981, 114-5) thinks was a genuine attempt to defuse the situation.
43. Greenhalgh (1981, 106-7; 283) and Seager (1979, 158) detect a hardening of attitude in Pompey, with the result that until 1 March 50 he would not consider the appointment of a successor to Caesar but after that date he would not hesitate, and would not tolerate Caesar as consul while also in command of an army. Caelius' letters to Cicero change their tone on this score (*Ad Fam.* 8.13; 8.14); for the first time he thinks war is coming, and the only way to avoid it would be to send either Caesar or Pompey to Parthia.
44. For the recall of the legions for the projected Parthian war, and Pompey's contribution of the legion he had lent to Caesar, see Appian (*BC* 2.29); Plutarch (*Pompey* 56.3; 57.4; *Caesar* 29). Pompey kept the two legions in Italy near Rome, which Cicero (*Ad Att.* 7.13) later judged to have been a ruse. Caesar was more generous when he said that it was Marcellus who detained them (*BG* 8.54-5; *BC* 1.9). According to Plutarch (*Pompey* 58) it was Curio who proposed that Caesar should give up his command, but Appian (*BC* 2.30.11) records that it was Marcellus; Seager (1979, 158-9) believes that Appian is more reliable. Marcellus' action in putting a sword in Pompey's hands is described by Plutarch (*Pompey* 59); Appian (*BC* 2.31); Dio (40.64.4; 40.66.1). Caesar (*BG* 8.52-5) naturally reports the build-up to the war rather differently, saying that the armed tyranny of Pompey was causing alarm in the Forum, and that the retention of the two legions that were destined for the Parthian war made it clear that the intentions of the Senate towards Caesar were unfriendly. Greenhalgh (1981, 284) doubts that Pompey would have been willing to accept the proposed compromise that Caesar should keep one legion with either Illyricum or Cisalpine Gaul, especially since Cicero reports that Pompey did not seem to desire peace and thought that Caesar would subvert the constitution even if he did not have an army at his back (*Ad Att.* 7.3; 7.4; 7.8). Pompey related to Cicero the virulent verbal attack on him by Antony, adding that if Caesar's subordinates spoke in such a fashion, how much worse would it be if Caesar himself were in command in the Senate (Cicero *Ad Att.* 7.8.5)?
45. Caesar's letter to the Senate and the proposals it contained are described by Caesar himself (*BC* 1.1); Plutarch (*Pompey* 59; *Caesar* 30); Appian (*BC* 2.32); Dio (41.1). Cicero (*Ad Att.* 7.9) outlines the alternatives open to the Senate and Pompey in dealing with Caesar. In his account of the lead up to the civil war, Caesar (*BC* 1.2-6) does not blame Pompey specifically for the refusal to compromise; he describes how, after the proposal of Metellus Scipio was vetoed by Antony and Cassius, Pompey summoned the Senate to a meeting with him, but Lentulus and Cato still would not back down. See also Greenhalgh (1981, 285); Seager (1979, 161-2). Plutarch (*Caesar* 31) says that the expulsion from the Senate of Antony and Cassius gave Caesar the excuse to make war, but as Greenhalgh points out (1981, 285) it was not strictly the sacrosanctity of tribunes that Caesar made his rallying cry, but the treatment of men of high rank. According to Appian (*BC* 2.33) Caesar's

army was declared *hostis*, an enemy of the state, while Pompey's was the protector. For the assembly of the Thirteenth legion and Caesar's speech to the soldiers, in which he said that Pompey had been led astray by his friends, see Caesar (*BC* 7-9).

6 Civil war

1. Greenhalgh (1981, 136-7) analyses Caesar's choices, and describes his infiltration of Ariminum after crossing the Rubicon; Gelzer (1968, 196) says that the military success of the invasion of Italy was offset by 'the undesirable consequence that the legitimate government fled' before Caesar. In all other respects Caesar wished to portray Pompey as the main cause of the war because of his reluctance to tolerate an equal. Seager (1979, 164-5) describes Caesar's sudden advance and says that it took Pompey by surprise, because he thought he would have more time to prepare. For an examination of why Pompey decided to fight see Pocock (1959); Wylie (1992b). Appian (*BC* 2.34) tells the story of Favonius, which Greenhalgh (1981, 138) suggests is more imaginary than true. Caesar himself (*BC* 1.1-10) is careful to outline all the wrongs done to him and the near illegality of the actions of the Pompeians in order to justify his invasion of Italy. He does not make any mention of the Rubicon. As Gelzer (1968, 193 n.3) points out, the story is elaborated in the later sources (Appian (*BC* 2.34; Plutarch *Pompey* 60; *Caesar* 32; Suetonius *DJ* 31). His quotation as he crossed the Rubicon, 'Let the dice fly high', is from the Greek poet Menander; although Caesar does not relay any details himself, the historian Asinius Pollio was among his followers, and Gelzer suggests that his work is the source used by the later historians.
2. Seager (1979, 166) maintains that Pompey intended to defend Rome but was forced to change his mind by the rapidity of Caesar's invasion. Dio (41.5.1; 41.6.1) says that the speed of Caesar's advance, the general hostility to war, and the lack of preparation contributed to Pompey's decision to leave the city. Greenhalgh (1981, 138-9; 141; 145) takes the opposite view, that Pompey always intended to abandon Rome and Italy, pointing out that Pompey had put the two legions that he drew from Caesar's Gallic army into winter quarters in Apulia, whereas if he had intended to defend Rome he would have kept them in readiness at Capua. Cicero's attitude varied between acceptance and reluctance for the abandonment of Rome; Seager (1979, 165) evaluates the references that Cicero made to the possibility of Pompey's withdrawal from Rome; in October 50 (*Ad Att.* 6.8) Cicero may have thought that Pompey would leave Rome for Spain, but later in December he spoke with Ampius Balbus and Pompey himself, discussed the possibility of leaving Rome and Italy, and then wrote to Atticus outlining the alternative strategies that were open to Pompey (*Ad Fam.* 2.16; *Ad Att.* 7.8). See also Cicero (*Ad Att.* 7.13; 7.14; 7.21); Plutarch (*Pompey* 59); Appian (*BC* 2.36).
3. Pompey left for Capua on 17 January, with the warning that all who did not follow him would be regarded as enemies (Caesar *BC* 1.14; Plutarch *Pompey* 60; *Caesar* 33; Dio 41.6.1; Appian *BC* 2.37; Suetonius *DJ* 75.1). According to Plutarch, the majority of people followed Pompey because they liked him, not necessarily because they wanted to fight for freedom. The appointment of magistrates is laconically described by Caesar (*BC* 1.6) who highlights the irregularity of the proceedings. See also Seager (1979, 162); Greenhalgh (1981, 134-5); Dio (41.3.3); Appian (*BC* 2.34).
4. Greenhalgh (1981, 140-1) says that if Pompey remained in Rome to face Caesar, the senators with him would probably decide to save their property by falling in with Caesar. Cicero reported to Atticus that it was almost certain that Labienus had deserted Caesar, and that it served no purpose

because there was no government to meet with (*Ad Att.* 7.12); and then when he knew that the rumour was true, he said that he thought Labienus a hero (*Ad Att.* 7.13); see also Tyrrell (1972); Greenhalgh (1981, 144).

5. The negotiations proposed by the two sides and relayed back and forth by Lucius Caesar and Roscius can be viewed in different lights. Seager (1979, 167-8) suggests that both sides were sincere in their offers of peace, and Caesar would have been happy if the terms that he offered had been accepted. Greenhalgh (1981, 147-8) describes the situation as more of an exercise in delaying tactics, without sincerity on either side, pointing out the discrepancy between the accounts of Caesar and Cicero. Caesar (*BC* 1.9) says that his offer was for both sides to abandon their armies, Pompey to go to Spain, arms to be laid down in Italy, and elections to be held. Then he reports (*BC* 1.10) that the Pompeian reply was that he should give up Ariminum and return to Gaul, a compromise that he would not make, because it involved giving up what he had gained; he complained of the unfairness of the demands (*BC* 1.11). Cicero (*Ad Att.* 7.14) reports that Caesar's terms were accepted, with the proviso that he should abandon the cities that he had occupied outside his province; then the government would return to Rome. Greenhalgh (1981, 147-8) says that Pompey felt safe in calling Caesar's bluff, and that neither of them had any intention of abiding by the peace terms they proposed.
6. Cicero began to realise after the fall of Picenum that Italy would have to be abandoned (*Ad Att.* 7.20; 7.21). On the Domitius episode see Burns (1966). Seager (1979, 169-71) says that Pompey would not have confided in Domitius any earlier than he had to his plans to leave Italy, but he did make it clear enough in the end. For Pompey's letters to Domitius see Cicero (*Ad Att.* 8.11a; 8.12b; 8.12c; 8.12d), reproduced in Greenhalgh (1981, 150-7). See also Caesar (*BC* 1.19).
7. Dio (41.5.1; 41.6.1) says that Pompey changed his plan when he heard that Caesar was advancing on Rome, because he had not enough troops to resist, and there was a lack of popular support for the war. Seager (1979, 166) takes this to mean that Pompey had intended to defend Rome but had to change his mind. See also Appian (*BC* 2.36). Seager also thinks (1979, 172) that Domitius stubbornly remained at Corfinium in the hope that he could blackmail Pompey into making a stand in Italy. By 17 January Cicero knew that Pompey was going to evacuate Italy, and the idea may have been discussed as a contingency plan in December. Greenhalgh (1981,133; 135-6; 138) thinks that Pompey's plan was always to evacuate Italy and fight elsewhere, but it was not good policy while trying to recruit soldiers to advertise this plan; Cicero could not conceive of leaving Italy, and when he did think of it, he imagined that Pompey would go to Spain. Seager (1979, 177) refers to the quotation attributed to Pompey that if Sulla could do it, then he could, arguing that Pompey was talking purely on military matters; see Cicero (*Ad Att.* 8.11; 9.7; 9.10).
8. See Greenhalgh (1981, 161) on Magius; Caesar (*BC* 1.26) expresses surprise when he reached Brundisium that Pompey had not sent Magius back to him with a reply to his message, but according to Cicero (*Ad Att.* 9.13), Pompey had in fact sent a reply via Magius. Caesar (*BC* 1.24-5) reports the capture of Magius, Pompey's *praefectus fabrum*, or chief engineer, and Cicero (*Ad Att.* 9.7c) includes a copy of a letter from Caesar to Oppius and Cornelius Balbus referring to the capture and release of Magius and another of Pompey's prefects, saying that 'if they have any gratitude they should exhort Pompey to prefer my friendship to that of the men who were his bitterest enemies both to him and to me'. On Pompey and Caesar at Brundisium see Greenhalgh (1981, 163-7); Seager (1979, 174-6). Caesar (*BC* 1.24-6) describes the scene at Brundisium, the siege works that he built and Pompey's response to them; he claims that he did not know whether Pompey intend-

ed to hold Brundisium indefinitely, or whether he wished to control the Adriatic and carry on the war from Greece. In a later passage, when describing how Pompey embarked and left Brundisium, Caesar adds (*BC* 1.27) that he was unsure whether Pompey was alarmed by the siege works, or left because he had planned to do so from the beginning of the war. Seager (1979, 174) dismisses this as propaganda, since Pompey was only waiting for the return of his ships.

9. After Pompey left Italy, Caesar says (*BC* 1.29) that he approved the plan to collect ships so as to follow him, but Pompey had gathered together so many that there were none to be had, and it would take too long to build more. Sea power was crucial to the war (Greenhalgh 1981, 168). Cicero reported to Atticus (*Ad Att.* 10.8) that Pompey's first care had always been for the fleet, and he considered that whoever controlled the sea would win the war. Sea power was also necessary for the control of the corn produce from Sardinia, Sicily and Africa, a factor which was recognised by both Pompey and Caesar; but Pompey could not persuade his legates to go out to gain the relevant provinces. He asked Cicero and then Cato to go to Sicily, but neither would co-operate, and by the time that Cato decided to stop lingering in Rome, waiting upon events, it was too late (Greenhalgh 1981, 166); see also Plutarch (*Caesar* 35); Dio (41.18); Appian (*BC* 2.40); Cicero (*Ad Att.* 9.2a). Caesar sent Quintus Valerius Orca to Sardinia with one legion and Curio to Sicily (*BC* 1.30); on Curio in Sicily see Greenhalgh (1981, 171-2); Gelzer (1968, 212); on Curio in Africa see Greenhalgh (1981, 187-9); Gelzer (1968, 212; 220); Caesar (*BC* 2.33-44); Appian (*BC* 2.44-6); Dio (41.41).
10. Dio (41.15) describes the meeting of the Senate called by the tribunes Antony and Cassius, which would be outside the city walls since Caesar was still in command of troops; see Gelzer (1968, 208-9). On the refusal of Massilia to open its gates, see Caesar (*BC* 1.33-6); Dio (41.19); Velleius Paterculus (2.50). Gaius Antonius was sent to Illyricum with troops to keep it open for Caesar to gain a foothold there if necessary (Caesar *BC* 3.10; Appian *BC* 2.47; Dio 41.40); see also Greenhalgh (1981, 186); Gelzer (1968, 212).
11. On the war in Spain see Caesar (*BC* 1.37-87); Appian (*BC* 2.42-3); Dio (41.18-24); Plutarch (*Caesar* 36); see also Greenhalgh (1981, 172-85); Gelzer (1968, 212-19); Fuller (1965, 192-206).
12. On the naval actions of Decimus Brutus and Dolabella see Greenhalgh (1968, 202); Gelzer (1968, 219-20). Dio (41.35) records the mutiny of Caesar's troops. Before giving an account of the war in Greece, Caesar (*BC* 3.4-5) documents Pompey's build up of ships from his various clients, and the recruitment of troops, including Gnaeus Pompey's efforts if Egypt in recruiting the Gabinian soldiers.
13. Plutarch (*Pompey* 64) elaborates on Pompey's training activities, claiming that at 58 years old he put the younger men to shame. On Pompey's supreme command, see Seager (1979, 181), who points out that although this bestowal of power ought to have made life easier, in fact Pompey still had difficulty in putting his ideas into operation. Wylie (1992b, 558) speculates as to why Pompey did not ask for supreme command in the first instance. See also Greenhalgh (1981, 193-4), who includes Appian's version (*BC* 2.50) of the speech that Pompey made to his troops on the occasion of the award of supreme command; Plutarch (*Pompey* 66); Appian (*BC* 2.65); Velleius Paterculus (2.52.1).
14. Dio (41.43) describes how the Romans had two sets of magistrates for the year, because Caesar arranged the elections in Rome, and the Pompeians carried on as they were with the current consuls and praetors in promagistracies. But as Dio points out, the consuls and proconsuls had little influence, because the real power lay with Caesar and Pompey; see also Greenhalgh (1981, 192-3). On Caesar's rapid legislation before he left for Greece see Gelzer (1968, 220-1); Greenhalgh (1981, 195); Caesar (*BC* 3.1-2); Plutarch (*Caesar* 37). The corn dole was the most important issue; see Appian (*BC* 2.48; 2.54) on the distribution of corn to the people, and on Caesar's use of his war-

ships to guard the sea routes and ports of Sardinia and Sicily. On the debt problem see Cicero (*Ad Att.* 7.18; 9.9; 10.11); Dio (41.38).

15. For the beginning of the war in Greece see Caesar (*BC* 3.2); Dio (41.44); Plutarch (*Caesar* 37); Suetonius (*DJ* 58); Appian (*BC* 2.54); Velleius Paterculus (2.51). On the race for Dyrrachium see Greenhalgh (1981, 199-200); Gelzer (1968, 224-5); and on Bibulus' blockade see Gelzer (1968, 225); Caesar (*BC* 3.8). Caesar (*BC* 3.11-13) records how he captured Oricum and Apollonia.
16. The skirmishing between the Pompeians and Caesarians is inferred from a remark of Dio (41.47), where he records an unsuccessful attack by Pompey, but gives no details; it is possible that among other things Pompey was trying to cut Caesar's supply lines; see Gelzer (1968, 227); Greenhalgh (1981, 199-200). Once the two armies were encamped on the Apsus, Caesar (*BC* 3.13) says that he decided to winter there and wait for the rest of his troops to arrive under Antony.
17. When Caesar occupied a coastal strip to prevent the Pompeian fleet from getting fresh water, Bibulus and Libo tried to arrange a truce with him, but failed; see Caesar (*BC* 3.15-17). Caesar also records (*BC* 3.18) that he sent Vibullius to Pompey to try negotiation, but Pompey did not let him speak, and replied that he would not live by Caesar's will; see also Gelzer (1968, 223-6); Greenhalgh (1981, 200-1).
18. Camped near to each other the Pompeians troops began to arrange meetings but Labienus put a stop to it, saying that only the delivery of Caesar's head would end the war (Caesar *BC* 3.19). When Antony landed at Nymphaeum with Caesar's remaining troops, the Greeks warned him of Pompey's ambush; thus foiled, Pompey withdrew to Asparagium (Caesar *BC* 29-30). Greenhalgh (1981, 205-7; 289) debates the theories as to where Antony and Caesar joined forces.
19. Caesar describes (*BC* 3.45-7) how his main concern at Dyrrachium was to confine Pompey, while Pompey's was to occupy the widest possible circuit; and in exercising these two conflicting aims there were several small battles. For the blockade see Greenhalgh (1981, 211-28); Gelzer (1968, 230-1); Fuller (218-27).
20. The ancient sources record Pompey's problems with his officers and the squabbling among themselves; see Plutarch (*Pompey* 67; *Cicero* 38.5); Cicero (*Ad Fam.* 9.9); Appian (*BC* 2.67); Caesar (*BC* 3.82). One of the foremost problems was the suspicion that even if Caesar were defeated Pompey himself might turn into a Dictator and it would be necessary to rid the Roman world of him too; once the war was over Pompey would be superfluous; see Greenhalgh (1981, 229-30, 244); Seager (1979, 177).
21. Caesar tried to cut the water supply by blocking the streams around Pompey's camp (Caesar *BC* 3.49). By a ruse, Caesar was induced to try to take Dyrrachium; different details are recorded by Appian (*BC* 2.60) and Dio (41.50). Caesar (*BC* 3.52-3) describes the attempt to take Dyrrachium and the other battles around the perimeter of the siege works; see also Greenhalgh (1981, 216-8). For the story of the two Gauls who defected to Pompey with details of the unfinished fortifications, and the resultant successful attack, see Caesar (*BC* 3.59-71); Dio (41.51) Appian (*BC* 2.61); Greenhalgh (1981, 219-20). The judgement that there could have been a complete victory if the Pompeians had been led by a victor does not come from Caesar's account, but from Plutarch (*Caesar* 39) and Appian (*BC* 2.61). It is possible that Pompey did not follow up the successful attack because he expected that Caesar would capitulate; see Greenhalgh (1981, 225-6); Appian (*BC* 2.63).
22. The choices facing Pompey were to continue the policy of attrition in order to wear Caesar down, which would mean prolonging the war, as advocated by Afranius; or invasion of Italy, but there was reluctance to abandon Scipio; see Cicero (*Ad Fam.* 4.9); Plutarch (*Pompey* 66-7; *Caesar* 40); Appian (*BC* 2.65-6); Dio (41.52); Velleius Paterculus (2.52). Greenhalgh (1981, 246) notes that Pompey

sent his fleet to attack Sicily and to blockade Brundisium, as though invasion of Italy was on the agenda. On Gomphi and Larissa see Caesar (*BC* 3.80-1).

23. The ancient sources concur in suggesting that Pompey was prevailed upon by his associates to risk everything on one battle. Plutarch (*Pompey* 67) says that Pompey was too much concerned with his good reputation and did not want to seem disrespectful to those who advised him to fight. Appian (*BC* 2.67) considers that some were tired of the war and wanted a quick decision. Caesar (*BC* 3.82) notes that Pompey was accused of prolonging the war in order to enjoy his command; see also Seager (1979, 181-2) on the difficulties that Pompey faced over his policy of trying to wear Caesar down. Greenhalgh (1981, 245-6) points out that the corn was ripening, as Caesar records (*BC* 3.81), which would mean that Caesar's army would no longer be under threat of starvation, and therefore the policy of attrition would no longer work.
24. Caesar (*BC* 3.88-97) describes the battle of Pharsalus, but his account differs from that of Plutarch (*Pompey* 69) and Appian (*BC* 2.75), who derived their information from the historian Asinius Pollio, who was present at Pharsalus (Greenhalgh 1981, 248). See also Gwatkin (1956; 1957); Pelling (1973). On the question of whether Pompey intended to go to Parthia for help, Plutarch (*Pompey* 76) and Appian (*BC* 2.83) both insist that Pompey discussed three choices of where to turn, claiming that he did not want to go to Africa or Egypt because he did not trust king Juba or Ptolemy, but that his preference was for Parthia. Seager (1979, 185) says that the story should be accepted, though the embassy of Hirrus was more likely to have been undertaken to arrange peace and neutrality. Greenhalgh (1981, 260-1) concurs that the main mission of Hirrus would probably have been to protect Syria from attack, but he doubts that Pompey seriously intended to claim assistance from or go to Parthia. Dio (42.2) rejects the tale, and Greenhalgh (1981, 261) points out that the source for the story is more vindictively Caesarian than Caesar himself, since he does not mention it. On Pompey's death see Plutarch (*Pompey* 77); Dio (42.5); Caesar (*BC* 3.103).

7 Legacy

1. Syme (1939, 51) thought that if Pompey had defeated Caesar he would have been assassinated. Most authors agree that Pompey did not seek a Dictatorship or a military dominance; see Gruen (1974, 44-5; 66); Seager (1979, 187-8); Greenhalgh (1981, 268-9); Meier (1990, 60). Full of admiration for Pompey, Wylie (1990, 455-6) suggests that he was genuinely high-principled, and that he modelled himself on 'Aristotle's concept of the great souled man'. Sallust (*Historiae* 3.48.23) says that Pompey wanted to be accepted by the senators, and to be the best of them. Livy was full of praise for Pompey, but as Yavetz points out (1990, 34) it did not demand great courage, because it was not forbidden. Augustus distanced himself from Caesar the Dictator, and cultivated the legacy of Pompey (Raaflaub and Samons 1990, 446); Syme (1939, 317) says that the tone of literary culture in Augustan times was Pompeian, rather than Caesarian. According to Dio (56.34.2-3) Pompey's image was displayed at Augustus' funeral.
2. The resemblance of Pompey to Alexander began in his early youth, and was remarked upon when he was put on trial just after the death of his father. Pompey's friend and client Theophanes compared him to Alexander (*F Gr Hist.* no.188), as did Sallust (*Historiae* 3.88) and Plutarch (*Pompey* 2.1-2; 12.3; 13.5). See also Greenhalgh (1980, 11) for personal descriptions of Pompey, with reference to his hairstyle and facial characteristics that reminded people of portraits of Alexander.

3. Seager (1979, 188) sums up the anomalies in Pompey's career: he held two triumphs as an equestrian, he entered the Senate as consul, and he was awarded military commands while a private citizen.
4. Seager (1979, 188 n.28) suggests that Pompey provoked crises in order to provide himself with causes to fight for. Dio (40.46) says that the tribunes, Pompey's cousin Hirrus and Vinicianus, were ready to present a bill to make Pompey Dictator, but his friends said that he did not want the office. See Ridley (1983) on Pompey's powers in the 50s. On Augustus' powers and the government of the Empire see Eder (1990, 97-8; 106-7) who points out that in order to govern the provinces, Augustus appointed legates just as Pompey and Caesar had done, so that the method was not an alien concept. After 27 BC, the constitutional basis for Augustus' command was unique, since he was consul every year as well as holding a command over troops and provinces; for this Ridley (1983) does not construe Pompey's sole consulship as a valid precedent.
5. On Pompey as politician see Leach (1978, 211), who says that he was a strategist rather than a tactician, and Gruen, (1974, 45), who says that not only was Pompey the greatest general in Rome, but also the greatest politician. Greenhalgh (1980, 68) describes Pompey as a military man rather than a politician, and points out that during his first consulship, Pompey more or less retired from view once the tribunician bill was passed and the law courts were reformed.
6. See Gruen (1974, 62-3) and Anderson (1963) for Pompey's followers.
7. Velleius Paterculus (2.53.4) and Lucan (2.562) both point out that Pompey had risen as high as any man could without becoming a monarch, and Lucan (1.125) adds that Pompey would not tolerate an equal. Tacitus did not like Pompey; he called him the maker and breaker of his own laws (*Annals* 3.28), and described him as no better than Marius or Sulla, just more devious (*Histories* 2.38). Galsterer (1990) reviews the opinions of successive authors as to what extent Augustus was the direct heir of Pompey.

Bibliography

Abbreviations

AJP	*American Journal of Philology*
ANRW	*Aufsteig und Niedergang der Römischen Welt*
CAH	*Cambridge Ancient History*
C & M	*Classica et Mediaevalia*
CJ	*Classical Journal*
CP	*Classical Philology*
CQ	*Classical Quarterly*
CR	*Classical Review*
CW	*Classical World*
F Gr Hist	*Fragmente der Griechischer Historiker* ed. F. Jacoby
ILS	*Inscriptiones Latinae Selectae* ed. H. Dessau, Berlin 1892-1916
JRS	*Journal of Roman Studies*
MAAR	*Memoirs of the American Academy at Rome*
RhM	*Rheinisches Museum für Philologie*
TAPhA	*Transactions of the American Philological Association*

Ancient sources

Appian	*Bella Civilia*
Appian	*Mithridatica*
Asconius	
Aulus	*Noctes Atticae*
Cicero	*Ad Atticum*
	Ad Familiares
	Ad Quintum Fratrem
	Brutus
	De Imperio Gn. Pompeii
	In Verrem
	Philippics
	Pro Balbo
Frontinus	*Strategemata*
Livy	

Orosius
Pliny *Naturalis Historia*
Plutarch *Lives*
Sallust *Bellum Catilinae*
Sallust *Historiae*
Strabo
Suetonius *Twelve Caesars*
Valerius Maximus
Velleius Paterculus

Modern works

Adcock, F.E. 1932, 'The legal term of Caesar's governorship in Gaul', *CQ* 26, 14-26
Adcock, F.E. 1966, *Marcus Crassus, millionaire*. Cambridge
Ameling, W. 1994, 'Augustus and Agrippa: Bemerkungen zu P. Köln VI 249', *Chiron* 24, 1-28
Anderson, W. 1963, *Pompey, His Friends, and the Literature of the First Century BC*. Berkeley: University of California Press
Astbury, R. 1967, 'Varro and Pompey', *CQ* 17, 403-7
Badian, E. 1955, 'The date of Pompey's first triumph', *Hermes* 83, 107-18
Badian, E. 1958, *Foreign Clientelae 264-70BC*. Oxford
Badian, E. 1959, 'The early career of A. Gabinius (cos. 58 B.C.)', *Philologus*, 103, 87-99
Beard, M. and Crawford, M. 1985, *Rome in the Late Republic*. London: Duckworth
Bellemore, J. 1999, 'Josephus, Pompey, and the Jews', *Historia* 48, 95-118
Berry, D.H. 1993, 'Pompey's legal knowledge, or lack of it', *Historia* 42, 502-4
Broughton, T.R.S. 1951, *Magistrates of the Roman Republic*. Vol. 1. New York
Broughton, T.R.S. 1952, *Magistrates of the Roman Republic*. Vol. 2. New York
Broughton, T.R.S. 1986, *Magistrates of the Roman Republic*. Supplementary volume. New York
Brunt. P.A. 1962, 'The army and the land in the Roman Revolution', *JRS* 52, 69-86
Brunt, P.A. 1971, *Social Conflicts in the Roman Republic*. New York and London: W.W. Norton and Co.
Burns, A. 1966, 'Pompey's strategy and Domitius' stand at Corfinium', *Historia* 15, 74-95
Carney, T.F. 1961, 'The death of Sulla', *Acta Classica: Proceedings of the Classical Association of South Africa* 4
Cuff, P.J. 1958, 'The terminal date of Caesar's Gallic command', *Historia* 7, 445-71
Davison, J.A. 1930, 'Cicero and the *lex Gabinia*', *CR* 44, 224-5
de Souza, P. 1999, *Piracy in the Graeco-Roman World*. Cambridge University Press
Deutsch, M.E. 1924, 'Pompey's three triumphs', *CP* 19, 226-9
Drummond, A. 2000, 'Rullus and the Sullan *possessores*', *Klio* 82(1), 126-53
Eder, W. 1990, 'Augustus and the power of tradition: the Augustan Principate as binding link between Republic and Empire', in Raaflaub and Toher 1990, 71-122
Ehrenberg, V. 1953, '*Imperium maius* in the Roman Republic', *AJP* 74, 113-36
Elton, G.R. 1946, 'The terminal date of Caesar's Gallic proconsulate', *JRS* 36, 18-42
Fantham, E. 1975, 'The trials of Gabinius in 54 B.C.', *Historia* 24, 425ff
Fletcher, W.G. 1939, 'The Pontic cities of Pompey the Great', *TAPhA* 70, 17-29
Freeman, P.W. 1994, 'Pompey's eastern settlement: a matter of presentation', *Collection Latomus* 227, 143-79

Frisch, H. 1948, 'The first Catilinarian conspiracy: a study in historical conjecture', *C&M* 9, 10-36

Fritz, K. von, 1942, 'Pompey's policy before and after the outbreak of the civil war of 49 BC', *TAPhA* 73, 145-80

Galsterer, H. 1990, 'A man, a book, and a method: Sir Ronald Syme's *Roman Revolution* after fifty years', in Raaflaub and Toher 1990, 1-20

Gelzer, M. 1959, *Pompeius*. Munich: F. Bruckmann Verlag, 2nd ed.

Gelzer, M. 1968, *Caesar: politician and statesman*. Cambridge, Mass.

Grant, M. 1973, *The Jews in the Roman World*. London: Weidenfeld and Nicolson

Greenhalgh, P. 1980, *Pompey: the Roman Alexander*. London: Weidenfeld and Nicolson

Greenhalgh, P. 1981, *Pompey: the Republican Prince*. London: Weidenfeld and Nicolson

Gruen, E.S. 1966, 'P. Clodius: instrument or independent agent?', *Phoenix* 20, 120-30

Gruen, E.S. 1968, *Roman Politics and the Criminal Courts*. Cambridge, Mass.

Gruen, E.S. 1969, 'Pompey, the Roman aristocracy, and the conference of Luca', *Historia* 18, 71-108

Gruen, E.S. 1971, 'Pompey, Metellus Pius and the trials of 70-69 BC: the perils of schematism', *AJP* 92, 1-16

Gruen, E.S. 1974, *The Last Generation of the Roman Republic*. Berkeley: University of California Press

Gwatkin, W.E. 1956, 'Some reflections on the battle of Pharsalus', *TAPhA* 87, 109-24

Gwatkin, W.E. 1957, 'Pompey on the eve of Pharsalus', *CB* 33, 39-41

Hadas, M. 1930, *Sextus Pompey*. Columbia

Hill, D.K. 1944, 'The temple above Pompey's theater', *CJ* 360-5

Hillman, T.P. 1997, 'Pompeius in Africa and Sulla's order to demobilize', *Latomus* 56, 94-100

Jameson, S. 1970a, 'Pompey's *imperium* in 67: some constitutional fictions', *Historia* 19, 539-60

Jameson, S. 1970b, The intended date of Caesar's return from Gaul', *Latomus* 29, 638-60

Keaveney, A. 1982, *Sulla: the last Republican*.

Knight, D.W. 1968, 'Pompey's concern for pre-eminence after 60 B.C.', *Latomus* 27, 878-83

Lacey, W. K. 1966, *Augustus and the Principate: the evolution of the system*. Liverpool: Francis Cairns

Lacey, W.K. 1978, *Cicero and the End of the Roman Republic*. London

Lazenby, J.F. 1959, 'The conference of Luca and the Gallic War', *Latomus* 18, 67-76

Leach, J. 1978, *Pompey the Great*. London: Croom Helm

Lintott, A.W. 1967, 'P. Clodius Pulcher – Felix Catilina?', *Greece and Rome* 14, 157-69

Leach, J. 1978, *Pompey the Great*. London: Croom Helm

Loader, W.R. 1940, 'Pompey's command under the *lex Gabinia*', *CR* 134-6

Luibheid, C. 1970, 'The Luca conference', *CP* 65, 88-94

Marshall, B.A. 1973, 'Crassus and the command against Spartacus', *Athenaeum* 51, 109-21

Marshall, B.A. 1976, *Crassus: a political biography*. Amsterdam

Mattingly, H.B. 1975, 'The *consilium* of Cn. Pompeius Strabo in 89 BC', *Athenaeum* new series 53, 262ff

McDermott, W.C. 1977, '*Lex Pompeia de tribunicia potestate* (70 BC)', *CP* 72, 49-51

Meier, C. 1990, 'C.Caesar Divi filius and the formation of the Alternative in Rome', in Raaflaub and Toher 1990, 54-70

Mitchell, T.N. 1973, 'Cicero, Pompey, and the rise of the First Triumvirate', *Traditio* 29, 1-26

Pelling, C.B.R. 1973, 'Pharsalus', *Historia* 22, 249-59

Pocock, L.G. 1959, 'What made Pompeius fight in 49 B.C.?', *Greece and Rome* 6, 68-81

Raaflaub, K.A. and Samons, L.J. 1990, 'Opposition to Augustus', in Raaflaub and Toher 1990, 417-54

Raaflaub, K.A. and Toher, M. (eds.) 1990, *Between Republic and Empire: interpretations of Augustus and his Principate*. Berkeley: University of California Press

Reynolds, J. 1962, 'Cyrenaica, Pompey and Cn. Cornelius Lentulus Marcellinus', *JRS* 52, 95-

Rickman, G. 1980, *The Corn Supply of Ancient Rome.* Oxford: Clarendon Press

Ridley, R.T. 1983, 'Pompey's commands in the 50s: how cumulative?' *RhM* 126, 136-48

Robinson, O. F. 1997, *The Sources of Roman Law: problems and methods for ancient historians.* London: Routledge

Sanders, H.A. 1932, 'The so-called First Triumvirate', *MAAR* 10, 55-68

Sanford, E. M. 1939, 'The career of Aulus Gabinius', *TAPhA* 70, 64-92

Seager, R. 1964, 'The first Catilinarian conspiracy', *Historia* 13, 338-47

Seager, R. 1965, 'Clodius, Pompey, and the exile of Cicero', *Latomus* 24, 519-31

Seager, R. 1979, *Pompey: a political biography.* Oxford: Blackwell

Sherwin-White, A.N. 1956, 'Violence in Roman politics', *JRS* 46, 1-9

Sherwin-White, A.N. 1984, *Roman Foreign Policy in the East, 168 BC. to AD 1.* London : Duckworth

Shotter, D. 1994, *The Fall of the Roman Republic.* Lancaster Pamphlets Series. London: Routledge

Siani-Davies, M. 1997, 'Ptolemy XII Auletes and the Romans', *Historia* 46, 306-40

Smith, R.E. 1957, 'The Lex Plotia Agraria and Pompey's Spanish veterans', *CQ* 51, 82-

Spann, P.O. 1987, *Quintus Sertorius and the legacy of Sulla.* University of Arkansas Press

Stevens, C.E. 1938, 'The terminal date of Caesar's command', *AJP* 1938, 169-208

Stocker, A.F. 1961, 'The *legis dies* of Caesar's command in Gaul', *CJ* 56, 242-8

Stockton, D.L. 1971, *Cicero: a political biography.* London

Stockton, D.L. 1973, 'The first consulship of Pompey', *Historia* 22, 205-

Sumner, G.V. 1966, 'Cicero, Pompeius and Rullus', *TAPhA* 97, 569-82

Syme, R. 1939, *The Roman Revolution.* Oxford University Press

Taylor, L.R. 1941, 'Caesar's early career', *CP* 36, 113-32

Taylor, L.R. 1949, *Party Politics in the Age of Caesar.* Berkeley: University of California Press

Twyman, B.L. 1972, 'The Metelli, Pompeius, and prosopography', *ANRW* I.1, 816-74

Twyman, B.L. 1979, 'The date of Pompeius Magnus' first triumph', *Collection Latomus* 164, 175-208

Ward, A.M. 1969, 'Cicero's support of the *lex Gabinia*', *CW* 63, 8-10

Ward, A.M. 1970a, 'The early relationships between Cicero and Pompey until 80BC', *Phoenix* 24, 119-29

Ward, A.M. 1970b, 'Cicero and Pompey in 75 and 70 BC', *Latomus* 29, 58-71

Ward, A.M. 1977, *Marcus Crassus and the Late Roman Republic.* Columbia and London

Wylie, G.R. 1990, 'Pompey *megalopsychos*', *Klio* 72, 445-56

Wylie, G.R. 1992a, 'The genius and the sergeant: Sertorius versus Pompey', *Collection Latomus* 217, 145-62

Wylie, G.R. 1992b, 'The road to Pharsalus', *Latomus* 51, 557ff

Yavetz, Z. 1990, 'The personality of Augustus: reflections on Syme's *Roman Revolution*', in Raaflaub and Toher 1990, 21-41

Index

Numbers shown in **bold** refer to illustrations